The Republic AND THE Riots

THE Republic AND THE Riots

Exploring Urban Violence in French Suburbs, 2005–2007

Matthew Moran

PETER LANG

Oxford · Bern · Berlin · Bruxelles · Frankfurt am Main · New York · Wien

Bibliographic information published by Die Deutsche Nationalbibliothek
Die Deutsche Nationalbibliothek lists this publication in the Deutsche Nationalbibliografie;
detailed bibliographic data is available on the Internet at http://dnb.d-nb.de.

A catalogue record for this book is available from the British Library.

Library of Congress Cataloging-in-Publication Data:

Moran, Matthew.
  The republic and the riots : exploring urban violence in French
suburbs, 2005-2007 / Matthew Moran.
     p. cm.
  Includes bibliographical references and index.
  ISBN 978-3-0343-0718-5 (alk. paper)
  1. Urban violence--France. 2. Violence--France--Clichy-sous Bois. 3.
Violence--France--Villers-le-Bel. 4. Riots--France. 5.
Suburbs--France. 6. France--Race relations. 7. France--Social
conditions--21st century. I. Title.
  HN440.V5M67 2011
  303.6'230944--dc23
                        2011038768

COVER IMAGE: 'Riots in the Le Mirail district of Toulouse, France on 6 November, 2005'.
Photographed by: AKSARAN. Image licensed by Getty Images.

ISBN 978-3-0343-0718-5

© Peter Lang AG, International Academic Publishers, Bern 2012
Hochfeldstrasse 32, CH-3012 Bern, Switzerland
info@peterlang.com, www.peterlang.com, www.peterlang.net

Printed in Germany

Contents

Acknowledgements

This book would not have been possible were it not for the help and support of a number of friends, colleagues and mentors. I am indebted to Philippe Marlière, who supervised this project as a doctoral thesis. Many thanks also to Michel Kokoreff for his help and guidance during my fieldwork in Villiers-le-Bel. For her insightful comments and criticisms I would like to thank Joanna Smyth.

On the home front, I would like to thank my family and friends for their ongoing support over the last number of years. My parents, in particular, have supported me in every possible way and for this I am truly grateful. I would also like to thank my wife, Éadaoin, who always offers a voice of reason when things seem uncertain.

Methodology

The research for this book comprised two methodological strands. First, the issues at stake were approached from a theoretical perspective, drawing on a wide range of studies relating to the French *banlieues*. This provided a historical and ideological context within which the events of 2005 and 2007 could be situated. Moreover, a review of existing literature provided a valuable insight into the socio-cultural dynamic that underlies life in the suburbs. However, analysis of life in the *banlieues* and, more specifically, the drivers and causes of large-scale collective violence in these areas must pass from the theoretical to the empirical. To deconstruct the socio-cultural processes in operation in these areas and gain a comprehensive understanding of the social dynamic at play in these areas, it is necessary to enter the world of the *banlieues* and study it from within. Consequently, the second methodological strand involved a qualitative case study of Villiers-le-Bel.

Lofland and Lofland state that qualitative research is of immense analytical value: 'the central reason for undertaking this ongoing witnessing of the lives of others is the fact that a great many aspects of social life can be seen, felt, and analytically articulated *only* in this manner'.[1] Moreover, Jorgensen states that 'it is not possible to acquire more than a very crude notion of the insider's world [...] until you comprehend the culture and language that is used to communicate its meanings'.[2] Direct observation of the research setting thus allowed me to gain a first-hand understanding of the actual social dynamic in operation as opposed to a perceived social dynamic (which may be influenced by media coverage or political discourse,

---

1   John Lofland and Lyn Lofland, *Analysing Social Settings: A Guide to Qualitative Observation and Analysis* (Belmont: Wadsworth Publishing Company, 1995), 3.
2   Danny Jorgensen, *Participant Observation: A Handbook for Human Studies* (Thousand Oaks: Sage, 1989), 14.

for example). Moreover, contact with the local population permitted access to the voices of those inhabiting the area and those at the source of the violence – the voices that are often submerged amid the wave of social commentary that inevitably accompanies instances of urban violence. The qualitative research was based on participant observation and semi-structured interviews and took place over a period of nine months.

The sample groups chosen for the interviews reflect the primary aims of the study: to explore the varying interpretations of the 2005 and 2007 urban violence and determine the underlying causes of these events. Representatives of four principal groups were selected for semi-structured interviews: local youths aged between eighteen and twenty-five; police officers who had worked in the area or in neighbouring suburbs; social workers working in the area; and the elected officials of Villiers-le-Bel.

The first group mentioned – local youths – represent an integral element of the study. In 2005, and again in 2007, it was primarily the youth of the suburbs that engaged in large-scale acts of violence and destruction. More significantly, despite the abundance of commentary on French urban violence that has been voiced in the public and political spheres in recent years, the voices of the young people of the suburbs have been conspicuously absent. Therefore, it is important to gain an understanding of these events from the perspective of the youth of the *quartiers sensibles*.

Over forty young people were interviewed over a period of nine months with approximately half of the interviewees claiming that they had been physically involved in the violence of either 2005 or 2007, or both. The level of involvement of the remaining interviewees could not be ascertained. Evidently, given the sensitive nature of the subject, it was not always easy to gain access to those young people that participated in acts of violence themselves. This is primarily due to their distrust of individuals coming from outside the immediate community network. The young people interviewed were suspicious of any attempts to obtain information and, inevitably, this proved to be a significant obstacle in terms of establishing trust between the researcher and the interviewees. Participant observation and access facilitated by local contacts allowed me to overcome this obstacle in most cases. However, certain interviewees were unwilling to speak of their personal role in the riots. The setting of these interviews varied: a quarter of the interviews took place in local youth centres while the remaining interviews took place in various locations chosen by the young people such as apartments, cafés and car parks. The distinction here is important in the sense that the interviews conducted outside the institutionalized environment of the youth centre usually produced more detailed information as well as often heated and emotionally charged dialogue.

Representatives of the forces of law and order constituted the second sample group. Given the prominent role occupied by police-youth relations in the development of the events of 2005 and 2007, as well as the persistent claims of discrimination and the tense day-to-day relations between these two groups, I felt it was important to obtain the point of view of those charged with upholding law and order in these areas, to understand their interpretation of life in the suburbs. This group proved difficult to access due to the sensitive nature of their work and an overriding fear of exposure. Consequently, the sample group here was made up of officers who had worked in neighbouring suburbs in the last two years. Another reason to omit officers currently working in Villiers-le-Bel was due to the tense nature of police-youth relations. In terms of establishing trust with the local youth, it was necessary to maintain a clear distance from the local police.

The third sample group – local social workers – was chosen based on the position of this group in the social hierarchy. In the *quartiers sensibles*, the majority of social workers occupy a place mid-way between the institutions and the local population. Moreover, social workers are professionally qualified to help the local population deal with the challenges and problems that they face on a daily basis. Consequently, the social worker must have an understanding of these problems and is thus qualified to provide reliable information regarding life in the locality. Social workers played a pivotal role in helping me gain access to the local young people.

Finally, the fourth sample group – elected officials – was chosen to provide the perspective of those in power and an insight into how urban violence is understood and managed in terms of the local administration.

All interview participants, apart from elected officials being interviewed in their official capacity and social workers being interviewed in their professional capacity, made confidentiality a condition of their participation. For this reason, real names are not used in the analysis in the fourth chapter. Young people and police officers, especially, demanded anonymity and in most cases did not permit the interview to be recorded. Certain youths were involved in legal proceedings, while others feared reprisal. In relation to the police, the majority of officers feared that their comments would lead to reprimand by their superiors if their identity was made public.

Introduction

Quartiers sensibles or *banlieues* – since the beginning of the 1980s, and the urban violence that took place in the Lyon suburb of Vaulx-en-Velin, these terms have rapidly become synonymous with certain French suburban landscapes. Characterized by severe social and economic problems, as well as a high proportion of inhabitants of immigrant origins, these areas exist at the limits of French society.

In the *quartiers sensibles* the social climate is dominated by high levels of unemployment, crime and delinquency.[1] Discrimination and marginalization form part of the daily life of inhabitants, whether it is through the tense relations with the police or the difficulties experienced by residents in securing employment due to their association with areas that are stigmatized due to their social and economic problems as well as intense media coverage of past instances of violence. The scene of sporadic and highly mediatized outbreaks of large-scale urban violence for over three decades, these suburban areas have been targeted by French urban policy – the *politique de la ville* – during that time in an attempt to integrate the *banlieues* into mainstream French society. However, despite numerous efforts, the suburbs have remained excluded, with further episodes of violence merely serving to reinforce the negative perception of these areas in a circular process that further distances them from mainstream society.

In 2005, the *quartiers sensibles* were propelled to the centre of attention in French, and indeed world, media as violence once again enveloped these areas. The death of two teenagers, electrocuted as they hid from the

---

1   While the term 'quartiers sensibles' is originally a policy term used in the context of French urban policy, this term is used interchangeably with the term 'banlieues' throughout the thesis. The usage here is at once descriptive and intended to highlight the overarching stigma that has become attached to both of these terms in the popular imagination.

police, in the Parisian suburb of Clichy-sous-Bois proved to be the spark that ignited the suburbs. For a period of three weeks cars were set alight, buildings were attacked, and *banlieusards* clashed with the forces of order. Moreover, the events of 2005 signalled a new stage in French urban violence. While past events had typically been limited to the immediate spatial surroundings of the *banlieue* in question, the events of 2005 went much further in terms of their scale and amplitude. During the second week, the violence spread to suburban areas further afield, eventually affecting *banlieues* right across the country. The gravity of the situation provoked the government to declare a state of emergency, invoking emergency laws dating from colonial times.[2]

The events that unfolded at this time affected all areas of French society and politics. However, the chain of events that was initiated in 2005 did not end with the three weeks of violence. In 2007, the death of two youths, aged sixteen and seventeen years, provoked three nights of rioting, the violence of which, while limited to the Parisian suburb of Villiers-le-Bel, proved to be beyond that of 2005 with regard to intensity. Essentially, it can be argued that the riots of 2007 constituted the aftershock of 2005, with both events, while temporally separated, taking place in the same context and under almost identical circumstances. In an insightful editorial published in *Libération* in 2007, two days after the deaths occurred, Laurent Joffrin stated that 'chacun peut [...] constater que la matrice sociale et psychologique des émeutes de 2005 est toujours à l'oeuvre'.[3] In terms of context, the memory of 2005 and the deaths of the two young resi-

---

2   A decree was approved at a special cabinet meeting on 8 November 2005, declaring a state of emergency in certain defined areas. Emergency powers were invoked under a 1955 law dating from the Algerian war of independence. The law bestowed wide-ranging emergency powers on the authorities including: the right to impose curfews in designated areas, the right to prohibit public gatherings; and the right to assume control of the media. This was the first time the law had been applied on mainland France and was seen by many as a drastic measure on the part of the government. See 'La loi permet "d'interdire la circulation des personnes ou des véhicules dans les lieux et aux heures fixées par arrêté"', *Le Monde* (8 November 2005).

3   'Matrice', *Libération* (27 November 2007).

dents of Clichy-sous-Bois were still fresh in the minds of the young people of Villiers-le-Bel, and indeed, youths of all other *quartiers sensibles* were touched in some way by the events of that time. The temporal distance separating the events of Clichy-sous-Bois from those of Villiers-le-Bel was not sufficient to efface the thoughts, feelings and emotions aroused in 2005. This is best illustrated by the choice made by young people in Villiers-le-Bel in the days following the tragedy to adopt the same slogan that was first seen on t-shirts and banners among the friends and family of the two dead *clichois* – 'Morts pour rien'. In the case of Villiers-le-Bel, *Le Monde* reported how 'l'après-midi, on a photocopié à la hâte les portraits de deux adolescents "morts pour rien": le même cri de ralliement qu'après le drame de Clichy-sous-Bois'.[4]

Beyond the more general context of the violent events which occurred two years apart, it was the circumstances surrounding the immediate cause of the 2007 violence that provided the strongest link to the riots of 2005, and the similarities here are striking. The events that took place in Villiers-le-Bel echoed those that occurred in Clichy-sous-bois two years previously: two young residents of the locality (of a similar age to the youths who died in 2005) died in an incident involving police officers. As was the case in 2005, the exact circumstances surrounding the incident were unclear and left room for speculation. And as in 2005, the narrative took two separate paths: the police immediately denied any wrongdoing, while local youths held the forces of law and order responsible for the tragedy. Thus it is clear that the events of 2007 are inextricably linked to those of 2005. During the 2007 riots, Francois Pupponi, Mayor of the neighbouring suburb of Sarcelles stated that 'c'est Clichy bis', thus acknowledging the link between the two instances of violence.[5]

4   'A Villiers-le-Bel, un meneur: "C'est pas du cinéma, c'est de la guerre"', *Le Monde* (28 November 2007).
5   'Un premier rapport de l'IGPN écarte la responsabilité des policiers', *Le Monde* (27 November 2008).

Both during and after the events of 2005 and 2007, various social and political commentators aired a range of interpretations regarding the causes of the riots: simple acts of destruction by delinquents; a fragmentation of society along ethnocultural lines; a manifestation of social crisis. However, these interpretations, formed for the most part without the benefit of critical distance, are reductive and do not adequately address the key issues at stake in the suburbs. While the suburbs have been perceived as a point of social rupture in French society since the first riots in the Lyon suburb of Les Minguettes at the beginning of the 1980s, the events of 2005 were unprecedented. The scale of the violence represented a turning-point in French urban violence as the violence and destruction progressively spread to all corners of the hexagon. The events of 2007 were also unique. While not provoking the same widespread violence engendered by the incident at Clichy-sous-Bois, Villiers-le-Bel crossed a new threshold in terms of intensity. The violence of 2007 represented the first time that firearms were widely used in clashes between the police and young *banlieusards*.

The new levels reached in 2005 and 2007 respectively, one in terms of scale, the other in terms of intensity, are indicative of a growing malaise in French *banlieues*. More generally, the violence of 2005, as well as the aftershock of 2007, revealed the extent of the social divide that is growing within the Republic. Media accounts have revealed that many young people living in these areas seemed to be angered by the failure of the Republic to treat them as the equals of people from more affluent areas. Could it be that these young people were attempting to address the blind spot of French republicanism? That is to say, the situation that is produced when the reality of the racial and social discrimination suffered in the suburbs on a daily basis is obscured by the abstract proclamation of 'universal equality' for all citizens as set out in the Declaration of the Rights of Man and Citizen. Did the riots constitute a rejection of French society and values at large, or, conversely, could the violence be seen as a call for social inclusion?

In light of these issues, this book will explore the causes and significance of the violent events of 2005 and 2007. To do this, I will use these instances of large-scale urban violence as a starting point to examine the social, cultural, and economic situation in the French suburbs. On a larger scale, my analysis situates the question of the *banlieues* within the broader context of the republican model and its supporting ideology. The book will examine the origins and nature of French republicanism before focusing on the validity and application of this model in contemporary French society. In working towards these goals, the question of policing in the *banlieues* will also be considered, given the frequent causal link between the forces of order and instances of large-scale violence in the suburbs, as well as the vital role of police in society as the immediate representatives of justice, guardians of the republican regime. The role of police is undoubtedly an issue of paramount importance in the question of integrating the *banlieues* into mainstream French society. Finally (although undoubtedly most importantly), the book will be supported by empirical evidence gleaned from a nine-month case study of Villiers-le-Bel, the scene of violence and destruction in both 2005 and 2007 and a suburb that is representative of all the social and economic problems that characterize the *quartiers sensibles*. The case of Villiers-le-Bel is particularly interesting. In 2005, while a significant number of cars were burned and clashes with police were recorded, this commune did not experience the levels of violence that occurred elsewhere despite its spatial proximity to Clichy-sous-Bois, the source of the riots.[6] However, in 2007, the considerable use of firearms on the part of the young rioters in Villiers-le-Bel went beyond anything recorded in 2005.

Thus, important questions are raised: why was the violence somewhat limited in 2005 in comparison to other areas further afield? And why in 2007 did the violence reach unprecedented levels of intensity, with a number of police suffering wounds inflicted by firearms? In this regard, the results of extensive fieldwork permit an in-depth assessment of the true nature and causes of both the 2005 riots and the aftershock of 2007. The fieldwork provides access to the voices of those inhabiting the *quartiers sensibles*, voices which are often rendered inaudible by the clamour of interpretations voiced by social commentators. Analysis of these seldom-heard perspectives will allow the research to go beyond the media-constructed 'reality' of life in the suburbs and reveal the social and cultural processes

6 Communes are the smallest administrative subdivision in France.

operating in these areas. In more general terms, the fieldwork will afford a unique insight into the questions of belonging and citizenship in the *banlieues*. The identity of the *banlieusards* that exists in the public sphere is often one that has been constructed and superimposed by social commentators and the media, perhaps with a particular political or financial agenda in mind. 'Emeutier', 'immigré', and 'délinquant' are some of the names given to the inhabitants of these areas. However, this attributed identity often bears little resemblance to the self-perception of identity held by the inhabitants themselves. Consequently, the qualitative research carried out in Villiers-le-Bel will explore the question of identity among local residents and, on a larger scale, how the inhabitants of the area perceive their relationship with French society and the Republic at large. The case-study of Villiers-le-Bel, while undoubtedly reflecting the local social dynamic, will provide a general frame of reference to which other similar areas may be compared. The conclusions drawn from research in the microcosm of Villiers-le-Bel will provide new information that will shed new light on the macrocosm of the *quartiers sensibles* in more general terms.

Ultimately, this book will provide the reader with a comprehensive understanding of one of the most pressing issues facing contemporary French society. Bringing together questions of immigration, citizenship, belonging and identity, the analysis will centre on issues which have dominated public and political life in France for three decades. The central focus of the book, the *banlieues*, sits on the point of convergence of all of these issues. The *banlieues* are widely perceived to represent a concentration of all the challenges facing the French Republic at the beginning of the twenty-first century. In this context, the suburbs can be regarded as a testing-ground for the Republic, a means of assessing the direction in which French society is heading. My analysis of the nature and causes of the riots will thus offer an insight into a broader triad of interconnections: the interplay between republican ideals and the reality of daily life in the *banlieues*; between national projections of unity and localized realities of disunity, and between figures of authority (political and policial) and citizens.

Reading the Riots:
Clichy-sous-Bois and Villiers-le-Bel

The violence that took place in Clichy-sous-Bois in 2005, as well as the after-shock of these events that occurred in Villiers-le-Bel in 2007, undoubtedly constituted an important moment in the evolution of the *quartiers sensibles*. The riots exposed a growing social divide within the Republic, a divide that poses a legitimate threat to social cohesion and challenges the fundamental values at the heart of French republicanism. The events that unfolded on these occasions, temporally somewhat separated but both sharing a strong contextual link and occurring under very similar circumstances, impacted upon all areas of French society and politics. This impact was compounded by intense media attention which served to magnify the violence, giving a global audience an insight into all aspects of the riots, from official per-spectives to the opinions of those involved in the violence.

Beyond the attention of traditional forms of media, the internet played an important role in the 'opening up' of the violence, as this relatively new form of communication provided the means to spread information and personal opinions on local, national and international scales previously unimaginable, transcending all borders and censorial controls through interactive webpages, blogs, and chatrooms, created and maintained by potentially anonymous members of the general public. Thus, both the events of 2005 and, to a lesser extent, those of 2007 were scrutinized by the national and global community through the prism of the media. Inevitably, the large-scale nature of the violence in the first case, and the intensity of the violence in the second, produced a plethora of opinions and debates originating from all areas of the political spectrum. In both instances, the aftermath of the violence saw various social commentators interpreting the events in many different ways. Some, for example, reduced the riots to simple acts of vandalism and destruction by delinquents and thugs; others evoked the threat of communitarianism, a fragmentation of French society along ethnocultural lines; and yet others claimed that the actions of those involved simply represented the reflection of a purely social crisis. However, the issues at stake in the suburbs are undoubtedly more complex than these readings would suggest.

Although the suburbs have, for many years, been labeled as a point of social rupture in French society, a theory reinforced by similar past events such as the violence at Les Minguettes in 1981, at Vaulx-en-Velin in 1990, at Les Yvelines in 2002, or at Nanterre in 1995, to give but a few examples, the 2005 riots were of an unprecedented scale and magnitude, affecting suburban areas throughout the country and resulting in the resurrection of emergency laws dating from colonial times. The extent of the destruction (by 14 November 2005 damage claims were estimated to be in the region of 200 million euros), combined with the duration and intensity of the violence, represented a clear indication of the profound malaise that dominates these areas, reflecting a complex web of social and economic issues that would appear to be far greater than the destructive tendencies of a minority of rebellious youths.[1] The riots of 2007, focused in Villiers-le-Bel, were also unprecedented. In this case, however, it was not the geographical scale of the riots which was unique, but rather the force of the violence – over the space of two nights of intense confrontations between youths and police, 130 police officers were injured, a number of whom were hospitalized with gunshot injuries.[2]

Before attempting to explore the socio-cultural issues underlying the violence that enveloped the *quartiers sensibles* on these occasions, it is first necessary to gain an insight into the various interpretations of the violence offered by social commentators, both during and in the immediate aftermath. This proves valuable in two respects: first, a knowledge of the different analyses circulated allows one to situate the events within contemporary discourse regarding the French suburbs; second, the interpretations of the

1 'EU offers France aid after riots', *BBC News* (14 November 2005).
2 'Dispositif de sécurité', *Le Parisien* (28 November 2007).

violence propagated by the media, as well as the media attention itself, must constitute a determining factor in the construction of the socio-cultural situation of the *quartiers sensibles* due to their impact upon the perceptions of these areas and their inhabitants which dominate the public and political spheres. Consequently, this chapter will begin by examining the events themselves, commencing with an exploration of the immediate causes of the 2005 riots, and then charting the progression of the violence, from its beginnings in the Parisian suburb of Seine-Saint-Denis to the national phenomenon that enveloped France in early November. The analysis will then examine the causes and development of the 2007 aftershock that was contained, for the most part, within the suburb of Villiers-le-Bel.

A Background to the Violence

The Sparks that Ignited the Suburbs

On the night of 27 October 2005, the death of two teenage inhabitants in the Parisian suburb of Seine-Saint-Denis proved to be the spark that ignited the profound malaise of the *quartiers sensibles*. These deaths, the tragic result of an attempt to flee police officers, set in motion a chain of events that culminated in widespread rioting and destruction in a number of urban areas across the nation. Although these deaths were undoubtedly the initial catalyst for the violence, as the riots progressed and grew in scale the anger at this tragedy was overtaken by a more profound anger and frustration on the part of the inhabitants of the *quartiers sensibles* at the socio-cultural situation that has evolved in the suburbs. To their friends, Zyed Benna and Bouna Traoré were the innocent victims of the police discrimination that forms part of daily life in the suburbs; 'Morts pour rien' was the slogan branded upon t-shirts worn by their families, who led protest marches in front of the media. For those living in similar suburban communities, while these deaths lacked a personal link, the tragedy constituted yet another example of the discrimination and humiliation that are primary factors in the social equation of these areas. The death of Zyed (seventeen) and Bouna (fifteen) proved to be the incident that opened the metaphorical floodgates, unleashing the anger of the suburbs and causing a situation that had long been in an extremely volatile state to explode.[3] However, before attempting to look beneath the surface and probe the complexities of life in the *quartiers sensibles*, it is worth examining in detail this series of events which resulted in the resurrection of emergency laws dating from colonial times.

On the night in question, Traoré and Benna died by electrocution at the site of an EDF electrical transformer in the Parisian suburb of Seine-Saint-Denis. Another teenager, Muhittin Altun (seventeen), sustained serious injuries. Despite the inquiry that was set up by the state prosecutor at Bobigny to investigate the charge of 'non-assistance à personnes en danger' and to clarify the circumstances surrounding the deaths of the teenagers, the exact details relating to the events of 27 October remain confused, with the version of events presented by police differing from that of the youths involved in the incident.[4] It has been established that, on the night in question, police responded to a call from a member of the public in relation to a possible break-in at a building site in the locality of Livry-Gargan. Six youths were subsequently arrested and brought to the nearby police station for identity verification, only to be released later without charge.[5] Meanwhile three teenagers, Zyed, Bouna and Muhittin,

---

3   In 2003, Stéphane Béaud and Michel Pialoux concluded their study of the *quartiers sensibles* with the words 'autant de "bombes à retardement"' in reference to the numerous social and economic problems facing the suburbs. In 2005, this ominous prophecy was fulfilled. See Stéphane Béaud and Michel Pialoux, *Violences urbaines, violence sociale. Genèse des nouvelles classes dangereuses* (Paris: Fayard, 2003), 410.

4   It is worth noting that the inquiry was not opened until the 2 November, five days after the death of the two youths and the same day that 'la plainte avec constitution de partie civile, signée par huit membres des familles de Benna, Traoré et Altun, est remise par leurs avocats au doyen des juges d'instruction au tribunal de Bobigny'. See Michel Kokoreff, *Sociologie des émeutes* (Paris: Payot, 2008), 57.

5   'Les circonstances de la mort des adolescents restent floues', *Le Monde* (5 November 2005).

evaded arrest by entering the EDF site. Initially, police claimed that there had been no pursuit involved in the arrest, in an attempt to distance themselves from any causal link to the deaths of the teenagers. Jean-Pierre Mignard and Emmanuel Tordjman, the lawyers representing the families of the deceased, highlighted this claim as a central element of 'le mensonge' that had an important impact on the subsequent scale of the riots.[6] The story told by the youths involved in the incident differs from this account. One of the teenagers, Sofiane, told the inquiry that she had been part of a group of youths returning from a game of football. Sofiane claimed that, on hearing police sirens, the group simultaneously began to run.

Though there was a discrepancy between the two versions of how the incident began, it was the role played by police in the deaths of the two teenagers that formed the central issue of the inquiry, and the officers involved were subsequently investigated for 'non-assistance à personnes en danger'.[7] The police officers involved denied any wrongdoing. However, the legal process took a new turn in December 2006 when the lawyers acting for the families registered a new complaint based on the final report of the *Inspection générale des services* (IGS), which was made public on 8 December 2006.[8] The report revealed that the police had indeed pursued the youths, thus negating their official response to the events. Moreover, the report highlighted a flaw in police procedure, stating that although radio messages had been transmitted, they had not been heard by almost two thirds of the officers present in the area. This fact is all the more important when one considers that if they had been alerted, EDF personnel could have intervened before the tragedy occurred. Subsequently, the judge presiding over the judicial inquiry, opened in 2005, recommended that two police officers be investigated for 'non assistance à personnes en danger'.[9]

6   Jean-Pierre Mignard and Emmanuel Tordjman, *L'Affaire Clichy: Morts pour rien* (Paris: Stock, 2005), 53.

7   Ibid., 57.

8   'Nouvelle plainte pour "mise en danger de la vie d'autrui"', *Le Monde* (7 December 2006).

9   'Clichy-sous-Bois: les familles soulagées après la mise en examen de deux policiers', *Le Monde* (8 February 2007).

This result did not spell the end of the initial legal process surrounding the tragedy; the file was later transferred to another judge who requested a reconstruction of events in 2008 due to contradictory evidence.[10] The case took another turn in late 2010 when the actions of two police officers investigated on charges of misconduct in 2005 were again brought into question.[11] Ultimately, a series of delays and postponements have meant that elements of the case are still ongoing over five years after the incident took place and a certain measure of confusion remains regarding the exact circumstances surrounding the deaths of the two teenagers.

Beyond the immediate nature of the tragedy, the legal follow-up, and its impact on those involved, the incident revealed a number of issues that are indicative of more fundamental problems in relation to the current social climate in the *quartiers sensibles*. First, if no crime had been committed, why did the group feel the need to run from the approaching police? Second, why did the police deem it necessary to arrest six youths and bring them to the local station for a simple identity check that could have been conducted on location? Third, did the police officers intentionally fail to help the teenagers knowing that they had indeed entered the EDF site and were in grave danger? These questions undoubtedly point towards more profound problems in terms of the relations between police and the youth of the suburbs, problems that certainly warrant further study.

Analysis of the beginnings of the 2005 riots reveals that, although the deaths of the two youths served as the primary catalyst for the violence that followed, there was in fact another factor that also played a decisive role in the outbreak and escalation of the violence. This incident took place on 25 October, a number of days before the start of the civil unrest, when the then-Minister of the Interior visited the Parisian suburb of Argenteuil. During a speech to local residents, Nicolas Sarkozy adopted his usual hard-line stance on crime and delinquency, promising inhabitants that he would 'les débarrasser des voyous [...] de la racaille', and using the metaphor of a

---

10   'Clichy-sous-Bois demande justice', *Libération* (28 October 2008).
11   'Clichy-sous-Bois: appel du renvoi des policiers', *Le Figaro* (27 October 2010). The police officers were acquitted of all charges on appeal; see 'Drame de Clichy-sous-Bois: non-lieu pour les policiers', *Le Figaro* (28 April 2011).

'Kärcher', or high-powered cleaning hose, when speaking of his intentions to clean the suburbs of the 'scum' inhabiting these areas.[12] These controversial comments were, at the time, immediately denounced by the Minister for the Promotion of Equality, Azouz Begag, himself a former inhabitant of the *quartiers sensibles*. Sarkozy's description of certain inhabitants of the suburbs was peceived as a direct insult by many residents, compounding the discrimination that permeates life in the suburbs by publicly verbalizing the stigma that has been attached to these areas by mainstream society. Although Sarkozy's statements did not directly result in rioting, his claims added to the frustration of the inhabitants of these areas, effectively moving the situation in the suburbs towards a context where the potential for civil unrest was markedly increased.

Throughout the violence Sarkozy's statements were frequently cited by the rioters as a primary reason for their personal involvement; comments such as 'Sarko has declared war so it's war he's going to get', 'we won't stop until Sarkozy resigns', and 'the main person responsible for this situation is [...] Sarkozy' were recorded by journalists throughout the riots.[13] Numerous internet blogs registered similar comments; these blogs were not initially subjected to any form of censorship and were created by the youths themselves, perhaps resulting in a more accurate reflection of the intensity of the emotions evoked by the words of the then Minister of the Interior: 'France should be ashamed of its incompetent government. Sarkozy is the one who should be cleaned with a Kärcher', 'I say yes to the riots, yes to Sarkozy's resignation', 'We will f**k this bastard Sarkozy and his policemen'.[14] In addition to the impact of Sarkozy's words in terms of the general development and progression of the violence, his subsequent attempts to explain the circumstances surrounding the deaths of the two teenagers served to

---

12 'Les dérapages de Villepin et Sarkozy', *Libération* (31 October 2005).

13 'Suburbs are ablaze with anger', *The Times* (3 November 2005); 'The man whose fate rests on a solution to the revolt', *The Times* (7 November 2005); 'Policiers – jeunes. Le cercle infernal', *Le Monde* (17 October 2006).

14 As authorities became aware of these internet forums and points of online protest they were shut down. Quotes cited in, 'Go home in the name of Allah, order imams with megaphones', *The Times* (8 November 2005).

further aggravate the situation. On 28 October, the day after the tragedy at Clichy-sous-Bois occurred, Sarkozy claimed that the two dead youths had been wanted for burglary.[15] In an analysis of the 2005 violence, Jean-Pierre Dubois denounces these 'mensonges officiels' articulated by those in power as an additional form of violence suffered by the inhabitants of the suburbs, exacerbating 'les violences sociales et les discriminations subies par l'ensemble de la population des "quartiers de relégation" et tout spécialement par la jeunesse qui y vit'.[16] More tellingly, Laurent Mucchielli confirms that there was a marked increase in the violence in the suburb of Clichy-sous-Bois following Sarkozy's statements which were perceived as yet another insult to the inhabitants of this area.[17]

Although the comments of the Minister of the Interior and the deaths of Benna and Traoré played a central role in the outbreak and escalation of the violence, the subsequent scale of the riots demands a more comprehensive explanation. Two days after the death of the two teenagers approximately 400 youths clashed with police at Clichy-sous-Bois.[18] The tension was increased the following day when, during violence between local youths and the CRS, a tear-gas grenade was allegedly fired in the direction of the local mosque.[19] This incident, the precise details of which remain unclear, raises interesting questions in itself: did the officer who fired the grenade know that the mosque lay in the line of fire? Or, conversely, was the officer in question ignorant of the local terrain? The answers to both of these

15   Jean-Pierre Dubois, 'Violences et politiques', in Véronique Le Goaziou and Laurent Mucchielli, eds, *Quand les banlieues brûlent. Retour sur les émeutes de novembre 2005* (Paris: La Découverte, 2006), 69–80 (70).

16   Ibid.

17   Laurent Mucchielli and Abderrahim Ait-Omar, 'Les émeutes de novembre 2005: les raisons de la colère', in Véronique Le Goaziou and Laurent Mucchielli, eds, *Quand les banlieues brûlent. Retour sur les émeutes de novembre 2005* (Paris: La Découverte, 2006), 5–30 (13).

18   Paul Silverstein and Chantal Tetreault, 'Urban Violence in France', *Middle East Research and Information Project* <http://www.merip.org/mero/interventions/silverstein_tetreault_interv.htm> accessed 10 June 2006.

19   The Compagnies Républicaines de Sécurité (CRS) constitute the branch of the French national police that deals with public disorder and rioting, among their other responsibilities.

questions raise more important issues in relation to the role and functions of police in the *quartiers sensibles*. These issues will be discussed in detail in Chapter 3. In any case, the report was seized upon and magnified by the media, fuelling the spread of the riots. By the night of 6 November, ten days after the deaths that had triggered the riots, the violence was at its peak, with riots occurring in many major French cities. Media reports detailed unrest of enormous magnitude as outbreaks of violence were recorded in all parts of the country. Violence erupted in Nantes, Orleans, Rennes and Rouen, while 'arsonists hit the Lille area in the North, Strasbourg in the East, Lyons in the southeast, Nice and Cannes on the Mediterranean and Toulouse and Bordeaux to the southwest'.[20]

The suburban violence of 2005, while comparable to similar events that have occurred in France since the 1980s, was undoubtedly an unprecedented phenomenon. With the Ministry of the Interior recording around 10,000 vehicles burned and hundreds of buildings damaged or destroyed, the scale of the destruction was enormous.[21] Over 1,400 cars were burned in a single night at the height of the violence, for example.[22] While previous events, such as the aforementioned violence of Les Minguettes in 1981 or Vaulx-en-Velin in 1990, developed under similar immediate conditions – that is, within a context where the police were perceived as having committed an injustice against local inhabitants – these instances of violence were largely contained within the city of origin.[23] In the case of the 2005 violence however, this format changed as the riots transcended all city and regional borders, developing as a national phenomenon that posed a serious and legitimate threat to what Nicolas Sarkozy termed 'Republican Order'.[24] Mucchielli stated that 'jamais des processus émeutiers n'avaient connu en France une telle durée et n'avaient pris une telle extension géographique'.[25]

20 'Flames spread to all corners as Chirac tries to keep control', *The Times* (7 November 2005).
21 Cited in Mucchielli and Ait-Omar, 'Les émeutes de novembre 2005: les raisons de la colère', 8.
22 'Violence subsides across France', *BBC News* (10 November 2005).
23 See Silverstein and Tetreault, 'Urban Violence in France'.
24 'France to fight back with more police and curfews', *The Times* (8 November 2005).
25 Mucchielli and Ait-Omar, 'Les émeutes de novembre 2005: les raisons de la colère', 9.

The extreme nature of the riots was illustrated by both the large-scale deployment of police forces and the reaction of the government to the violence. In terms of police resources, the large number of clashes between inhabitants of the suburbs and the police necessitated the deployment of fifty-seven out of France's sixty CRS riot police units to the *banlieues* by the second and third weeks of the violence. With regard to the political reaction to the events, on 8 November decrees number 1386 and 1387 (applying the law of 3 April 1955) declared a state of emergency, giving departmental prefects extensive powers including the right to impose curfews, to forbid public gatherings and to place citizens under house arrest. Following a visit to the suburb of Aulnay-sous-Bois, another *banlieue* that witnessed riots violence, the then Prime Minister, Dominique de Villepin, acknowledged the serious nature of the situation as he told deputies in the French parliament that France faced a situation of 'unprecedented gravity'.[26]

The Aftershock: Villiers-le-Bel

The nationwide riots that began in Clichy-sous-Bois ended in official terms when the state of emergency was lifted on 3 January 2006. However, there was another link in the chain of events initiated in autumn 2005 that was yet to be seen. On 25 November 2007, two youths from the suburb of Villiers-le-Bel died when the motorbike they were riding collided with a police car. Moushin Sehhouli and Larami Samoura were fifteen and sixteen years old respectively. Although the practical circumstances of the tragedy were slightly different from those of 2005, the end result was the same: the deaths of two teenagers provoked widespread anger among local youths, resulting in intense, albeit brief, violence. As has been discussed in the introduction, in the case of Villiers-le-Bel the memory of 2005 played a significant role in the development of the violence and immediate parallels were drawn by

26   'France MPs back emergency powers', *BBC News* (15 November 2005).

local politicians and the media and, most importantly, the local residents themselves.[27] The official version of events publicized by the *Préfecture de police* denied that the police were at fault; police sources claimed, rather, that the two youths, who were not wearing helmets, had not been obeying the rules of the road at the junction where the crash occurred.[28] A preliminary report by the *Inspection générale de la police nationale* (IGPN) absolved the police of blame. This report claimed that the motorbike was travelling at high speed and that the police car was travelling between forty and fifty km/h without emergency lights or siren on a routine patrol.[29] However, in a situation similar to that of 2005, the official version of events was contested by witnesses. Two days after the initial incident, *Le Parisien* newspaper quoted a number of young people from the area who expressed their disbelief in the account presented by police:

> Pour les jeunes du quartier, il ne fait aucun doute qu'il s'agit d'une bavure. 'Ils les ont tamponnés', raconte l'un d'eux. 'Ils voulaient les bloquer sur le trottoir. Ils ont déjà fait cela', poursuit un autre. Selon un habitant de la ZAC [...] les policiers auraient coupé la route à la moto.[30]

Moreover, this doubt was not limited to the younger inhabitants of Villiers-le-Bel. *Libération* reported that 'A Villiers-le-Bel, il n'y a personne pour trouver l'accident "normal"', citing Serge, a resident who spoke of murder.[31] Incidentally, the initial report by the IGPN was challenged by the evidence of a technical expert as part of the inquiry that followed the deaths. A technical examination of the police vehicle revealed that, contrary to the

---

27   A number of national and international newspapers evoked 'Le spectre des émeutes de 2005' including *Libération, La Libre Belgique*, and *Le Parisien*, for example. The role of memory will be discussed in greater detail in Chapter 5.

28   'Echauffourées à Villiers-le-Bel après la mort de deux adolescents', *Le Monde* (25 November 2007).

29   'Un premier rapport de l'IGPN écarte la responsabilité des policiers', *Le Monde* (27 November 2007).

30   'Cinq questions autour du décès de Larami et Moushin', *Le Parisien* (27 November 2007).

31   'La colère ne s'arrête pas à Villiers-le-Bel', *Libération* (27 November 2007).

claim of the IGPN, the car was travelling at a speed of 64.3 km/h at the moment of impact.[32] Moreover, the status of the police car concerned at the time of the crash was brought into question as the circumstances of the tragedy came under intense scrutiny by the lawyers representing the families of the dead youths. It appears that there were in fact two police cars in the immediate area of the collision and both were responding to a reported theft.[33] However the Ministry of the Interior presented a conflicting statement which said that 'monté par un équipage de la BAC (brigade anticriminalité), [la deuxième voiture] partait en mission pour des "roulottiers et empruntait alors un itinéraire proche de celui du véhicule de patrouille qui entrera en collision avec la moto"'.[34] If indeed the car involved in the tragedy was participating in a pursuit, the fact that no siren was used to alert the public of the status of the police cars would be significant.[35] This theory of a pursuit is supported by the fact that analysis of the anti-lock braking system (ABS) revealed that the police car was accelerating at the time of the collision.[36]

Again, these questions highlight some of the issues associated with police working in the *quartiers sensibles* in terms of their credibility as representatives of justice. Demands for truth and justice were a primary concern for many of the involved in some way in the events of both 2005 and 2007, and yet, in both cases, the initial account of police was proved to be flawed. Beyond the specific conditions relating to the actual collision, the circumstances of the immediate aftermath were also somewhat unclear. Following the incident itself, residents of the locality remained at the scene in attempt to preserve the integrity of the site until a technical examination could be carried out. However, the IGPN claimed that the police car had

32   'Villiers-le-Bel: la parole policière mise en cause', *Le Monde* (1 July 2008).
33   See 'Villiers-le-Bel: une deuxième voiture de police sur les lieux?' <http://www.20minutes.fr/article/202331/France-Villiers-le-Bel-une-deuxieme-voiture-de-police-sur-les-lieux.php> accessed 10 November 2008.
34   Ibid.
35   At the time of writing, the police officers involved in the incident at Villiers-le-Bel had been acquitted of any wrongdoing.
36   'Villiers-le-Bel: la parole policière mise en cause', *Le Monde* (1 July 2008).

been attacked with iron bars following the incident and that consequently the state in which it was photographed by the media was not solely the product of the accident. This claim was subsequently proven incorrect by amateur video footage shot by a local resident minutes after the crash took place. This footage, showing the full extent of the damage to the police car, matched photographs published in the media. The IGPN subsequently revised their conclusions and acknowledged that the damage to the car had been caused by the initial impact of the crash.[37] In any case, the causal link, perceived or actual, implicating police officers in the deaths of the two adolescents once again proved to be the spark that ignited the riots when a significant number of local youths took to the streets. As night fell on 25 November young people from the surrounding area gathered on the streets and set fire to a number of cars and rubbish bins. Then, as the violence began to intensify, public and private buildings, including a car dealership and a police station, were set on fire, while approximately three hundred youths clashed with the forces of order throughout the evening.

Following the first night of riots, initial reports claimed that around twenty police officers and firemen were injured 'lors des échauffourées ou par des tirs de grenaille'.[38] This figure was later revealed to be much higher, with forty members of the police force alone reported injured. Almost 200 police reinforcements were deployed in Villiers-le-Bel and the surrounding suburbs of Garges-lès-Gonesse and Sarcelles over the course of the evening, in an attempt to prevent the spread of the violence. The gravity of the situation was not lost on police, with one source quoted as saying 'cela faisait longtemps qu'il n'y avait pas eu autant de forces de police rassemblées [...] même en 2005, cela ne s'était pas vu. La ville était entièrement quadrillée'.[39] The rapid and comprehensive response, in terms of manpower, reflected the dominance of the memory of 2005 in light of an almost identical situational context, that is, the deaths of two local youths

---

37   'L'IGPN révise ses conclusions', *Le Monde* (30 November 2007).

38   'Villiers-le-Bel en état de siège après la mort de deux jeunes', *Le Parisien* (26 November 2007).

39   'Un premier rapport de l'IGPN écarte la responsabilité des policiers', *Le Monde* (27 November 2007).

following an incident involving police. The following day a silent march held in honour of Moushin and Larami took place. The march, attended by the families of the deceased, as well as some 250 youths from the area, represented a demand 'que "justice soit faite, dans le calme et la sérénité".[40] During the march, a number of marchers wore t-shirts branded with the slogan 'Morts pour rien', illustrating the perceived continuity between the two sets of events, the influence of 2005 on the collective imagination of the youth of Villers-le-Bel.

Despite the calls for calm, Villiers-le-Bel was again the scene of violence and destruction on the night of Monday 26 November. Sixty-three cars were burned, the local library was set alight and a number of private buildings were damaged. The town hall narrowly escaped destruction after a Molotov cocktail was thrown into the porch. As the night progressed, material destruction was overshadowed by the intense clashes taking place between police and groups of young people from the area. The police were initially the focus of various projectiles such as bottles and rocks. Witnesses also reported seeing 'fusils à pompe et de fusils à chasse dans les mains de jeunes'.[41] The police responded with Flash-balls and tear gas.[42] Over the course of the evening, 160 reinforcement officers were drafted in to help establish control. But despite the influx of officers, 'peu après 22 heures, on dénombrait trente-huit blessés parmi les forces de l'ordre, dont un policier atteint à l'épaule par un tir de gros calibre qui a transpercé son gilet pare-balles et vingt-cinq autres touchés par des tirs de grenaille'.[43]

The violence also spread to neighbouring *quartiers* including Goussainville, Ermont, Garges-lès-Gonesse and Sarcelles. However, despite these outbreaks, the violence was spatially limited, for the most part, to

40   'Nouveaux face-à-face entre jeunes et forces de l'ordre', *Le Parisien* (27 November 2007).
41   '22 heures, la bibliothèque disparaît dans les flammes', *Le Parisien* (27 November 2007).
42   'Flash-ball' is the brand name of a French-manufactured, non-lethal, hand-held weapon used by French police.
43   'Nouveaux face-à-face entre jeunes et forces de l'ordre', *Le Parisien* (27 November 2007).

the suburbs of Villiers-le-Bel and its immediate surroundings – a repeat of the widespread diffusion of 2005 was avoided. Moreover, the riots at Villiers-le-Bel were concentrated within a time period of two nights, and by 27 November the violence had largely run its course. This was due in part to the overwhelming police presence in the area, estimated by several media sources to be in the region of one thousand police officers and gendarmes. Nevertheless after only two days of violence, eighty-two officers were reported injured, four seriously.[44] A doctor who worked in the emergency department of a hospital in Val d'Oise during the events compiled a dossier describing the injuries treated by the surrounding hospitals. Based on this information the doctor 'juge "impressionnant" que "95 pour cent des policiers accueillis aient été blessé par balles. Pour la plupart d'entre eux, ce n'est pas grave, juste du plomb, mais on n'avait jamais vu ça"'.[45]

Questioning the Riots

In terms of the socio-cultural climate that has developed in the suburbs, the riots of 2005 and 2007 raise interesting questions, both as individual events and as a combined moment in the historical and social development and progression of urban violence in France. On the one hand, the magnitude of the 2005 riots raises a number of far-reaching questions regarding the extent and depth of the socio-cultural and economic exclusion that dominates in the *banlieues*. With no personal link to the two dead teenagers, or to each other (in the national context), why did young people in other *quartiers sensibles* become involved in the large-scale destruction and violence? Why did these young people, a significant number of whom had no previous dealings with the law, decide to violently oppose the police, representatives of the French state and guardians of civil order? On the

---

44 'Les armes font surface', *Libération* (29 November 2007).
45 Ibid.

other hand, why did the 2007 riots in Villiers-le-Bel reach new levels of violence in terms of the clashes between young people and the forces of order? The conflict between these two groups was marked by an unprecedented intensity in this instance. This intensity was expressed through the significant use of firearms by local youths, marking a new development in the violence that often takes form in the *banlieues*. These events were also marked by a significant number of injuries on the part of police; the media highlighted the fact that 'les violences en banlieue de 2007 marquent une escalade avec l'utilisation d'armes à feu contre les policiers'.[46] For Patrice Ribeiro of the police union *Synergie*, 'un cap a été franchi dans l'intensité des violences avec l'apparition des armes. D'après nos collègues sur le terrain, la situation est bien pire qu'en 2005'.[47]

In the wake of the violence various social commentators interpreted events in different ways, with some viewing the events as the work of experienced delinquents, while others evoked an ethnocultural withdrawal from mainstream society on the part of inhabitants of the suburbs. Others still interpreted the violence as a purely social crisis stemming from 'determining' factors such as unemployment and socio-economic relegation. These interpretations were diffused to the national and international public by the media, who maintained a significant presence in the suburbs throughout the violence, effecting intensive coverage of events as the riots progressed. However, before attempting to examine and deconstruct the various interpretations propagated in relation to the violent events of 2005 and 2007 respectively, it is worth pausing to explore the role played by the media in the development of the violence. This is important for a number of reasons. First, the media have a direct input into the construction of the socio-cultural framework of the *quartiers sensibles* given that the media often constitute the sole link between members of the general public and these areas of relegation. The media have the ability to offer an insight into life in the suburbs. These organizations thus impact upon the formation of the collective identity of the *banlieues* in the popular imagination, with

46   'Les armes font surface', *Libération* (29 November 2007).
47   Ibid.

the potential to add to or dispel some of the stigma attached to these areas through the nature of their coverage. Second, the fundamental interplay at the heart of the media industry, that is profit versus the ideal goal of the media (balanced and objective coverage of national and international events), leads to a power struggle that frequently results in the prioritization of sensationalist material. This phenomenon has important consequences in terms of the development and escalation of instances of urban violence in French *banlieues*. In a consumer society that has become dependent on the media for information and attention, acts of violence or large-scale destruction have become a means of securing a national and international platform for issues that would otherwise remain obscure and localized. Third, a direct link exists between the media and those involved in the violence, given that a number of the rioters used the internet, the largest and most freely accessible branch of the media in terms of publication and censorial control, to publicly express their feelings on the violence and, on a larger scale, the pressing social issues at stake in the *banlieues*. This was achieved through the creation of blogs, or interactive web pages, maintained and controlled by their creator while allowing virtually uncensored communication by means of text messages posted on the site by other internet users. In this context, during the 2005 riots for example, the internet afforded those who availed themselves of it a means of potentially communicating directly with their countrymen, and indeed the entire world.[48] It is important to note, however, that the majority of these blogs were shut down by the authorities when they became aware of them in order to prevent rioters rallying support in other suburbs. Thus these forums of uncensored communication were in fact limited to a certain extent in terms of their lifespan.

A notable example of this development could be seen on the interactive website of French radio station, Skyrock, where a number of separate blogs were shut down as a result of comments posted by users calling for young

---

48 Evidently linguistic limitations restricted the size of the audience that could potentially be engaged through the internet. The language barrier eliminated, for example, those users who did not have an understanding of French or, in some cases, 'verlan' (the slang used by youths in the suburbs).

people to unite against the police. Two blogs, one named 'Sarkodead', the other named 'Hardcore', called for others to join in the riots. In both cases, the authorities succeeded in tracing the creators of the blogs: a sixteen-year-old youth from the suburb of Seine-Saint-Denis was placed under investigation for 'inciting harm to people and property over the internet' while a fourteen-year-old youth from Aix-en-Provence was questioned.[49] However, numerous other blogs analysing the violence, and even expressing support for those involved in the violence, appeared throughout the riots and remained accessible online. Examples of these interactive webpages include: blogs set up on the Skyrock site – a significant number of musicians denounced police violence as well as the repressive actions of Nicolas Sarkozy; <blogstory.over-blog.com>, which included a blog featuring comments from both residents of the affected areas and comments from people living in areas other than the suburbs; <http://paris.indymedia. org>, which featured a comment calling for a gathering in Bobigny on 7 of November to support the rioters being tried almost immediately following their arrest; and <http://yahoo.bondyblog.fr/>, a webpage initially set up by the Swiss magazine *L'Hebdo*, dedicated to 'giving a voice to the suburbs' through the writings of a number of young people 'representing the diversity of France and residing in Seine-Saint-Denis'.[50]

49   See 'French bloggers held after Paris riots', *The Guardian* (9 November 2005).

50   See <www.skyrock.com>; <http://blogstory.over-blog.com>; <http://paris. indymedia.org/article.php3?id_article=45642> all accessed 2 June 2007; and <http://20minutes.bondyblog.fr/qui_sommes_nous.shtml> accessed 10 April 2006.

Power Relations and Representation: The Power of the Media

Constructing Reality: The Role of the Media

Throughout history the media have developed as one of the cornerstones of modern society. The coverage offered by the media provides the public with the means to look beyond the immediate and localized sphere of daily life and gain an insight into events unfolding in locations all around the globe. The plethora of images, interviews, reports and commentaries that are dispersed and broadcasted on a continual basis by the various media organizations form a worldwide network of information, a link between members of the public and the global community. According to Todd Gitlin, the media have come to represent 'a central condition of an entire way of life'.[51] Undoubtedly, the power of these organizations is immense. Denis McQuail claims the media constitute 'an essential element in the process of democratic politics by providing an arena and channel for wide debate [...] and for distributing diverse information and opinion'.[52] On a larger scale, the media are important agents of transformation and change in society. Ignacio Ramonet acknowledges that the media 'have been a recourse against abuses of power within the democratic structures of our societies' and 'have often seen it as a duty to denounce [...] violations of human rights'.[53] In cultural and social terms, the media can play an important role in breaking down the barriers that separate populations of a different cultural heritage or social status. The media afford the public an insight into the customs and traditions of other cultures, as well as the challenges faced by different social groups. They provide a means of engaging with people of different origins. Thus, it is clear that the media have the potential to

---

51   Todd Gitlin, *Media Unlimited* (New York: Metropolitan Books, 2002), 210.
52   Denis McQuail, *McQuail's Mass Communication Theory* (London: Sage, 2000), 4.
53   Ignacio Ramonet, 'Set the Media Free', *Le Monde Diplomatique* (English Edition) (October 2003).

greatly benefit society. However, alongside the many benefits, it is of course necessary to acknowledge the equal potential of the media to negatively impact upon society by creating or adding to social and cultural divisions through biased or incomplete coverage that fails to transmit the entire truth of a situation, whether it be through genuine error or other ulterior political or financial motives. In this respect, Eoin Devereux claims that the media are 'inextricably bound up with the capitalist project and [...] play a centre-stage role in the reproduction and continuation of various kinds of social inequalities at local, national and global levels'.[54]

Considering the omnipresence of the media in contemporary society, and the powerful position occupied by these organizations in terms of cultural production and mediation, it is useful to briefly examine the underlying mechanisms and processes influencing media production in the public sphere. This will provide a more general theoretical framework within which the specific relationship between the media and the socio-cultural situation in the suburbs can be analysed and understood. Of course, this exploration is not intended as a fully fledged sociological study of the nature of the media; rather, this section aims to give a theoretical insight into the workings of the media in order to better understand the various forces and relationships influencing cultural production in this domain. This structural study of the media will be based on Pierre Bourdieu's analysis of the media which focuses particularly on the concept of the 'journalistic field' and the power relations in operation both within this field and between this and other fields of cultural production.[55] While Bourdieu's critique of the media centres largely upon the medium of television, the issues raised, especially those relating to the journalistic field, can undoubtedly be applied more broadly across the media spectrum. Philippe Marlière reveals that, essentially, Bourdieu's theoretical analysis of the media incorporates two main arguments: '[f]irst, his observations on the way television deals with news (i.e. the search for "sensational events", "scoops", the homogeniza-

---

54   Eoin Devereux, *Understanding the Media* (London: Sage, 2007), 13.
55   Pierre Bourdieu, *On Television and Journalism*, trans. Priscilla Ferguson (London: Pluto Press, 1998), 39.

tion of programmes, the importance given to sports and entertainment programmes, etc.) and the way in which speakers [...] are obliged to speak. [...] Second, his stigmatization of "the journalists" as an undifferentiated category'.[56] In order to explore the mechanisms of the media through the prism of Bourdieu's critique, it is first necessary to consider the idea of the 'journalistic field', a concept at the centre of the Bourdieusian analysis and one that plays a pivotal role in gaining an understanding of the rules and rationale that govern the media sphere.

Pierre Bourdieu and the Journalistic Field

Bourdieu describes the journalistic field as 'a microcosm with its own laws, defined both by its position in the world at large and by the attractions and repulsions to which it is subject from other such microcosms'.[57] The journalistic field is made up of complex and ongoing relationships of power and inequality as 'all the individuals in this universe bring to the competition all the (relative) power at their disposal. It is this power that defines their position in the field and, as a result, their strategies'.[58] Thus to fully understand what journalists do and are able to do, the various parameters of the field, such as relative position of the particular news medium and the positions occupied by journalists themselves within the environment of their respective newspapers or networks, must be considered. In the context of this idea of the journalistic field, three key, and often overlapping, influences can be identified in the processes and structures governing media production. First, Bourdieu's analysis broaches the question of economic and market forces and their impact on the process of media production. For Bourdieu, it is not enough to study the impact of external economic forces on media production because the material or images

---

56 Philippe Marlière, 'The Rules of the Journalistic Field: Pierre Bourdieu's Contribution to the Sociology of the Media', *European Journal of Communication*, 13 (1998), 219–234 (223).
57 Bourdieu, *On Television and Journalism*, 39.
58 Ibid., 40.

produced by a particular medium or media cannot be explained solely by their ownership by a particular conglomerate. At the same time however, Bourdieu acknowledges that an explanation of media structures would not be complete without considering the impact of external economic issues. In this respect, Rangan Chakravarty and Nandini Gooptu reveal that 'the media, in their structures of production and transmission, are driven by certain imperatives of power, domination and control'.[59] Thus, to gain a complete understanding of the mechanisms at work behind the scenes in the media production process, the issue of ownership must be considered. The politics of ownership must influence, to some extent, the direction of the organization. In spite of this, it is important not to overestimate the question of ownership in the journalistic field because, beyond this, media organizations must be considered in terms of what Bourdieu terms their 'relative weight'.[60] In other words, attention must be paid to the relative symbolic power of the organization, its position in relation to other organizations in the journalistic field, and indeed in other fields. Bourdieu uses the television station TF1 to illustrate this fact:

> To understand what goes on at TF1, you have to take into account everything that TF1 owes to its location in a universe of objective relations between the different, competing television networks. You also have to recognize that the form this competition takes is defined invisibly by unperceived power relations that can be grasped through indicators like market share, the weight given to advertising, the collective capital of high-status journalists, and so on [...] you have to take into account the totality of the objective power relations that structure the field.[61]

Thus it is clear that external factors form an intricate web linking various levels and degrees of influence on cultural production in the media sphere. However, while there are numerous external factors impacting upon media production, the influence of the market is arguably the factor that has the most immediate and decisive effect on the journalistic field. Bourdieu states,

---

59 Rangan Chakravarty and Nandini Gooptu, 'Imagi-nation: The Media, Nation and Politics in Contemporary India', in Elizabeth Hallam and Brian Street, eds, *Cultural Encounters. Representing 'Otherness'* (London: Routledge, 2000), 89–107 (90).
60 Bourdieu, *On Television and Journalism*, 39.
61 Ibid., 40.

for example, that the ratings systems, or indeed the circulation figures in the realm of print media represent the 'hidden god of this universe, who governs conduct and consciences'.[62] In relation to this capitulation to the powers of capitalism, he draws attention to the paradoxical development that has taken place in terms of media legitimation: 'Only thirty years ago, and since the middle of the nineteenth century [...] immediate market success was suspect. It was taken as a sign of compromise with the times, with money [...] Today, on the contrary, the market is accepted more and more as a legitimate means of legitimation'.[63] Essentially, the interplay that exists between the traditional 'ideal' role of the media – to diffuse information in an objective, truthful manner – and the commercial goal of this industry, namely profit, has shifted in favour of the commercial benefits which can be gleaned from the markets.[64] Certainly, in an industry where competition has increased in scale and intensity, business-related goals have resulted in an ever-growing demand for sensationalist material to attract an audience and maintain levels of profit.

The impact of economic and market forces upon the journalistic field is closely linked to, and often overlaps with, the second key element in Bourdieu's analysis of the media: the question of censorship. According to the Bourdieusian interpretation, cultural production in the media is inextricably linked to the idea of censorship. Censorship influences all stages of media production and plays a decisive role in shaping the information received by the public. This is largely due to the conditions imposed on media actors. On the macro-scale, censorship is related to the relative position of a given medium within the journalistic field; the political affiliations of the medium; and 'its specific location between the "intellectual"

---

62 Ibid., 27.
63 Ibid.
64 McQuail speaks of the 'objectivity concept' in relation to the news media, the main features of which are: 'adopting a position of detachment and neutrality towards the object of reporting (thus an absence of subjectivity or personal involvement); lack of partisanship (not taking sides in matters of dispute or showing bias); attachment to accuracy and other truth criteria (such as relevance and completeness); and lack of ulterior motive'. McQuail, *Mass Communication Theory*, 145.

and "market" poles'.[65] The political position of a particular newspaper or television station, for example, can influence, to a certain extent, what is diffused through that medium, what 'fits' with the medium's position in the journalistic field. Incidentally, Marlière reveals a lacuna in Bourdieu's analysis of the media in his failure to give adequate consideration to the potentially significant impact of the political field on media production. Marlière states that 'Bourdieu takes very little notice of the negative role played by the political field itself in the subjection of television to the rules of the market [...] This is all the more striking because France – the object of Bourdieu's case study – is probably one of the few European countries in which the journalistic field is still not totally independent of political power.'[66] Marlière effectively shows how the French media, despite some moves towards a democratic system, still remain 'somewhat subordinated to political power.'[67]

The subtle forms of censorship that exist on the macro-scale of media organizations and their place in the field as a whole are multiplied and augmented as the focus moves towards the micro-scale – that is, the multitude of influences and limitations, perceived or otherwise, in operation at the grass-roots level of the journalist. At this micro-level, in tandem with those forces operating from above, the concept of censorship can be understood in terms of what Bourdieu calls the 'circular circulation of information', that is to say, competition within the journalistic field has the paradoxical effect of homogenizing production.[68] Essentially, Bourdieu claims that in the journalistic field, 'to know what to say, you have to know what everyone else has said.'[69] This maxim makes a review of the daily press an essential tool for the successful journalist; this circular process stems directly from the market influences exerted on the journalistic field.

Journalists operate in an atmosphere of constant pressure, an environment built around the ongoing search for exclusivity that will allow a particular medium to stand out from its competitors and afford a journalist

65   Bourdieu, *On Television and Journalism*, 69.
66   Marlière, 'The Rules of the Journalistic Field', 225.
67   Ibid.
68   Bourdieu, *On Television and Journalism*, 23.
69   Ibid.

recognition within and beyond the field. Thus the influence of the markets ensures that a potent form of censorship underlies the media industry, with the result that the extraordinary, the sensational, is always given priority. In other words, journalists are bound to a certain extent by invisible parameters which dictate the stories that will be diffused in the public sphere. In order to progress or gain recognition in the industry a journalist must enter into this circular process, at least until such a time as he or she has amassed sufficient symbolic capital to achieve success independent of the censorship process, that is, through large-scale recognition by the public or by peers (and even then, actors may never be entirely free of the market constraints influencing the field). The concept of censorship thus constitutes an integral element of the journalistic field, dictating how journalists operate within the boundaries of this field. Citing the work of Patrick Champagne, Bourdieu states that journalists select and prioritize information according to their 'perceptual categories', that is, the invisible structures such as background, training and the particular form of reasoning required by the industry, to name but a few.[70] And once again, the parameters within which this process of selection and prioritization occur are based on the search for the sensational.

The third element of Bourdieu's analysis of media structures and processes is based on the effects and impact of censorship and market influences on society in terms of the information diffused by the media. In this context, Bourdieu speaks of the 'reality effect', or the specific cultural effect achieved by the processes governing media production in the public sphere.[71] Essentially, Bourdieu claims:

> The power to show is also a power to mobilize. It can give life to ideas or images, but also to groups. The news, the incidents and accidents of everyday life, can be loaded with political or ethnic significance liable to unleash strong, often negative feelings, such as racism, chauvinism, the fear-hatred of the foreigner or, xenophobia. The [...] very fact of reporting, of putting on record as a reporter, always implies a social construction of reality that can mobilize (or demobilize) individuals or groups.[72]

70 Ibid., 19.
71 Ibid., 21.
72 Ibid., 21.

The media thus 'produce "reality effects" by creating a "media vision" of reality which, in turn, tends to create the reality which the media claim to describe'.[73] This is not to suggest that the media fabricate events; however, it does show that the vision presented by the media can distort the reality of a given event. The emphasis given by the media to certain aspects of an event or situation inevitably requires the omission of other aspects that might be considered equally, or indeed more, important in another context. This process will be illustrated in the context of the suburbs further on. Ultimately, in terms of the social identities of social actors or groups, the reality effects produced by the media can result in a specific form of symbolic violence. Bourdieu defines symbolic violence as 'violence wielded with tacit complicity between its victims and its agents, insofar as both remain unconscious of submitting to or wielding it'.[74] In other words, the reality produced by the media under the visible and invisible structural influences acting upon and within the journalistic field, and absorbed by the public sphere which accepts it as such, unaware of those same influences, can result in the symbolic oppression of a particular social actor or group. This symbolic oppression can have negative implications for those concerned in terms of marginalization, stigmatization and exclusion if the reality effects of the media are left unchallenged.

In general terms, Bourdieu's analysis offers an insight into the fundamental mechanisms and processes governing the media. Of course, Bourdieu's interpretation is not flawless, nor is it exhaustive. Marlière points out, for example, the problems encountered in presenting journalists as a 'monolithic category'.[75] In speaking of 'journalism', Bourdieu seems to 'refer to a unified category created by the illusion that it necessarily speaks and acts as one individual world'.[76] This interpretation reveals a 'lack of in-depth analysis of the different types of journalism and of the different categories of journalist (including those who dominate and those who are dominated)'.[77]

73   Marlière, 'The Rules of the Journalistic Field', 221.
74   Bourdieu, *On Television and Journalism*, 17.
75   Marlière, 'The Rules of the Journalistic Field', 223.
76   Ibid., 223.
77   Ibid.

Nonetheless, the central theoretical concerns raised by Bourdieu address the fundamental structures and power relations having a direct impact on the question of cultural production in the media. Moreover, this theoretical analysis allows for a better understanding of the role of the media in the social construction of the situation in the *quartiers sensibles*. It has already been mentioned, in general terms, how the mechanisms that shape the journalistic field lead to the prioritising of sensationalist material; Bourdieu reflects on the consequences of such processes in terms of the reality effects and the potential ethnic and political significance of media coverage. The relationship between the relentless pursuit of the sensational and the result-ant negative effects in terms of cultural production is particularly relevant in the context of symbolic oppression in the *quartiers sensibles*. Marlière succeeds in encapsulating the key issue at stake here: this unilateral process of symbolic oppression that exists in the suburbs and the fact that it stems in large part from the sensationalist-oriented goals of media coverage in these underprivileged areas:

> The media tend to create an image of social problems for the public consumption which emphasizes the 'extraordinary', that is, violent actions, fights between young-sters and the police, acts of vandalism, juvenile delinquency, the overconcentration of immigrant populations, etc. Media portrayal of these suburban areas 'stigmatizes' the people living there in all aspects of their everyday lives, thereby extending the bad reputation of a place to its inhabitants.[78]

Sensationalism and Media Censorship: Influencing Urban Violence?

In the context of the *quartiers sensibles* and the violence of both 2005 and 2007, it can be argued that the public and political attention brought to the suburbs by the presence of the media served to highlight and provoke action in relation to the urgent social issues hindering the development of these areas. The political pressure produced succeeded in releasing funds

---

78   Ibid., 221.

destined for rehabilitation projects and social development initiatives. On 8 November 2005, for example, under media and political pressure, Dominique de Villepin announced an increase in funds for social associations in the suburbs – a decision that reversed the move made by the government in 2002 to reduce funding to these organizations.[79] However, Champagne, speaking ten years earlier, claimed that this type of interpretation is excessively optimistic as it fails to consider the symbolic impact of media presence on populations that are 'culturellement démunies'.[80] Following the outbreak of the riots, the media descended on the *banlieues* in droves; the violent events which were unfolding promised to provide sensational images and headlines, thus boosting all-important audience ratings and satisfying the demands of the market. As a result, coverage focused on the violence and destruction, the clashes between youths and the police, with little attention being given to the underlying social problems facing these areas. Through analysis of a wide range of articles published by the written press, Mathieu Rigouste has effectively categorized the dominant images emerging more generally in the media in relation to the *quartiers sensibles*.[81] He determined four distinct categories, each one describing a dominant and generalized representation of the suburbs appearing through the coverage of the written press:

1) A 'sick' element of society needing to be restored to health
2) A space at war that must be pacified
3) A savage space that must be civilized
4) An invasive space that must be contained

In the context of the 2005 violence, and again in 2007, two of these categories were especially prevalent within media discourse relating to the suburbs. First, that relating to a social space at war with the state, with reports highlighting the clashes between youth and the forces of order and evoking a social

---

79   'Pourquoi un tel fiasco de la politique de la ville?', *Le Monde* (11 November 2005).
80   Patrick Champagne, 'La vision médiatique', in Pierre Bourdieu, ed., *La misère du monde* (Paris: Seuil, 1993), 61–79 (p.72).
81   Mathieu Rigouste, 'Le langage des médias sur "les cités". Représenter l'espace, légitimer le contrôle', *Hommes et Migrations*, 1252 (2004), 74–81 (75).

space torn by civil war. An article particularly representative of this type of discourse appeared in *Le Figaro* on 9 November 2005.[82] From the beginning of the article, the author suggests that the suburbs have, for a number of years, been in the grip of a civil war that the forces of order are losing: 'la loi des bandes, avec ses codes, ses rites et son vocabulaire, s'impose peu à peu dans certaines zones'. The author places emphasis on the anarchy which, for him, characterizes the *quartiers sensibles* where 'racket, rixes, razzias, guet-apens, trafic en tout genre' form part of daily life. The military language employed by the author throughout the article is especially striking; the words and phrases used evoke the image of a battle-field: 'Le quartier devient le territoire. On le défend. On le quadrille.'[83] This idea was taken up again during the coverage of the 2007 violence, with a number of journalists evoking warlike images.[84] Second, the category relating to the idea of the suburbs as an invasive space that must be contained, with a significant portion of the coverage evoking an ethnic dimension to the riots, essentially linking the history of immigration that exists in these areas, notably the presence of a significant Muslim population, to the outbreak and escalation of the violence. Rigouste's analysis holds that 'selon la presse, les "cités" envahissent la France de manière générale et les centres-villes en particulier'.[85] He goes on to say that 'le registre de l'invasion représente les "cités" comme des portes ouvertes sur l'étrangeté et la menace, à l'intérieur de l'espace national mais issues de l'extérieur.'[86] Thus a specific interpretive framework is imposed upon the *quartiers sensibles* through sensationalist coverage; these areas are placed in a one-dimensional descriptive matrix that offers no alternative to the violent and destructive images evoked. As a result, inhabitants are stigmatized through their position as residents of these areas; they are incorporated into the reputation attached to the territory. This idea will be discussed again in the context of the reality effects further on.

---

82 'De la loi des bandes à la jungle urbaine', *Le Figaro* (9 November 2005).

83 Ibid.

84 See, for example, 'A Villiers-le-Bel un meneur: "C'est pas du cinéma, c'est de la guerre"', *Le Monde* (28 November 2007).

85 Rigouste, 'Le langage des médias sur "les cités". Représenter l'espace, légitimer le contrôle', 80.

86 Ibid.

Apart from the idea of the stigmatization of populations, the priority given to sensationalist material in contemporary society is a fact that in itself raises interesting questions regarding the subject of urban violence, once again especially relevant in the context of the *quartiers sensibles*. Could it be that this formula for media attention that relies more and more upon sensationalism has perhaps encouraged violence in areas where dialogue has failed, where voices have been ignored, since violence provides a certain means of attracting media, and by extension, public attention, on a national and international scale?

During the violence of 2005, Patrick Lecocq, editor-in-chief of the television station *France 2* drew attention to this issue when he posed the question: 'Do we send teams of journalists because cars are burning, or are the cars burning because we send teams of journalists?' at the News Xchange conference in Amsterdam.[87] In relation to the continuous stream of visual imagery, through photographic and television coverage of the riots, that was transmitted to the national and international public as the 2005 events unfolded, Jean-Jacques Wunenburger explores the idea of media imagery as 'un simple effet d'amplification, de chambre d'écho des violences', due to the instantaneous diffusion of graphic images of urban violence by the media. In this context, Wunenberg asserts that the media become involved in the event as actors, aiding its growth and progression:

> Les jeunes émeutiers des banlieues contemporaines, enfants de la télévision et du mobile, pratiquent une violence sous l'œil des caméras, devant des micros [...] La captation et la transmission de la violence deviennent ainsi des opérateurs inclus dans le processus de décharge [de la violence]. On détruit et on enflamme, en se sentant inséré dans un réseau d'images et même dans une compétition d'images avec d'autres groupes qu'on suit par des télécommunications.[88]

---

87   'French TV bosses admit censoring riot coverage', *The Guardian* (10 November 2005).

88   Jean-Jacques Wunenburger, 'Imaginaires de la violence: du fondement symbolique au fantasme destructeur', in Raphaël Draï and Jean Francois Mattéi, eds, *La République brûle-t-elle? Essai sur les violences urbaines françaises* (Paris: Editions Michalon, 2006), 69–86 (81).

Undoubtedly, their position as the source of information for the general public gives various media organizations the power to influence our opinions, even our thoughts. Consequently, the manner in which the media present information to the public influences, to a certain extent, public perceptions of an event, or a social or cultural agent or group. That is not to suggest a 'hypodermic model where media messages can simply be injected into the mind of the audience to influence their views and visions of the world directly'.[89] However, in providing a link, often the only link, between marginalized communities, such as those of the *quartiers sensibles*, and mainstream society through words and images that portray the inhabitants of these areas in a certain manner, the media plays a significant role in the construction of the socio-cultural situation of the *quartiers sensibles* within the broader context of French society as a whole. Jennifer Kelly claims that 'youths can be viewed as drawing on various media-saturated discourses that are socially shaped but also socially shaping in terms of identities, social relations and systems of knowledge'; however it can be argued that this statement applies to all of society, as the media frequently provide the reference point for the 'other', that part of society which the audience has no contact with or knowledge of.[90] These organizations can affirm, to a certain extent, the social and cultural identity of the inhabitants of the suburbs in the popular imagination.

Media Representations: Defining the 'Reality' of French Suburbs?

In general terms, the media attention surrounding the instances of rioting in 2005 and 2007 depicted a social space dominated by violence and destruction – a stark contrast to mainstream society. The pressing social and ethnic issues in these areas were submerged by the wave of sensationalism that was transmitted from the suburbs to the general public. In an astute

---

89   Chakravarty and Gooptu, 'Imagi-nation: The Media, Nation and Politics in Contemporary India', 105.
90   Jennifer Kelly, *Borrowed Identities* (New York: Peter Lang, 2004), 195.

analysis of the 2005 violence, Françoise Blum claimed that 'les moyens que [les émeutiers] utilisent sont sans doute les seuls efficaces en ces temps où les médias font et défont l'actualité'.[91] However, in expressing their frustration at their current socio-cultural situation, those involved in the riots assisted in a process by which the suburbs are further stigmatized by the media. This process occurs through a unilateral representation that places these areas in opposition with mainstream society and fails to acknowledge any positive aspect of these marginalized areas, such as the solidarity that exists between inhabitants brought together through common hardships. Champagne encapsulates the role of the media in the violence of 2005 in a paradoxical statement, claiming that these organizations have stigmatized the suburbs since the riots of Vaulx-en-Velin in 1990 with 'Dix ans d'intensification d'une forme de violence qui en rendant visible la violence visible n'en rendait que plus invisible la violence invisible'.[92] The events of 2007 constitute yet another step in this process. Essentially, media treatment of urban violence in the *quartiers sensibles* exemplifies the Bourdieusian concept of the symbolic violence inflicted by the media on society, a product of the reality effects that result from the influence of the journalistic field. A limited representation of these instances of urban violence that focuses on the highly visible spectacle of the violence rather than the 'invisible' causes motivating such acts, that is, the underlying social and economic issues, has effectively separated the acts of violence from the related social causes:

> On assiste à un processus de brouillage qui va autonomiser la violence, celle-ci apparaissant de plus en plus comme gratuite, comme un défi à l'ordre républicain [...] comme des actes liés au trafic de drogue, bref comme autant de comportements inexcusables ou criminels qui ne méritent qu'une répression accrue tant sur le plan policier que sur le plan judiciaire.[93]

---

91   Francoise Blum, 'Ils sont entrés en politique', *Le Monde* (11 November 2005).
92   Champagne, 'La vision médiatique', 73.
93   Ibid.

As the violence is detached from the social problems to which it is inextricably linked, it becomes, in terms of the media, the property of those inhabitants involved at the grass-roots level, the young people burning cars and engaging in confrontations with police. The youths are denounced as refusing to integrate, and the violence is no longer associated with the underlying social issues:

> La violence devenait ainsi progressivement une propriété de la jeunesse immigrée ou issue de l'immigration, de jeunes perçus comme 'inassimilables' par la France alors que nombre de ces comportements devaient beaucoup à un refus d'intégration par le France de ces populations.[94]

Evidently, this separation has impacted negatively on the social issues that dominate the *quartiers sensibles*. The media have contributed to the superimposition of a specific and artificial 'reality' onto these marginalized areas of the Republic. The focus of those in power is directed to the immediate repression of the violence and destruction, diverting attention from the true causes of the violence and thus hindering the development of long-term strategies aimed at combating the social deterioration that is taking place in these areas. Residents of the suburbs see their areas portrayed as ghettos, with inhabitants characterized as delinquents. Thus it is that the frustration and anger that motivated the youth of the suburbs to engage in acts of violence and destruction serve to reinforce, through media coverage, popular stereotypes that give the public a superficial glance at the events unfolding but that do not consider the issues underlying the spectacle. As a result, beyond the pressing socio-economic problems that dominate in the *banlieues*, inhabitants must also contend with an extremely negative public image that is produced by the media and often does not reflect the reality of life in these areas.

Both during and after the violence, the coverage diffused by the various media provided a point of reference for those social or political commentators who publicized their opinions in the public sphere. However, it has been shown that the 'reality' constructed by the media during the

94   Ibid.

violence represented a selective portrait of the situation in the suburbs. As a result, certain interpretations articulated in the wake of the 2005 riots, which incorporated or were built around the 'reality' constructed by the media, themselves failed to account for the complexities of the situation in the suburbs. Having considered the role of the media in the development of the 2005 violence and, on a larger scale, the construction of the socio-cultural situation in the *banlieues*, it is now necessary to examine and deconstruct the interpretations articulated by social commentators in the wake of the riots.

Interpreting Violence in the *banlieues*

Crime, Delinquency and the Law of the Street: The Dominant Interpretation of French Urban Violence

In contemporary French society, two themes have occupied a primary position in political and media discourse in recent years: insecurity and urban violence. Mucchielli affirms that the preoccupation with urban violence dates from the beginning of the 1990s, when the topic became a permanent fixture in the discourse of journalists, politicians, security professionals and numerous intellectuals following the first series of 'urban riots', which began with those of Vaulx-en-Velin in October 1990 and continued with riots in Parisian suburbs between March and July 1991.[95] He goes on to state that, in recent years, the expression 'urban violence' has become trivialized to the point of becoming almost a daily fixture in the various media. Moreover, a review of coverage by the written press in relation to the suburbs over the last twenty years shows that the themes of 'insecurity' and 'urban violence' have engendered a particular vocabulary that explicitly links the suburbs to

---

95   Laurent Mucchielli, *Violences et insécurité. Fantasmes et réalités dans le débat Français* (Paris: La Découverte, 2001), 7.

the threat of insecurity and urban violence. Terms such as 'jeunes des cités' and 'jeunes de banlieue' explicitly associate the activities of certain young people in the suburbs with the cause of the security problem facing French society; expressions and terms such as 'fracture sociale'; 'violence gratuite'; 'zones de non-droit'; and 'la haine des banlieues' have constructed a stereotype of the suburbs as a menace to mainstream society.[96] Finally, and most importantly, Mucchielli states that the use of this vocabulary is inseparable from a general representation according to which French society is faced with an inexorable rise in crime and violence, with adolescent delinquents becoming more and more violent at a younger age.[97]

The discourse articulated in the wake of the riots of 2005 and 2007 constituted a continuation of this trend that depicts a society threatened from within, with the values and ideals of the Republic being placed in stark contrast to the menace of the *quartiers sensibles*. Significantly, this discourse found voice, for the most part, among police and certain political sources, as represented by the then Minister of the Interior, Nicolas Sarkozy. The status of these commentators as prominent figures in the political and public arenas gave an additional weight to their commentary and ensured that it was widely spread in the media, making this viewpoint the dominant interpretation of the riots. Moreover, the abundance of alternative interpretations, all vying for attention in the public sphere, effectively served to render them inaudible, thus reinforcing the dominant position of the security-oriented discourse. This point will be further discussed in the following section. Essentially, the security-oriented interpretation viewed the riots as the actions of 'voyous' and 'racaille': experienced delinquents expressing a hate for French society and the Republic.[98] The picture painted by Sarkozy was one of a social space dominated by a 'peur des bandes, des caïds', areas ruled by mafia-like organizations where even the police are

---

96 The review of newspaper articles mentioned here comprised of a study of more than 300 articles from three major French newspapers – *Le Monde, Le Figaro, Libération* – spanning the period 1987–2007.

97 Mucchielli, *Violences et insécurité*, 7.

98 Cited in 'Nicolas Sarkozy continue de vilipender "racailles et voyous"', *Le Monde* (11 November 2005).

afraid to go.[99] Moreover, the now President of the Republic dismissed the
importance of a number of social issues, such as discrimination and problems with the education system in the suburbs, as he cited the activities of
criminal gangs as the principal cause of the violence and, more generally,
the despair that reigns in the *banlieues*:

> La première cause du chômage, de la désespérance, de la violence dans les banlieues,
> ce ne sont pas les discriminations, ce n'est pas l'échec de l'école. La première cause du
> désespoir dans les quartiers, c'est le trafic de drogue, la loi des bandes, la dictature de
> la peur et la démission de la République.[100]

Sarkozy's interpretation of the violence found support among a number
of politicians. On 5 November 2005, Gérard Gaudron, Mayor of Aulnay-
sous-Bois, led a protest march against the violence, telling media report-
ers that the march was 'neither a provocation nor a demonstration of
force, but a republican response to acts of delinquency'.[101] Claude Pernes,
Mayor of Rosny-sous-Bois denounced a 'veritable guerrilla situation, urban
insurrection'.[102] Elsewhere, the then Prime Minister, Dominique de Villepin,
who despite refusing to align himself fully with Sarkozy's security-oriented
discourse, instead calling for caution and urging ministers not to stigmatize
vast areas, voiced his opinion that those involved in the riots were delinquents during an interview on the French television station, TF1.[103]

Statements issued by various police bodies and unions in the wake of
the 2005 violence also supported this interpretation. Jean-Claude Delage,
for example, General Secretary of *Alliance Police Nationale* (the right-wing
majority union of police officers), presented the striking image of 'la canaille
[des banlieues] en guerre contre l'état' at the union's fifth National Confer-

99   Ibid.
100 Philippe Ridet, 'M. Sarkozy durcit son discours sur les banlieues', *Le Monde* (22
     November 2005).
101 Alex Duval Smith, 'The week Paris burned', *The Guardian* (6 November 2005).
102 'Unrest spreads across France', *Al Jazeera* (6 November 2005).
103 See 'Fresh violence hits Paris suburbs', *BBC News* (3 November 2005).

ence in November 2005.[104] The warlike discourse of *Alliance Police Nationalale* was compounded by Frédéric Lagache, national secretary of the union, who called for 'l'éradication de ceux qui pourrissent la vie des habitants des cités et instrumentalisent les jeunes contre les forces de l'ordre'.[105] The minority right-wing union *Action Police CFTC* was another voice much quoted by the media during the 2005 violence due to its sensationalist interpretation of events. Michel Thooris, general secretary of the union, claimed that France was seeing a civil war unfolding in her suburbs: 'there is a civil war under way in Clichy-sous-Bois at the moment'.[106] These declarations all form part of an established trend evoking the menace of the *quartiers sensibles*, the threat of these areas to the prospect of a cohesive French society, and asserting the need for repressive police action against the 'army' of delinquents who threaten social order.

The events of Villiers-le-Bel provoked a renewal of this interpretation of the suburban violence as nothing more than the work of delinquents. Once again, this interpretation emanated from the top of the French political hierarchy, with President Sarkozy denouncing the 'voyoucratie' of the *banlieues* in a statement to the press on 28 November 2007. Sarkozy adopted a hard-line approach, similar to 2005, that was extremely critical of interpretations evoking the social problems at stake in the suburbs. Sarkozy explicitly stated that 'ce qui se passe à Villiers-le-Bel n'a rien à voir

104 'Violences: Sarkozy annonce une prime pour les forces de l'ordre', *Alliance Police Nationale* (17 November 2005) <www.alliance-police-nationale.fr> accessed 12 June 2006.

105 '"Il faut reconquérir les quartiers par le dialogue"', *Libération* (21 October 2006).

106 'Fires of "civil war" erupt in Paris', *The Guardian* (30 October 2005). Note: *Action Police* are no longer affiliated with the *Confédération Française des Travailleurs Chrétiens*. On 24 February 2007, *Libération* reported the decision made by the CFTC to withdraw their mandate from *Action Police*. The decision was made on the grounds that the behaviour of *Action Police* 'was not acceptable in terms of union independence'. The decision was believed to reflect disapproval at the links between *Action Police* and the political party of Philippe de Villiers, Mouvement pour la France. See 'Le syndicat Action Police quitte la CFTC', *Libération* (24 February 2007).

avec une crise sociale, ça a tout à voir avec la voyoucratie'.[107] Furthermore, the president went on to claim: 'Je réfute toute forme d'angélisme qui vise à trouver en chaque délinquant une victime de la société, en chaque émeute un problème social'.[108] He dismissed what he termed the 'donneurs de leçons' who 'ignorent eux ce que c'est d'être en uniforme et face à une bande d'enragés'.[109] Sarkozy's remarks represented a continuation of the security-oriented discourse that characterized the official response to the 2005 riots, and the president's interpretation was supported by a number of his ministers. The Minister of the Interior, for example, acting on the recommendation of Sarkozy, called on residents of the *banlieues* to isolate the delinquents involved in the violence.[110] In this way, Michèle Alliot-Marie reinforced the reductive interpretation put forward by Sarkozy, further legitimising the repressive response of which Sarkozy is a firm advocate. Those involved in the riots were positioned as a population apart, as delinquents refusing to remain within the parameters of mainstream society. Fadela Amara, the State Secretary responsible for the *politique de la Ville*, said in an interview with *Le Parisien*:

> Ce qui s'est passé, ce n'est pas une crise sociale. On est dans la violence urbaine, anarchique, portée par une minorité qui jette l'opprobre sur la majorité. Cette minorité, ce petit noyau dur, utilise le moindre prétexte pour casser, brûler, tout péter dans le quartier.[111]

Thus the political sphere subscribed to a security-oriented interpretation that failed to look beyond the immediate acts of violence and destruction carried out by local youths. This viewpoint also found resonance among police officers. Two days after the tragedy that sparked the violence, *Alliance*

107   'Villiers-le-Bel: Sarkozy dénonce une "voyoucratie"', *Libération* (28 November 2007).
108   Ibid.
109   Ibid.
110   'Emeutes urbaines: Sarkozy monte en premier ligne', *Le Figaro* (27 November 2007).
111   'Fadela Amara: "Le respect de la police, c'est très important"', *Le Parisien* (29 November 2007).

Police National issued a statement in which they offered their condolences to the families of the dead teenagers but said that it was 'unacceptable for a gang of delinquents to use this tragedy as an excuse to set the town on fire.'[112] *Synergie*, the second largest union of police officers, demanded 'la plus grande sévérité contre ces casseurs et ces criminels s'attaquant aux policiers.'[113] Olivier Damien, representative of yet another police union, the *Syndicat des commissaires*, said 'ce 'n'est plus l'expression d'un malaise, c'est du banditisme. On a à faire à des bandes qui n'attendent qu'un prétexte pour en découdre. La vérité sur ce tragique accident, ils s'en fichent.'[114] In all of these cases, the comments published rejected any link between the violent events and the social, economic and cultural problems facing the *quartiers sensibles*. The riots were primarily viewed as an excuse for delinquents to engage in acts of large-scale destruction. Once again, this discourse implied the need for increased repressive action in order to deal with the threat posed by gangs of delinquents to social order and unity.

However, the supposition that is implicit in this discourse – that of the existence of a core of hardened delinquents, directing their destructive tendencies at French society and the Republic at large – was called into question as the facts surrounding these episodes of violence emerged. In relation to the 2005 violence, for example, as time elapsed, allowing the events to be studied with a greater degree of critical objectivity, it emerged that the facts behind the events did not support this rhetoric. In fact, the opposite was true. A study undertaken by sociologists Stéphane Beaud and Michel Pialoux revealed that, contrary to Sarkozy's claim that 80 per cent of the young people brought before the courts were already known to police, the immediate appearances of the 'rioters' before the court at Bobigny showed that the majority had no prior history and thus could

112 'Dozens of policemen injured', *France 24* (27 November 2007) <http://www.france24.com/france24Public/en/special-reports/20071127-banlieues-riots-france-Villiers-le-Bel/20071126-banlieue-suburbs-violence-riot-villiers-bel-cars-burnt-police-teenagers-8-police-dead.php> accessed 12 November 2008.

113 'Un cap franchi dans la violence', *Le Figaro* (27 November 2007).

114 'Des émeutiers ultraviolents', *Le Parisien* (28 November 2007).

not be classed as delinquents.[115] Furthermore, in the case of those minors brought before the Bobigny children's court for their actions during the violence, Judge Jean-Pierre Rosenczveig revealed that, out of ninety-five minors brought before the court, only seventeen were already known to police.[116] These revelations call into question the rhetoric of insecurity that dominates popular discourse regarding the suburbs. For Beaud and Pialoux, this reductive discourse regarding urban violence effectively imposes a simplistic, binary view of the situation in the *quartiers sensibles* that fails to acknowledge the underlying social issues at stake:

> Ce discours sécuritaire [...] se nourrit d'une étiologie sommaire du phénomène de violence qui repose, au fond, sur une dichotomie rassurante: il y aurait, d'un côté, un noyau de 'violents', d'"irréductibles', de 'sauvages', dont on n'ose pas dire qu'ils sont irrécupérables et non rééducables (ce que pensent pourtant nombre de responsables), et de l'autre, les jeunes 'non violents', qui se laisseraient entraîner et qu'il conviendrait de protéger contre la contamination des premiers.[117]

It is worth noting that this situation was repeated in Villiers-le-Bel where, in spite of Sarkozy's criticism of the 'voyoucratie' in place in the area, it was revealed that of the first youths to be brought before the courts in Pontoise, only one already had a criminal record (the offence in question being a suspended driving license).[118] Moreover, as more information emerged following the end of the large-scale violence in 2005 and the return of 'normality' in the *banlieues*, the rhetoric of insecurity was again challenged by further evidence uncovered in a confidential report authored by the *Renseignements Généraux* (*RG*) dating from 23 November 2005.[119] This report, uncovered by the French daily newspaper *Le Parisien*, and published on 7 December

---

115   Stéphane Beaud and Michel Pialoux, 'La "racaille" et les "vrais jeunes": critique d'une vision binaire du monde des cités', in Clémentine Autin, Stéphane Beaud et al., eds, *Banlieue, lendemains de révolte* (Paris: La Dispute, 2006), 17–28 (19).
116   Ibid., 20.
117   Ibid., 18.
118   'Villiers-le-Bel: les premiers émeutiers condamnés sévèrement en comparution immédiate', *Le Monde* (29 November 2007).
119   The RG form the intelligence arm of the French national police.

2005, explicitly stated that the violence had not been organized or directed by criminal gangs or Islamist groups.[120] This statement undermined and contradicted the claims of a number of political figures that the riots were the result of the destructive trajectory of criminal gangs. This evidence was particularly damaging in relation to the public statements made by the then Minister of the Interior, given the significant role played by the RG in providing the Ministry of the Interior with information and statistics relating to the development of urban violence in cities.

The Threat of Communitarianism: Ethnocultural Fragmentation

Certainly, the interpretation that reduced the riots to the work of delinquents and thugs was not the only one to be voiced by social commentators. Another interpretation that was aired in the wake of the riots was ethnic-oriented, with advocates viewing urban violence in terms of communitarianism and a fragmentation of the Republic along ethnocultural lines. This viewpoint is closely linked to the aforementioned interpretation of the violence as the work of delinquents and thugs and is also to be found within the general critique that views the *banlieues* as a threat to mainstream French society. Since the 1960s and the development of the enormous HLM apartment blocks that dominate the skyline in many of the *quartiers sensibles*, the suburbs have always been home to large populations of immigrant origins, many of whom have roots in the Maghreb countries of northern Africa and subscribe to the Muslim faith. According to a report compiled by the National Institute for Statistics and Economic Studies in France following the 1999 French census, almost a quarter of the population of the 'sensitive urban areas' in the Ile-de France area is comprised of immigrants, with over a third of all immigrants in this area linked to coun-

---

120 'Selon les RG, les émeutes en banlieue n'étaient pas le fait de bandes organisées', *Le Monde* (7 December 2005).

tries where the predominant religion is Islam.[121] However, this statistic is reductive as it excludes those inhabitants of immigrant origins who have acquired French citizenship. More generally, research has shown that the French Muslim population is among the largest in Europe.[122] It is important to note that, in spite of this, no precise statistics exist in relation to ethnic origins due to the assimilationist nature of French social policy.

Following the events of 2005, Alain Finkielkraut proved to be one of the main proponents of the communitarian-oriented interpretation, publicising his opinions during a controversial interview with *Haaretz* on 18 November 2005. In the course of this interview, Finkielkraut clearly evoked an ethnocultural fragmentation of the Republic:

> In France, they would like very much to reduce these riots to their social dimension, to see them as a revolt of youths from the suburbs against their situation. The problem is that most of these youths are blacks or Arabs, with a Muslim identity [...] it is clear that this is a revolt with an ethno-religious character.[123]

The philosopher spoke of the 'anti-Republican pogrom' that has developed in the *quartiers sensibles* and the 'hate' that has grown against the Republic, a hate that stems from cultural and religious issues: '[the riots] are directed against France as a former colonial power, against France as a European country, against France, with its Christian or Judeo-Christian tradition'.[124] Finkielkraut made an analogy between the French Republic and Europe, both under attack from parts of the Muslim-Arab world, thereby explicitly linking the Muslim population of the suburbs to the menacing image of the *banlieusards* physically manifesting a religiously motivated hate for the Republic. Following the publication of this interview in *Haaretz*, Finkielkraut was widely criticized, all the more so given his former position as a leading voice for the political left; he subsequently published an apology in *Le Monde* on 27 November 2005. However, the ethnic-oriented

---

121 Source: *INSEE – Service Etudes et Diffusion.* <http://www.insee.fr/fr/insee_regions/idf/rfc/analyse.asp?theme=2&nbdoc=91&first=41> accessed 25 June 2006.

122 'Muslims in Europe: country guide', *BBC News* (23 December 2005).

123 'What sort of Frenchmen are they?', *Haaretz* (18 November 2005).

124 Ibid.

interpretation initially voiced by Finkielkraut found support in certain academic circles where it was claimed that in attempting to explain the violence of 2005, it was not enough to evoke 'les difficultés de la vie sociale et économique', difficulties that 'sont vécues par la plus grande partie de la population française' on a daily basis.[125]

Robert Redeker constitutes another academic commentator subscribing to the interpretation of the riots as a fragmentation of the Republic along ethnic and cultural lines. In his analysis of the events of 2005, Redeker rejects any interpretation of the violence in social terms, presenting instead a viewpoint that denounces what he terms the 'nihilist' violence of the suburbs, a violence that is rooted in 'une haine de la France' and cultural issues stemming directly from immigration.[126] From the outset, Redeker forges a definitive link between immigration, more specifically the refusal of immigrants to integrate into French society, and the malaise of the *quartiers sensibles*. He lists a number of events that he views as indicative of the violence that was to erupt in 2005, most notably mentioning a France-Algeria football match that took place in 2001 where, according to Redeker, youths from the suburbs waved the Algerian flag, chanted 'Ben Laden, Ben Laden, Ben Laden...' and hurled missiles at the ministers of the Republic.[127] Through this example, Redeker immediately imposes an identity on those involved in the riots of 2005, not as French citizens but as immigrants, and indeed potential fundamentalists, firmly rooted in the culture of their origins, and expressing a refusal to integrate into their host society. Throughout his analysis Redeker reinforces this identity as he specifically categorises the malaise of the *quartiers sensibles* as the malaise of a certain portion of the population of these areas, namely individuals of African origins. Moreover, Redeker directly evokes the threat of Islam

125 Raphaël Draï and Jean Francois Mattéi, 'Préface', in Raphaël Draï and Jean Francois Mattéi, eds, *La République brûle-t-elle? Essai sur les violences urbaines françaises* (Paris: Editions Michalon, 2006), 17–23 (17).

126 Robert Redeker, 'Le nihilisme et l'assourdissant silence des émeutes banlieusardes', in Raphaël Draï and Jean Francois Mattéi, eds, *La République brûle-t-elle? Essai sur les violences urbaines françaises* (Paris: Editions Michalon, 2006), 27–36 (27).

127 Ibid.

in the suburbs, propagating what Henri Rey terms 'la peur de l'autre', as he
states that the violence of 2005 was based on 'le modèle de l'islamisme –
s'attaque aux proches, à leurs personnes, et à leurs biens, de même qu'elle
détruit les infrastructures destinées à faciliter la vie commune'.[128]

During the course of his analysis, Redeker attempts to speak directly
to the youths involved in the riots; he calls upon the 'l'enfant étranger et
pauvre' to integrate into French society, to absorb French culture and cher-
ish it as their own. He claims that these 'immigrés' have 'rien à exiger mais
tout à mériter: quand on dîne à la table d'autrui, on remercie'.[129] Redeker
essentially chastises the inhabitants of the suburbs for asking anything of
the society that has taken them in, for withdrawing from the Republic and
its universal values. Thus, for Redeker, the solution to the problems posed
by the suburbs to mainstream French society is not to be found in the social
dimension: he views the social response of increased aid for the suburbs as
'la rassurante illusion des élites intellectuelles et politiques de notre pays. Le
discours du "plus" pour les banlieues est l'opium des décideurs et commen-
tateurs du temps présent'.[130] The author firmly believes that development
in the suburbs requires an urgent reorientation of the cultural policy at
play in the suburbs. For Redeker, 'ce n'est pas la pauvreté, c'est-à-dire une
situation sociale, qui engendre la violence anomique et insensée, c'est le
nihilisme, c'est-à-dire une construction culturelle'.[131]

Once again however, the facts of the violence told a different story.
Throughout the course of the 2005 riots a significant Muslim presence on
the streets was recorded by journalists. Yet journalists also documented that
the majority of these inhabitants actively engaged in discouraging the violence, in some cases even attempting to form barriers between youths and
police.[132] Moreover, the *Union of Islamic Organisations of France* (UOIF)
issued a *fatwa* during the violence forbidding Muslims from taking part

128   Ibid., 30. See also Henri Rey, *La peur des banlieues* (Paris: Presses de Sciences Po,
      1996).
129   Ibid., 33.
130   Ibid., 28.
131   Ibid., 36.
132   'Clichy-sous-Bois cristallise les tensions politiques et sociales', *Le Monde* (2 November
      2005).

in the violence, while other local Muslim organizations organized night patrols in an attempt to calm those involved in the violence.[133] Further evidence to contradict this cultural or ethno-religious interpretation of the riots was also revealed with the publication of the aforementioned confidential report by the RG, published in *Le Parisien*. The report stated that Muslim fundamentalists had 'aucun rôle dans le déclenchement des violences et dans leur expansion.'[134] Indeed, the RG confirmed that this group had every interest in a rapid return to calm in order to avoid damaging comparisons.

Urban Violence as the Reflection of a Social Crisis

At the other end of the spectrum, certain commentators placed emphasis not on the perceived cultural or ethnic element underlying the violence, but rather focused solely on the social issues in question. This interpretation involves viewing the riots of 2005, and indeed urban violence in more general terms, as a direct result of the social processes in operation in these areas. Unlike the ethno-religious viewpoint, which prioritizes a rejection of French society by groups of certain ethnic origins, this analysis draws on a number of tangible social problems with which the *quartiers sensibles* are faced. This social interpretation of urban violence is at the centre of the work of researchers such as Beaud and Pialoux, who laid the groundwork for this interpretation in their 2003 text *Violences urbaines, violences sociale: Genèse des nouvelles classes dangereuses*. In this work, they claimed that the '"émeute urbaine" selon l'expression consacrée, peut être comprise, dans un premier temps, comme le révélateur d'une lente dégradation des relations sociales dans la ZUP [Zones à urbaniser en priorité]'.[135] Essentially, Beaud and Pialoux see instances of urban riots as a symptom of the 'déstructuration et de décomposition du groupe ouvrier – groupe qui structurait et

---

133 'An underclass rebellion', *The Economist* (10 November 2005).
134 'Selon les RG, les émeutes en banlieue n'étaient pas le fait de bandes organisées', *Le Monde* (7 December 2005).
135 Beaud and Pialoux, *Violences urbaines, violences sociale*, 10.

agrégeait autour de lui [...] les autres fractions des classes populaires'.[136] This destructuring of the working class is, according to Beaud and Pialoux, the culmination of a number of social processes at work among the 'classes populaires':

> [U]n ensemble de phénomènes de durée et d'importance variables, situés dans des sphères différentes de la vie sociale, qui affectent en priorité depuis vingt ans les classes populaires: chômage de masse et précarité, affaiblissement des mécanismes de défense collective au travail, effondrement d'une représentation politique proprement ouvrière, déstabilisation des familles populaires, constitution de lieux de relégation spatiale.[137]

In other words, the riots in French suburbs must be understood in the context of the long-term social processes that have impacted upon the social situation of inhabitants of the *banlieues*, with the actions of the rioters reflecting the underlying social mechanisms at play. Beaud and Pialoux reaffirmed this interpretation in their analysis of the 2005 riots, emphasizing the impact of structural phenomena such as unemployment, increased urban segregation, discrimination in terms of employment, and the destructuring of working class families inhabiting the HLM apartment blocks.[138] Regarding the widespread nature of the 2005 events, the authors proposed an interpretation based on 'social despair'. According to Beaud and Pialoux, this social despair 'autrefois réservé aux membres les plus dominés du groupe [...] semble bien avoir gagné d'autres fractions du groupe des jeunes de cité – les jeunes ouvriers et les "bacheliers" – qui en étaient jusqu'alors un peu mieux protégées'.[139]

As one would expect, Beaud and Pialoux were not alone in proposing a social interpretation of the violence. Sociologist Laurent Bonelli adopted a similar approach in an article published in *Le Monde Diplomatique* one month after the 2005 riots. In his assessment of events, Bonelli stated that 'cette crise des milieux populaires est [...] profondément sociale'.[140] The

---

136 Ibid., 16.
137 Ibid.
138 Stéphane Beaud and Michel Pialoux, 'La "racaille" et les "vrais jeunes"', 18.
139 Ibid., 23.
140 Laurent Bonelli, 'Révolte des banlieues: Les raisons d'une colère', *Le Monde diplomatique* (December 2005).

sociologist emphasized the role played by the destructuring of the working classes during the post-industrial period in the emergence of urban
violence, and, more specifically the events of 2005:

> En toile de fond de ces violences figure d'abord une crise de reproduction des milieux
> populaires, qu'ont affectés en profondeur les conséquences de la crise économique
> amorcée dans la seconde moitié des années 1970 et les transformations induites par le
> passage à un modèle postfordiste de production. Automatisation, informatisation et
> délocalisations ont généré un chômage de masse, qui s'est conjugué avec la généralisa-
> tion du recours aux intérimaires et aux emplois temporaires. Ces deux facteurs ont
> accru la précarisation des conditions des milieux populaires.[141]

For Bonelli, large-scale urban violence in the suburbs is a reflection of the
underlying and enduring social processes at play in these areas with regard
to employment, urban development, education and social policy, to name
but a few. Additionally, Bonelli claims that this phenomenon particularly
affects the young people of the *banlieues*. Consequently, he concludes that
the riots of 2005 should not have caused surprise. The question, rather, is
why the *banlieues* did not explode sooner.

An Alternative Interpretation

Fighting to be Heard: Inaudible Interpretations

As previously mentioned, the riots that erupted in French suburbs in 2005,
as well as the aftershock that occurred in Villiers-le-Bel in 2007, represented
the product of a complex socio-cultural situation. These events resulted
from the combination of a wide range of social, economic and cultural
factors, all playing a part in the construction of the *quartiers sensibles* as a
setting for the production of large-scale urban violence. Given the range
of elements which have an impact on the development and progression
of events, and the fact that the riots themselves had no clear leaders or

---

141 Ibid.

organizational structure, the riots 'laissent libre cours aux interprétations les plus opposées, interprétations le plus souvent surchargées de considérations politiques et idéologiques'.[142] In other words, 'chacun y voit une confirmation par l'événement de ce qu'il "sait" déjà ou de ce qu'il "pensait"'.[143]

The communitarian-oriented interpretation that revolves around an ethno-cultural fragmentation of French society reduces the situation in the *quartiers sensibles* to its ethnic dimension, focusing on what Dubois terms the 'real or supposed origins' of the inhabitants of the suburbs.[144] However, the cultural reality of the *banlieues* reveals a fundamental flaw in this interpretation. The immigrant population of the suburbs has reached its third, and in some cases fourth, generation. Issues of national identity and cultural belonging have evolved with the birth of new generations, and questions of identity are no longer the same ones faced by the immigrant population of a decade ago. This is a central issue that will be examined in more detail in the next chapter. Citing immigrant origins and a strong adherence to those origins provides commentators with a relatively uncomplicated means of attributing blame for urban violence and destruction. This viewpoint does not reflect the truth of the situation however. The majority of youths in the suburbs are French nationals, born and raised in France, with little or no connection to the past of their ancestors. They are French, especially in their own eyes, even if they are labelled otherwise by certain commentators. The problems they face on a daily basis are the product of social, cultural and economic issues, among others; ethno-religious communitarianism is not the source of the *malaise des banlieues*. This reductive perception of the situation in the suburbs means that advocates of the communitarian-oriented interpretation fail to acknowledge the impact of the social and economic issues that weigh heavily in these areas.

If the ethno-religious interpretation fails to provide an adequate explanation for the riots, so too does the interpretation of the violence as the reflection of a purely social crisis. Nevertheless, while the ethno-religious

---

142   Didier Lapeyronnie, 'Révolte primitive dans les banlieues françaises. Essai sur les émeutes de l'automne 2005', in *Déviance et Société*, 30 (2006), 431–448 (432).

143   Ibid., 434.

144   Jean-Pierre Dubois, 'Violences et politiques', in Clémentine Autin, Stéphane Beaud et al., eds, *Banlieue, lendemains de révolte* (Paris: La Dispute, 2006), 69–79 (73).

interpretation is rendered inadequate due to a number of significant factual inaccuracies, the social interpretation touches on fundamental issues that are at the heart of the *malaise des banlieues*: unemployment and education being two of the most important. These elements undoubtedly play a major role in the social construction of the *quartiers sensibles*. The problem here is that this point of view is limited; the social interpretation fails to give adequate consideration to those other elements having an equally important impact on the production of violence in the suburbs. Kokoreff states that '[l'émeute] ne résulte pas seulement de phénomènes structurels qui en détermineraient les conditions de possibilité parce que trop extérieurs aux diverses situations observées: affrontements avec la police [...], pillages, dégradations et destructions de biens matériels ou d'équipements collectifs'.[145] In other words, the social interpretation alone does not fully explain the violence in French suburbs. For her part Andrea Rea claims that it is necessary to highlight 'le réductionnisme de l'interprétation sociale des émeutes. Comme le soulignait Robert Kerner, les émeutiers comptent également des jeunes disposant de ressources, des jeunes diplômés'.[146] Thus, to fully understand the reasons for the riots of 2005 and the aftershock of 2007, the macro-scale in its entirety must be considered, that is to say, all the elements having an influence on the situation in the *banlieues*. A comprehensive analysis of the violent events of 2005 and 2007 requires that the questions of race and ethnicity, among others, and the impact of these issues on life in the suburbs, be considered. The political dimension to the riots is another issue that must be taken into account when attempting to deconstruct these instances of suburban violence; while many would reduce the riots to nihilistic violence, Didier Lapeyronnie claims that 'Sans faire des émeutiers les porteurs d'un movement social, il est [...] nécessaire de [...] lire d'abord l'émeute comme une forme d'action collective et politique'.[147]

---

145   Michel Kokoreff, 'Sociologie de l'émeute. Les dimensions de l'action en question', in *Déviance et Société*, 30 (2006), 521–533 (523).

146   Andrea Rea, 'Les émeutes urbaines: Causes institutionnelles et absence de reconnaissance', in *Déviance et Société*, 30 (2006), 463–475 (465).

147   Lapeyronnie, 'Révolte primitive dans les banlieues françaises', 432.

Essentially, a significant proportion of the interpretative wave that emerged both during and after the violence of 2005 and 2007 represented selective and often conflicting viewpoints. Commentators attempted to interpret events in the context of different analytical frameworks, 'l'émeute apparaissant comme une sorte de film muet dont il incomberait aux observateurs et chercheurs d'en écrire la bande-son'.[148] There was a rush to propose interpretations and analyses which were often conflicting. This phenomenon had two important consequences. First, the production of so many differing interpretations in the public sphere provoked conflict and confusion in terms of credibility, resulting in a paradoxical situation. With proponents of different interpretations fighting to be heard and to establish their analysis in the public sphere, these viewpoints were effectively rendered inaudible. The security-oriented interpretation, benefiting from the support of leading figures in the French political landscape as well as officials and 'experts' from the security world, imposed itself as the dominant interpretation.[149] All other interpretations were lost under the weight of this reading of the violence and became marginalized in the public sphere. Thus, the security-oriented interpretation was reinforced even as other viewpoints were sidelined. Second, the proliferation of interpretive voices had a determining impact on the underlying message of the riots. Essentially, the message of those involved was submerged amid the many partial and conflicting analyses of the riots: 'Autant de "lectures" interdisant de faire entendre les émeutiers, voire refusant de les entendre'.[150]

Reason Amid the Chaos: The Underlying Message of the Violence

In an analysis of the 2005 violence published in *Le Monde Diplomatique*, Dominique Vidal draws attention to the fundamental paradox that surrounds the question of the 'quartiers sensibles' and their integration into

---

148   Kokoreff, 'Sociologie de l'émeute. Les dimensions de l'action en question', 523.
149   This issue will be further discussed in Chapter 3.
150   Lapeyronnie, 'Révolte primitive dans les banlieues françaises', 432.

mainstream society. Vidal claims the term 'integration', which, since the 1980s, has replaced that of 'assimilation' in popular discourse, is misleading:

> Il séduit [...] il semble admettre le respect de la culture, des traditions, de la langue et de la religion [...] Mais, à l'usage, il s'avère piégé. Dès lors que l'intégration ne fonctionne pas, c'est en effet vers les jeunes des banlieues que se pointe un doigt accusateur, comme pour leur demander: *'Pourquoi ne faites-vous pas l'effort de vous intégrer?'* Au lieu de se tourner vers une société incapable d'assurer l'égalité des droits et des chances à tous ses enfants, quelles que soient leur origine, la couleur de leur peau, la consonance de leurs prénom et nom.[151]

In this statement, Vidal succeeds in articulating one of the fundamental concerns in the debate on the *quartiers sensibles*. The violence of 2005 constituted a rupture in the fragile social equilibrium that holds sway in the *banlieues*, balancing the discrimination and marginalization suffered by the inhabitants of these areas on a daily basis with their growing anger and frustration at the injustices imposed upon them. The riots thus expressed the profound dissatisfaction that prevails among *banlieusards*, especially the young, in relation to their current socio-cultural situation. Inhabitants of the suburbs are ordered to integrate into a society that does not treat them as equals, a society that does not afford them the same opportunities as others. The lack of educational support, the lack of social services, the lack of facilities, and widespread discrimination in terms of employment are all issues that have resulted in a spiral of despair – for the young people of the suburbs, despair and hopelessness overshadow many dreams of upward social mobility. This despair is compounded by a loss of faith in the justice system as a result of continued police discrimination. In the *banlieues*, the deterioration of relations between the police and the public over a prolonged period has resulted in a relationship characterized by conflict and tension. The police are viewed as enemies, representative of a justice system that appears corrupt to the inhabitants of these areas, rather than a positive social element. Since 2002, the situation in these areas has further deteriorated, with reductions in government funding for develop-

---

151　Dominique Vidal, 'Casser l'apartheid à la française', *Le Monde Diplomatique* (December 2005).

ment projects in the suburbs. Beaud and Pialoux highlight the example of the *emplois-jeunes*, the government initiative aimed at creating jobs for unemployed youths. These jobs played an important part in the positive development of the *quartiers sensibles*, offering many youths a valuable opportunity, allowing them to 'regain confidence in themselves, giving them status, an income, and the chance to establish themselves and dream of a better future'.[152] Inhabitants of these areas feel isolated, physically and metaphorically, from a state that is failing to address the problems of the suburbs, from the Republic whose values and ideals do not appear to extend to these areas. These arguments are supported by a number of facts that emerged as the riots continued.

Throughout the violence, an extremely low level of civilian casualties at the hands of the rioters was sharply contrasted to the large number of attacks on of cars and buildings – this fact alone gives a significant insight into the motivations behind the riots. The widespread destruction of cars represented what Alec Hargreaves terms as an attack on the symbols of a 'social mobility and modes of consumption from which the rioters know they are excluded through structural inequalities and discriminatory practices'.[153] Attacks on buildings were centred on state-owned buildings such as schools and police stations, symbolic of a selective education system and a justice system that appears discriminatory to the inhabitants of the suburbs.[154] In this respect Kokoreff claims that:

> Rester dans sa cité pour mettre le feu à des véhicules, s'en prendre à des établissements scolaires ou à des équipements culturels témoigne bien d'une expérience de la relégation et de l'injustice qui ne semble dicible que du lieu ou elle prend corps.[155]

---

152   Stéphane Beaud and Michel Pialoux, 'La "racaille" et les "vrais jeunes"', 23.

153   Alec Hargreaves, 'La révolte des banlieues à travers les livres', *Le Monde Diplomatique* (November 2006).

154   During the riots Christian Demuynck, the UMP Senator of Seine-Saint-Denis, claimed that the national education system was at the heart of the problem in the *quartiers sensibles*. He stated that 'Trop de jeunes sortent du système sans diplôme ou sont orientés vers des filières qui ne mènent à rien'. Cited in 'Pourquoi un tel fiasco de la politique de la ville?', *Le Monde* (11 November 2005).

155   Kokoreff, 'Sociologie de l'émeute. Les dimensions de l'action en question', 528.

In addition, as the violence developed and progressed, the material destruction was eclipsed by the continued clashes between rioters and police, the intensity of the confrontations an indication of the extreme tension that exists between these two groups 'n'ayant aucun dialogue, aucune capacité de négotiation, de régulation, de médiation'.[156] Finally, the sheer magnitude of the events proved that the violence was linked to a profound and wide-ranging discontent, much greater than the destructive intentions of any one community, whatever its motivation. Following the initial outbreak of the unrest in Paris, similar instances of violence erupted in suburban areas across the entire nation.

Beyond the Violence: A Plea for Integration?
An Alternative View of Urban Violence

Following the riots there was widespread criticism of the Republican model and its failure in relation to the integration of the *quartiers sensibles*. However, closer examination of the situation in the suburbs reveals that it is not necessarily the nature of the Republican model that is in question here, but rather the application of this model that poses a challenge to the integration of the suburbs. At present, it appears that French society is witnessing a selective application of the values and ideals upon which the Republic is built. The suburbs exemplify this, representing the blind spot of the Republic, a social space in which all of the challenges that face contemporary French society – immigration, discrimination (both racial and other), unemployment, education and justice, to name but a few – are concentrated. The RG report published in *Le Parisien* on 7 December 2005 revealed that young people living in the suburbs feel oppressed by their poverty, their skin colour and their names. The report went on to claim that the young people of these areas are marked by 'l'absence de perspectives

---

156 Laurent Mucchielli, 'Il faut changer la façon de "faire la police" dans les "quartiers sensibles"', in Clémentine Autin, Stéphane Beaud, et al., eds, *Banlieue, lendemains de révolte* (Paris: La Dispute, 2006), 93–105 (93).

dans la société française', evoking 'une perte de confiance totale envers la République'.[157] The youth of the suburbs are asked to integrate into a society that refuses them access, and to adhere to ideals and values that do not appear to apply to them. Azouz Begag emphasized this point during the riots, claiming that 'les jeunes détruisent un espace public auquel ils n'ont pas le sentiment d'appartenir'.[158] This paradox of integration that dominates life in the suburbs was confirmed in the speech made by Jacques Chirac on 14 November 2005, following his prolonged silence as violence enveloped suburban areas across the country. In his statement, the then president claimed that 'nous devons tous être fiers d'appartenir [à la communauté française]'. Chirac spoke directly to the youth of the suburbs: 'Je veux dire aux enfants des quartiers difficiles, quelles que soient leurs origines, qu'ils sont tous les filles et les fils de la République'.[159] Yet how can the youth of the suburbs feel proud to be part of a community that excludes them and denies them access?

While the youth of the suburbs are indeed French, especially in terms of their own perception of their individual identity, they are not afforded the same chances as their peers from more affluent areas. Chirac's statement effectively highlighted the disparities that exist in terms of words and actions on the part of those in power, in terms of the application of abstract Republican ideals and values to all parts of a continuously evolving social and cultural reality. Thus, while the former President succeeded in publicly reaffirming the values and ideals of the Republic, his appeal could not reach the rioters directly, positioned as they are at the limits of the national community, officially linked through nationality but socially excluded. A gap has developed between the ideals and values of the Republic and the reality of contemporary French society, a gap related to the failure on the part of those in power to ensure the application of the values of the Republic to all parts of society. In an analysis of the riots published in *Le*

---

157 'Selon les RG, les émeutes en banlieue n'étaient pas le fait de bandes organisées', *Le Monde* (7 December 2005).

158 'Les déchirements du ministre Azouz Begag', *Le Monde* (8 November 2005).

159 'Jacques Chirac défend le modèle d'intégration à la française', *Le Monde* (14 November 2005).

Monde Diplomatique in August 2006, Denis Duclos highlighted one of the fundamental causes of the violence:

> La cause fondamentale [...] tient presque tout entière dans l' 'irrespect', ou la 'non-reconnaissance' de la personne, et notamment du jeune, comme sujet culturel et politique, et cela du fait presque exclusif des représentants de la République elle-même.[160]

In this context, the violence could be viewed as a plea for integration on the part of those who inhabit the suburbs, a plea for access to the same values and ideals that are available to other parts of society. This idea can be summed up through the words of Mokrane Hamadouche, a twenty-one-year-old resident of the *banlieues*, who asked: 'Je suis né ici, je parle français, je consomme français. Qu'est-ce que je dois faire de plus?'.[161] Mokrane believes that he does not need to integrate into society for, in his eyes, he is 'autant français que Sarkozy'.[162] This young man, along with other youths in similar situations, experiences a profound frustration when he is asked to integrate into French society, when he is denounced as 'inassimilable'. Essentially, this attitude stems from the fundamental paradox that permeates the question of the suburbs. The previously mentioned separation of the violence from its underlying causes due to intense media coverage of the riots – the isolation of the spectacle of the violence in the media, and consequently the public sphere – has helped foster the belief that the inhabitants of the suburbs were rejecting the Republic and all of its values. However, perhaps the opposite is true. While the events of 2005 did not constitute a social movement (due to the lack of leadership and coherent manifestos or demands, among other things), the violence that enveloped the nation did indeed represent a revolt by the youth of the *banlieues* against their socio-cultural situation. Angry and frustrated at their treatment by a society of which they are a part, could the spreading of violence have symbolized a widespread and spontaneous denunciation

---

160   'Retour sur la grande révolte des banlieues françaises', *Le Monde Diplomatique* (August 2006).
161   'Les as de la banlieue', *Le Monde* (25 December 2005).
162   Ibid.

by suburban communities across the nation of this selective social climate that has fostered a divided French society? Throughout the violence there were no formal calls for the end of the Republic, for this is not the desire of those involved in the riots. It would appear that the youth of the suburbs were simply asking to be recognized for what they are: citizens of France, and to be incorporated into mainstream French society.

Republicanism, Citizenship and Integration

The different interpretations of the 2005 violence reflect the diverse and opposing opinions that have been expressed in popular and intellectual discourse regarding the *quartiers sensibles* and their inhabitants. However, having deconstructed these readings of the riots, it is necessary to extend the analysis beyond the immediate causes and events of the violence and move the focus to the fundamental issues underlying both the events and the resultant interpretations. Consequently, to gain a comprehensive insight into the socio-cultural situation in the *banlieues* at the time of the riots, it is necessary to move away from the present and look to the past to explore the complex notion of French republicanism and, more specifically, the relationship between the Republic and the suburbs in terms of the integration of these areas and their inhabitants into mainstream society. This will provide an understanding of the development of these areas in recent years in social and cultural terms, and the accumulation of frustration and anger that facilitated the scale and intensity of the 2005 violence. The republican model has provided a framework for the development and progression of French society as a whole since the revolutionary period around 1789. As a result, an investigation into the origins and evolution of the Republic and its supporting ideology will provide the historical, political and social context within which the French model of integration, and the dynamic between this model and the particular socio-cultural construction presented by the *quartiers sensibles*, can be situated. This line of inquiry leads the researcher into an intricate web of social, political and identity issues that links questions of citizenship, national identity and integration with the historical development of the Republic and its accompanying narrative.

Throughout history, the ideological concept of the Republic has evolved as a philosophical and political entity beyond the power or reach of any one regime or government. The Republic and its supporting ideology are symbolic of a utopian vision of French society where the ideals of liberty, equality and fraternity form the cornerstones of what is perceived in France as a universally applicable social system. However, this does not mean that the interpretation and application of this vision have always been flawless. The continuing degradation of the social situation in the suburbs, for example, has highlighted in recent times the gap between the theory of the republican model and its practical application. Accordingly, questions have been raised in relation to the enduring relevance of French Republicanism. Can the abstract ideals of French republicanism be reconciled with the challenges of a rapidly evolving social and cultural reality at the beginning of the twenty-first century? Or has the proclaimed universal nature of the republican model become obsolete with the passage of time, if indeed this universal element ever existed in practice at all? These questions, which affect all aspects of French society, are especially relevant in the *banlieues*, areas which are proving to be a testing-ground for the Republic of the future, given their position as urban spaces in which many of the challenges facing contemporary French society are concentrated.

In light of these issues, this chapter will examine the nature of French republicanism, exploring this complex notion first in the context of the ideological origins of the republican model, forged during and after the French Revolution, and then in the more specific context of the republican model of integration and its development in the post-World War period.[1] Since the 1970s, particularly, issues relating to immigration and integration have consistently been at the centre of political debate due to the impact, perceived or otherwise, of immigration on traditional ideals and values of national unity and social cohesion. This focus on immigration has aroused great interest in the questions of citizenship and belonging, 'framed, in particular, as the reconciliation of cultural pluralism and political membership'.[2] These questions have been especially relevant in the

---

1   Robert Gildea, *France Since 1945* (Oxford: Oxford University Press, 2002), 132.
2   Adrian Favell, *Philosophies of Integration: Immigration and the Idea of Citizenship in France and Britain* (Basingstoke and New York: Palgrave, 2001), 22.

banlieues, areas mostly populated by immigrant populations stemming from the large-scale immigration that occurred in France during the post-war period of reconstruction, a historical development in which the current socio-cultural situation in the *banlieues* is undoubtedly rooted. The new challenges brought by the massive fluctuation in migratory trends at this time impacted upon republican ideas of citizenship, belonging and national unity and have, since then, continued to challenge the republican model in terms of its ongoing relevance and validity, with issues arising from these questions of immigration and integration inextricably linked to the social problems of the *banlieues* in the popular imagination.

The Republican Tradition

La République Française: A Multifaceted Concept

Before attempting to explore the nature and relevance of the republican model, it is necessary to pose a warning of sorts, that is, to acknowledge the position of this monumental concept as a multifaceted idea that can be interpreted in many different ways. An understanding of the multilayered and complex nature of the Republic, a concept that evokes consensus and opposition in almost equal measure within the citizenry, must precede any study attempting to explore the nature and ideological structure of the republican model, given the perennial and ongoing debate surrounding fundamental questions such as belonging, citizenship and integration, to name but a few. While the ideals and values that have emerged as dominant elements underlying the republican model are those frequently used to exemplify the republican narrative, it is necessary to bear in mind the fact that the evolution of the republican model has been an extended and fiercely contested process. Since its very creation, the French Republic has evoked different and often opposing ideas, thoughts and images for different people, with the differing interpretations often reflecting the

period of history within which they are situated. This plurality of ideological and historical viewpoints can be exemplified through a preliminary and cursory glimpse at the idea of equality, a cornerstone of French
republicanism that is enshrined in the triptych of the nation. In the wake
of the 1789 Revolution and the publication of the *Déclaration des Droits
de l'Homme et du Citoyen*, the idea of equality was contested vigorously
among politicians and social commentators alike, with the debate revolving
around two principal interpretations of this primary motivating principle.
The first interpretation considered equality strictly in civil and judicial
terms, while the second approached the idea of equality as a social and
political concept, and, although each pointed towards a very different
form of governance, both viewpoints constituted valid interpretations
of this founding ideal. Ultimately, the idea of equality was to progress in
terms of the judicial understanding of the word, formally documented and
enshrined in the *Déclaration des Droits de l'Homme et du Citoyen*. However,
'l'ambiguité entre les "deux" égalités est, depuis la grande Révolution, au
coeur de l'histoire française', and the relevance of this debate to contemporary society can be seen in opposing political ideologies of recent years:
'le social allant souvent de pair avec le dirigisme économique' while civil
and judicial equality facilitate arguments for economic liberalism.[3] Thus
it is clear that different meanings and understandings can be gleaned from
various aspects of the Republic and its supporting principles. Consequently,
it is possible for different political authorities and political groups, whose
members share the same ideas and viewpoints, 'to appropriate a specific
heritage, and in doing so to marginalize and even exclude others from it',
achieving this by giving privilege to a particular historical narrative over
competing versions.[4]

In further developing this idea of the Republic as a concept of multiple
layers and faces, it is useful to examine a statement made by Charles Péguy,
where he evokes the memory of a republic and a time 'quand le peuple était

---

3   Denis Sieffert, *Comment peut-on être (vraiment) républicain?* (Paris: La Découverte,
       2006), 15.
4   Sudhir Hazareesingh, *From Subject to Citizen. The Second Empire and the Emergence
       of Modern French Democracy* (Princeton: Princeton University Press, 1998), 3.

grand, quand les républicains étaient héroïques et que la République avait les mains pures.'[5] The image conjured up by Péguy in this statement is that of a new order, pure and untarnished, progressing towards a utopian vision based on liberty and equality. This claim reveals an essential characteristic of the Republic: the universal and perennial issues that it embodies ensure that subjective interpretations of this ideological concept will inevitably be infused with a certain degree of emotion and passion, stemming from and depending on personal history as well as historical, social and political influences and knowledge. In this respect, Denis Sieffert says: 'la République qu'il [Péguy] investit de sa passion n'est pas une construction objective [...] L'idée républicaine tire sa force de sa plasticité et de son aptitude à renvoyer à chacun une image singulière.'[6] In other words, the abstract ideals and values of the republic interact with the subjective history and experience of each individual citizen to form a potentially unique interpretation of the French Republic. In this context, it is possible to say that the word 'republic' belongs at once to everybody and to nobody as there is not one republic but several, each an ideological interpretation supported by certain aspects of the political and social history of the nation since the time of the Revolution.

Inevitably, this plurality of interpretations leads to problems of definition, the setting down of one all-encompassing definition of the French Republic. However, while debate has continued to rage around the nature of the Republic and the resultant republican model, there are certain constants that have held sway over the course of time. The fundamental values and ideals that emerged both during and after the Revolution of 1789 have become intrinsic elements of the nation's historical, cultural and political fabric. Although the matter of their interpretation has continuously engendered debate and political oppositions, these values of liberty, equality, national unity and the secular state have remained the cornerstones of the republican model, merging together to form a broader ideological framework that occupies a sacred position in the French popular imagination.

---

5   Charles Péguy, *Notre jeunesse* (Paris: Gallimard, 1957), 10.
6   Cited in Sieffert, *Comment peut-on être (vraiment) républicain?*, 5.

Conceiving the Nation-State:
The Origins of the French Idea of Nationhood

In France, the revolutionary period of 1789 represented a turning point in
the history of the French nation. The Revolution represented a break with
the past, substituting a 'doctrine of national sovereignty and [...] the link
between citizenship and nationhood' for the absolutist, monarchic regime
that had gone before.[7] The ideals, values and concepts forged during the
Revolution would be the template for the republics of the future, a blueprint for all societies and peoples seeking to build a nation on the foundations of liberty, and equality. However, it is important to acknowledge
that this monumental change from monarchal rule to sovereign nation did
not occur *ex nihilo*. Rogers Brubaker reveals that the process of nation-
building in France is part of an extended narrative stretching back before
the Revolution.[8] French society under the *Ancien Régime* was a society
operating under a strict social hierarchy of which the supreme power of the
absolutist monarchy was the pinnacle. The populace was strictly divided
according to social position and class, and, although the different regions
were controlled by the nobility and the clergy under the remnants of the
feudal system, the overall distribution of power was constituted around a
single political centre – Paris, the base of the bureaucratic and hereditary
monarchy, ruling the state by divine right. It was the monarchy which possessed the sovereign power to 'reform taxation in the name of the French
nation', for example, and which constituted the highest authority of the
legal system.[9] Thus the concept of national belonging, of nationhood, at
this time progressed and was understood for the most part in political and
territorial terms. The development of this idea is best illustrated through a
summary comparison with the relative situation in Germany at the same
time, where the 'disparity in scale between supranational [Holy Roman]

7   Rogers Brubaker, *Citizenship and Nationhood in France and Germany* (Cambridge,
     MA, and London: Harvard University Press, 1994), 35.
8   Ibid.
9   Martin Evans and Emmanuel Godin, *France 1815–2003* (London: Hodder-Arnold,
     2004), 7.

Empire and the sub-national profusion of sovereign and semi-sovereign political units' resulted in the development of an ethnocultural rather than political conception of nationhood.[10] A multitude of autonomous political units made the idea of German nationhood, in terms of national self-perception, a concept that was firmly rooted in the notion of race and cultural belonging rather than allegiance to a centralized source of political power.

In contrast, under the *Ancien Régime* the 'nation and the kingdom were conceptually fused in France' and situated within the 'spatial and institutional frame of the developing territorial state'.[11] State-membership under the *Ancien Régime* revolved primarily around political rather than cultural concerns; what mattered 'as a determinant of one's rights and obligations, was not, in the first instance that one was French or foreign: it was that one belonged to a *seigneurie* [...] or that one was a noble or a clergyman [...] or that one was a member of a guild' under the supreme authority of the monarch.[12] The distinction between Frenchmen and foreigners was not sharply defined or overly antagonistic in practice; Brubaker states that 'the distinction between citizens and foreigners had neither ideological nor practical significance [...] foreigners suffered few disabilities, and the most significant of these, in the domain of inheritance, had been largely removed by the eighteenth century'.[13] Thus state membership revolved on political rather than cultural axes, a system forming the historical matrix for the assimilationist self-understanding that would come to characterize the republican model. Paradoxically, with the coming of the Revolution, although the revolutionaries were motivated by the desire to undertake fundamental reforms and would ultimately break with the system of privilege established under the old order, this political construction of centralist governance established under the rule of the monarchy remained and became a central element of the new nation-state as it emerged, as did the political conception of membership instituted during the *Ancien Régime*.

10   Brubaker, *Citizenship and Nationhood*, 4.
11   Ibid., 3.
12   Ibid., 36.
13   Ibid., 39.

In relation to this continuity of the centralized political regime, Hayward states that in historical terms 'the political regime has retained a precedence over the political community that is derived from [...] its historic precedence. France is a unitary state superimposed upon a multinational society, the authority of Paris having been established under the monarchy [...] and reinforced by the republics'.[14]

While certain continuities existed between the *Ancien Régime* and the nation-state that emerged from the process of the Revolution, it is evident that the new order represented the emergence of a new political system that would forever change the face of French, and indeed European, society. The events of the Revolution produced shockwaves that reverberated throughout the established order of Europe. As new ideas reflecting the intellectual currents of the Enlightenment emerged and were circulated, traditional concepts of authority began to be challenged. Frederick Artz claims that the Enlightenment:

> [T]ook a new world view; it involved the reevaluation of all values, established a new order of thought [...]. The leaders [...] turned from otherworldly and pessimistic ideas to a secular view of life [...]. Knowledge took the place of grace, and the Philosophes appealed to all reasonable men to [...] accept the rule of reason.[15]

The main readership of the Enlightenment scholars was the discontented middle classes who were unhappy with the privileges enjoyed by the nobility and the Church. These scholars were members of the Third Estate; however, in this social stratum they were positioned towards the wealthier end of the spectrum and possessed a high level of what Bourdieu would term 'social capital'.[16] Artz states that the 'fervour of [these] reformers seemed

---

14 Jack Hayward, *The One and Indivisible French Republic* (London: Weidenfeld & Nicolson, 1973), 17.

15 Frederick Artz, *The Enlightenment in France* (Kent, OH: Kent State University Press, 1968), 30.

16 Bourdieu defined social capital as 'the sum of resources, actual or virtual, that accrue to an individual or a group by virtue of possessing a durable network of more or less institutionalized relationships of mutual acquaintance and recognition'. See Pierre Bourdieu and Loïc Wacquant, *An Invitation to Reflexive Sociology* (Chicago: Chicago University Press, 1992), 119.

to be constructing "a new religion of which reason was God, Newton's ideas the Bible, Voltaire and others the prophets".[17] One of the primary beliefs of the Enlightenment thinkers held that the state had a duty to promote the interests of its citizens. Enlightenment scholars believed that men should be allowed to govern themselves through their own reason and knowledge. The influence of writers such as Condorcet, Voltaire and Rousseau penetrated French society and impacted upon popular opinions and beliefs. The concomitant growth in the printing industry and levels of literacy meant that ideas advocating change reached a much wider audience than before: 'although literacy only dropped from 71 percent in 1700 to 63 percent in 1790, most people could read and write in Paris and other big cities'.[18] The influential pamphlet written by Sieyès in 1789 served as a precursor to the fundamental changes to come as the author questioned the very nature of a nation: 'What is a nation? A body of associates living under a common law and represented by the same legislature.'[19] Sieyès' pamphlet, developing ideas put forward in Rousseau's *Social Contract* of 1762 questioned the political system in place, articulating bold new ideas that pointed towards profound alterations in the hierarchy of power. In proposing a system where representation in terms of governance would extend to include all individuals forming part of the nation, Sieyès placed himself in direct opposition with the existing power structure of the *Ancien Régime*. Sieyès also emphasized the notion of civil equality before the law, elaborating on another Enlightenment idea set forth by Rousseau, thus posing a direct challenge to the supreme and 'divine' authority of the ruling monarch. Consequently, when the Third Estate proclaimed itself the national assembly in 1789, a process of shifting power relations was set in motion that would fundamentally change the political and social composition of the French nation. As the events of the Revolution unfolded, political sovereignty was transferred from the monarchy to the nation as the privileges of the *Ancien Régime* were swept away.

17   Ibid., 33.
18   Jack Censer and Lynn Hunt, *Liberty, Equality, Fraternity. Exploring the French Revolution* (University Park: Pennsylvania State University Press, 2001), 17.
19   Emanuel Sieyès, *What is the Third Estate?*, trans. M. Blondel (New York: Praeger, 1963), 126.

The publication of the *Déclaration des Droits de l'Homme et du Citoyen* in 1789 – a document that formed the basis for the first, and indeed, successive constitutions – encapsulated the foundations of the new system. At the core of this document was the transfer of power that would establish France as a nation-state and form the framework for the Republic to come. Article Three of the Declaration stated that 'The principle of all sovereignty rests essentially in the nation', thus officially proclaiming the transfer of power from the monarchy to the sovereign people, the members and the source of the new nation-state's power.[20] This new power dynamic would translate into the creation of 'modern national citizenship'.[21] The Declaration swept away 'the tangled skein of privilege – regional liberties and immunities, corporate monopolies, fiscal exemptions, vestigial seigneurial rights, and so on', creating a framework within which political citizens, rather than subjects, were viewed as equal before the law.[22] Needless to say, the application of these newly declared principles of equality was not immediate, nor did it go unchallenged by the vestiges of the *Ancien Régime*, and in the years following the Declaration, questions relating to who was included in the definition of 'man and citizen' were among those to dominate the debate on equality.[23]

Women, in particular, illustrated the limitations associated with this concept of equality, following the creation of the Declaration. Under the *Ancien Régime*, the role of women was strictly confined to the private sphere, with women having no place in the political arena. This deeply rooted perception of the status of women did not change with the publication of the Declaration of Rights. Landes states that 'despite the proclamation of the rights of man in 1789, the institution of universal manhood suffrage in 1792, […] women remained second-class citizens of the nation,

---

20 *La Déclaration des droits de l'homme et du citoyen.* Translation cited in Lynn Hunt, ed., *The French Revolution and Human Rights: A Brief Documentary History* (Boston: Bedford/St Martin's, 1996), 77–79.

21 See Rogers Brubaker, 'The French Revolution and the Invention of Citizenship', *French Politics and Society*, 7 (1989), 30–49.

22 Brubaker, *Citizenship and Nationhood*, 39.

23 See Hunt, *The French Revolution and Human Rights*, 16.

deprived of fundamental political rights'.[24] Certain public figures, such as Condorcet, believed that women should share political rights with men. Unfortunately, those sharing Condorcet's opinions were in the minority and, for the most part, the idea of political rights for women was greeted with incredulity. Under the constitution of 1791, women were categorized as passive citizens along with those men whose status was determined by their financial position. However, an important women's movement grew out of the Revolution, with groups such as the *cercle social* launching a campaign for women's rights in 1790–1791.[25] One of the most important developments in the fight for equality for women was the Declaration of the Rights of Woman, modelled on the original Declaration, penned by Marie Gouze in 1791 under the pseudonym Olympe de Gouges. In spite of this, the struggle of women to gain rights 'made few inroads into masculine prejudice against the female franchise'. Gouze was sent to the guillotine in 1793 and, in the same year, deputies of the National Convention 'resolutely rejected not only political rights for women but even their right to engage in any form of organized politics'.[26]

This example serves to underline the ambiguous nature of the concept of equality both during and after the Revolutionary period. However, despite the ongoing debate and conflict in relation to the meaning, scope and nature of 'equality', the *Déclaration des Droits de l'Homme et du Citoyen* played a vital role owing to the fact that it institutionalized and elaborated on the ideas and beliefs articulated by Sieyès in relation to the concept of nationhood. This document fundamentally altered both the socio-political structure of the nation, and the conception of the relationship between the nation and its people in terms of membership and allegiance. The focus on liberty and equality before the law that underpinned the Declaration would serve as the foundations of the new Republic, which was declared

---

24 Joan Landes, *Visualizing the Nation: Gender, Representation and Revolution in Eighteenth Century France* (Ithaca, NY: Cornell University Press, 2001), 4.

25 Hunt, *The French Revolution and Human Rights*, 27.

26 See Malcolm Crook, *Elections in the French Revolution: An Apprenticeship in Democracy, 1789–1799* (Cambridge: Cambridge University Press, 1996), 35; and Hunt, *The French Revolution and Human Rights*, 29.

in 1792 following the fall of the monarchy. These values were held up as emblematic of the Revolution and the resultant French nation-state, and would come to occupy a sacred position in the history and culture of French republicanism, inextricably linked with self-understanding in the French popular imagination.

The system of power relations established by the Revolution, that is, an 'immediate, direct form of state-membership', had a far-reaching effect on the dynamic existing between the nation and its members. The previous unilateral dynamic of power, under which state members were first and foremost subjects of the monarch, was replaced by a bilateral relationship revolving around the interaction between the sovereign nation and the citizens, who constituted the source of the nation's power. Any sub-state notion of belonging that had previously existed within the broader political construction of the sovereign state was abolished, and a new bond was formed, a national bond linking citizens politically through their interaction with and participation in the nation-state. By 1792, access to political rights had been extended to include the majority of the male population; this development cemented the idea of a direct interaction with the nation-state, firmly establishing the national bond in political terms. Gérard Noiriel refers to Rousseau's *Social Contract* when he defines citizenship as 'the ability of an individual member of a given national community to partake – albeit indirectly – in the elaboration of laws that he or she must then obey'.[27] In general terms, the creation of the sovereign nation-state and the inherent link between this institution and the citizenry implemented the idea of a greater sense of belonging to a national and theoretically egalitarian community.

27   Gerard Noiriel, *The French Melting Pot: Immigration, Citizenship and National Identity*, trans. Geoffrey Laforcade (Minneapolis and London: Minnesota University Press, 1996), 16.

The Universal Nation-State:
Towards an Assimilationist Self-Understanding

The new concept of the nation that emerged from the Revolution was characterized by a strong belief in the universal nature of the new order. For the revolutionaries of the period, and for those who followed, the French model forged around 1789 was much greater than the geographical limits of the nation; the 'Republic' was rather 'the word destined to designate a universal model, thought of through the exemplary nature of the singular'.[28] Marc Sadoun states that, in the light of the Revolution, and despite the internal oppositions rooted in opposing ideologies, 'with this passion, these values and this word [...] France lived her own history as that of the entire world'.[29] The rights and values forged in the heat of the Revolution would serve as a beacon for citizens of all nations, symbols of hope and progress. Although the revolutionary process was bitterly contested by those who remained loyal to the *Ancien Régime* – primarily the aristocracy and the clergy – others celebrated a new age of liberty. And this enthusiasm was not limited to France. The poet William Wordsworth celebrated the universal values born of the Revolution when he wrote: "twas a time when Europe rejoiced, France standing on top of golden hours, And human nature seemed born again'.[30] Once again, it was the *Déclaration des Droits de l'Homme et du Citoyen* that epitomized the universal aspirations of the new order. The generic nature of the document's title contained an inherent implication as to the universal quality of the rights and values it listed. It goes without saying that the rights contained therein applied to the society of origin. However, the abstract nature of the document, which proclaimed the general and inalienable rights of man without grounding the document in the political specifics of a particular government or regime, or indeed the national specifics of the French nation, gave the

---

28 Pierre Bouretz, 'La démocratie francaise au risque du monde', in Marc Sadoun, ed., *La Démocratie en France. Idéologies* (Paris: Gallimard, 2000), 27–137 (27).
29 Ibid., 2.
30 Cited in Censer and Hunt, *Liberty, Equality, Fraternity*, 55.

Declaration the ability to transcend national borders and temporal restrictions. As a result, this blueprint for modern democracy was able to travel through time, outlasting the challenges posed by various regime changes and internal political divisions, a model that could potentially be applied to any political regime, at any time. On the occasion of the bicentenary of the Revolution in 1989, President Mitterrand spoke of the 'Revolution of the Rights of Man' in recognition of the universal dimension inherent in the republican model.

The new concept of nationhood that emerged from the revolutionary period around 1789, characterized by this universal dimension, resulted in the concomitant development of an assimilationist self-understanding. Liberty, equality and fraternity were the values that would form the triptych of the Republic, and France was positioned as an ideal society that would embrace those seeking to benefit from this universal model. This assimilationist self-understanding stemmed from the theoretically universal element of the new regime: the expression of the fundamental desire for liberty held by all of mankind. In this respect, Brubaker cites the politician Vergniaud, who said: 'It is not for ourselves alone; it is not for that part of the globe that one calls France, that we have conquered Liberty'.[31] For all that, this ideological dimension of the republican philosophy was also motivated by more practical reasons. At the close of the eighteenth century, France was at war with a number of major European powers. Consequently, the revolutionaries needed to reconcile the notion of a universal, egalitarian society with the military advancement and territorial gains made in the aftermath of the Revolution. Thus, the concept of 'self-determination' was invoked by the revolutionaries, a concept based on reason and the idea of freedom of choice in terms of attachment to a particular political community or nation.[32] Brubaker refers to the works

---

31   Brubaker, *Citizenship and Nationhood*, 44.
32   Of course, like all aspects of the Revolution, the concept of self-determination was fiercely contested. Not all who lived in those areas incorporated into France desired to become French. However, the idea of universalist self-determination has become cemented as one of what Alec Hargreaves terms 'the founding myths' of the Republic.

of Albert Soboul and Jacques Godechot in affirming that the concept of self-determination 'was invoked to justify the territorial gains of 1791–1793, and even to reinterpret retrospectively the terms of the accession of Alsace to France in the seventeenth century'.[33]

This idea of self-determination effectively positioned France as a liberating force, embracing all those wishing to break free from the oppression of absolutist regimes. In this context, national boundaries became secondary to the universal desire for liberty. Brubaker highlights the fact that this idea of self-determination was not invoked in order to 'permit the projection of ethnocultural identity onto the political plane'; it was, rather, 'to give expression to the universal desire for liberty and thus – how could it be otherwise? – for incorporation into France'.[34] Race and ethnicity were thus dismissed as valid criteria for the conception of a nation, with emphasis instead being placed on the idea of a voluntary attachment to the political system of values offered by the French model. The line between Frenchman and foreigner became somewhat blurred as the political concept of citizenship emerged as the dominant criterion for national belonging. Tallien's remark in 1795 summed up this political definition of belonging: 'the only foreigners in France are the bad citizens'.[35] According to Tocqueville, '[the French Revolution] created a common intellectual fatherland whose citizenship was open to men of every nationality and in which racial discriminations were obliterated'.[36] These ideas of self-determination were embodied in Renan's 1882 speech at the Sorbonne. In expounding his understanding of the theoretical conception of a nation, Renan eliminated race, religion, language and geographical frontiers as suitable criteria for 'the foundation and legitimising of nations', claiming instead that a nation must be thought of as 'a soul, a spiritual principle', formed of two elements.[37] On one hand,

33 Brubaker, *Citizenship and Nationhood*, 7.
34 Ibid.
35 Cited in Brubaker, *Citizenship and Nationhood*, 7.
36 Cited in Michael Rapport, *Nationality and Citizenship in Revolutionary France* (Oxford: Clarendon Press, 2000), vi.
37 Cited in Maxim Silverman, *Deconstructing the Nation. Immigration, Racism and Citizenship in Modern France* (London: Routledge, 1992), 20.

Renan claimed that a nation is formed through the association of individuals who voluntarily affirm their desire to live together as a national community. This concept of the nation encapsulates the assimilationist universalism that characterized the birth of the Republic, and necessitates a political understanding of membership in the nation-state, given the incompatibility of assimilation with all 'consistently "organic" conceptions of membership' where ethnocultural boundaries are considered 'prior to and determinative of national (and ideally) state boundaries'.[38]

On the other hand, Renan's idea of the nation was also based on the concomitant acceptance, by the citizens, of the heritage of the nation; that is, the acceptance of 'shared memories' and the 'lived' history of those who had gone before.[39] Of course, Renan's theory of the nation is not without problems. Silverman, in particular, asserts that while Renan's theory does not reflect 'a biologistic essentialism [...] it often seems to verge on a cultural essentialism or absolutism'.[40] Silverman suggests that, as a result, the concept of culture in Renan's text remains ambivalent. However, in more general terms, Noiriel states that 'all individuals, regardless of the social formation to which they belong, aspire to fit into a coherent narrative of the past, even if it is more or less mythical', and if we consider this statement in the context of the intellectual fatherland evoked by Tocqueville, Renan's underlying meaning is clear.[41] Essentially, in setting out the acceptance of heritage, alongside self-determination, as one of the criteria for participation in a nation, Renan attempts to fulfil this basic desire for a coherent narrative through the evocation of an intellectual fatherland where the concept of culture is at once both a fixed and a fluid concept. 'Fixed' in the sense that this intellectual fatherland has formed and progressed due to the input of those members who have gone before, and 'fluid' in the sense that this political and intellectual association of individuals is constantly evolving as it incorporates and adapts to the 'lived history' and shared

---

38   Brubaker, *Citizenship and Nationhood*, 8.
39   Cited in Noiriel, *The French Melting Pot*, 11.
40   Silverman, *Deconstructing the Nation*, 20.
41   Noiriel, *The French Melting Pot*, xxviii.

memories of its members, both past and present. Naturally, while this concept of assimilationist universalism would come to form a central element of the revolutionary legacy and a cornerstone of republican ideology, the legitimacy of this idea did not pass through history unchallenged by the actions of those in power. As the new order consolidated its position, the line separating the offer of assimilation into a society that was proclaimed the home of equality and liberty, and the imposition of the French system upon unwilling populations became blurred, and the republican virtue of universal liberty soon degenerated into the oppression of imperial expansion. Colonialism, presented in the guise of the positive values and ideals that had emerged with the Revolution, would constitute a paradox threatening the virtue of the republican model and its self-created reputation as the source of liberty and equality.

In the immediate aftermath of the Revolution, French patriots 'took their role seriously as the instructors of nations, as the protectors of the oppressed.'[42] However, the original ideals became distorted when the republican idea of assimilationist universalism was appropriated by those in power in order to justify the aggressive territorial expansion and economic progression of the French Empire. Hargreaves states that:

> Officially designated as the ultimate objective of the colonial project, assimilation appeared to promise equal political rights to the indigenous inhabitants of the overseas territories. In practice, political equality would have destroyed the very foundations of the colonial system, and it was refused to all but a tiny elite among the indigenous populations.[43]

Colonialism was thus viewed through a prism formed from the positive elements of the Revolution: France had a duty to offer its model of liberty and equality to other nations and assimilate them, and their concomitant economic potential, into the utopian system that the French had fought to establish. By the later part of the nineteenth century, this interpretation of

---

42   Cited in Rapport, *Nationality and Citizenship in Revolutionary France*, 6.
43   Alec Hargreaves, *Multi-Ethnic France: Immigration, Politics, Culture and Society* (London and New York: Routledge, 2007), 149.

republican universalism was firmly established as 'la mission civilisatrice'.[44] In 1885, Jules Ferry justified French colonial expansion through his claim that 'il y a pour les races supérieures un droit, parce qu'il y a un devoir pour elles. Elles ont le devoir de civiliser les races inférieures'.[45] Ferry later replaced the phrase 'race inférieure' with 'culture inférieure' following political indignation at the use of such a term by a public figure in the nation that professed to be the home of equality. However, Ferry had provided a significant insight into the racism that permeated colonial expansion, revealing a manipulation of republican values that opposed the ideals made sacred by the Revolution. Inevitably, the effects of migratory trends, stemming in large part from the colonial period, have played, and indeed continue to play, a central role in the evolution of the ideas of citizenship and belonging in the modern French Republic. Nevertheless, despite the misappropriation of republican ideals in those geographical regions that would become colonies of France, and the subjugation of indigenous populations, it was the positive aspect of French universalism that would become cemented as one of the central ideologies of the French Republic as it progressed through history.

The One and Indivisible French Republic

The Republic born of the 1789 Revolution had broken with the past and created the modern nation-state, a new model of the nation that redefined its citizens as the source of the nation's power. Sieffert claims 'c'est peu dire que la Révolution va redéfinir l'identité française en léguant à la Ire République et à ses suivantes la notion de citoyenneté, et un nouveau rapport au sol et au sang'.[46] However, the weight of the past and the shadow of the Ancien Régime loomed over the new changes, and the new order faced

---

44   Ibid.
45   Gilles Martinet, *Une certaine idée de la gauche (1936–1997)* (Paris: Odile Jacob, 1997), 126.
46   Sieffert, *Comment peut-on être (vraiment) républicain?*, 18.

the constant threat of being overtaken by the memory of the old system. Weber affirms that in France, 'the political nation of the *Ancien Régime* functioned side by side with traditional community and social structures. The ideological nation of the Revolution had to compete with these'.[47] The new order brought about by the Revolution was still in the early stages of its development, still finding its footing among the remains of the deep-rooted *Ancien Régime*. Consequently, this profound alteration in the hierarchy of power necessitated a concomitant national unity to ensure the legitimization and continuation of the fledgling Republic.

In political terms, this path towards national unity was set in 1792 when, amid fierce debate over the nature of the new regime – federalist and decentralized, or united and centralized – Danton proclaimed 'les mots qui allaient figurer dans toutes les constitutions à venir: "La République française est une et indivisible"'.[48] Citizens were required to renounce any regional loyalties in favour of the greater national identity. This idea of national unity and an indivisible republic would evolve as one of the cornerstones of French republicanism. The Republic was to be a place where 'chaque citoyen a pour sa patrie la même sollicitude qu'un chef de maison porte à sa famille'.[49] On a larger scale, this need for national unity became interlaced with the assimilationist self-understanding that was a product of republican universalism. The Republic would absorb all those who yearned for liberty, strengthening itself through numbers, and feeding on a shared desire to create an egalitarian society. Those who were assimilated into the Republic, French or foreign, would strengthen it due to their desire to belong to the new order. But more than this, the young Republic needed a specific cause around which to build this national identity, a means of evoking a national fraternity that was greater than political unity alone. War would prove to be this unifying factor.

---

47 Eugen Weber, *Peasants into Frenchmen. The Modernization of Rural France 1870–1914* (London: Chatto & Windus, 1977), 113.

48 Jules Michelet, *Histoire de la Révolution (Tome IV)* (Paris: Elibron Classics, 2006), 27.

49 Sieffert, *Comment peut-on être (vraiment) républicain?*, 28.

As has previously been mentioned, by 1793 France was at war with a number of major European powers. Brubaker reveals that the wars that followed the Revolution were unique in that the battles revolved as much around ideas – that is, the ideological clash between the absolutist regimes of other European states and the French idea of universal liberty and equality – as they were about territorial gain.[50] In this context, paradoxically, the proclaimed universalism of the newly created Republic, which facilitated the emergence of an assimilationist self-understanding that transcended national borders, had also sharpened discord between nations. In any case, Brubaker confirms that only from 1792 on 'when the new order felt itself besieged by enemies within and enemies without, did there develop [...] justified by the doctrine of the "patrie en danger", elements of a xenophobic nationalism at home'.[51] Once again, it is important to emphasize that this nationalism was political rather than ethnocultural, a product of the philosophical debate that accompanied the Revolution and that was influenced by the Enlightenment. French soldiers fought for 'la patrie', for a nation and 'a revolution that they and their brothers and sisters had helped make'.[52]

However, if war provided an immediate means of galvanising the national identity in the aftermath of the Revolution when a reversion to the system of the *Ancien Régime* was an ever present threat, the military and the educational system provided the long-term framework within which the government would consolidate the national identity. Weber claims that 'the school, notably the village school, compulsory and free, has been credited with the ultimate acculturation process that made the French people French'.[53] And it was a series of reforms introduced by Jules Ferry in the 1880s that initiated these 'great engines of assimilation, welding France for the first time into a unified nation'.[54]

---

50   Brubaker, *Citizenship and Nationhood*, 44.
51   Ibid., 8.
52   Censer and Hunt, *Liberty, Equality, Fraternity*, 91.
53   Weber, *Peasants into Frenchmen*, 303.
54   Brubaker, *Citizenship and Nationhood*, 15.

Between 1881 and 1886 all fees and charges in primary schools were abolished, primary education was made compulsory, and 'an elementary teaching program was instituted, along with elaborate provisions for inspection and control'.[55] Mendras and Cole state that 'the main goal of the founding fathers was to transform backward conservative peasants into educated citizens, dedicated to the defence of the Republic'.[56] Essentially, education was 'a form of social engineering, since a national education system would be a tool for disseminating democratic ideas within the traditionally conservative villages, as well as a means of breaking the grip of traditional conservative notables over the local peasantry'.[57] The concept of a unified national identity, of France as united and indivisible, was instilled in an entire generation of young minds through the work of the teachers.

As might be expected, this process of cultural unification progressed slowly and did not go unchallenged. Regional identities persisted, a fact illustrated by Weber who reveals that news of a *levée en masse* in Brittany in 1870 gave rise to fears of separatism, provoking Léon Gambetta to plead with the Bretons 'I beg you to forget that you are Bretons, and to remember only that you are French'.[58] However, despite these challenges and setbacks, the education system slowly but surely inculcated the youth of the nation with the positive values and ideals that had emerged from the 1789 Revolution, inextricably linking these ideals with the ideas of *la patrie* and national unity. In this way, the negative aspects of the republican narrative were crushed under the weight of 'la machine unificatrice', and the idea of a unified French nation was fixed as a symbol of democratic progress in the popular imagination.[59]

---

55   Weber, *Peasants into Frenchmen*, 309.
56   Henri Mendras and Alistair Cole, *Social Change in Modern France: Towards a Cultural Anthropology of the Fifth Republic* (Cambridge: Cambridge University Press, 1991), 91.
57   Ibid.
58   Weber, *Peasants into Frenchmen*, 303 & 318.
59   Sieffert, *Comment peut-on être (vraiment) républicain?*, 22.

The military provided the other major axis along which the idea of national unity was developed and the national identity consolidated. Once again, however, this process was a difficult and extended one. Although conscription in France dates back to 1798, throughout most of the nineteenth century exemptions ensured that those who could afford to pay were substituted, a reality which was greatly resented by the lower classes. As a result, 'conscription was seen not as a duty owed to some larger community or nation, but as a heavy tribute exacted by an oppressive and alien state'.[60] Moreover, the exemption of foreigners from conscription was another source of much resentment among the general populace; it was claimed that foreigners claimed the benefits of French laws while avoiding the duties shouldered by citizens. It was not until 1889, when the exemptions were abolished, and participation in military service was extended, that attitudes towards the military began to change for the better. Brubaker reveals that this abolishment of exemptions went hand in hand with a more expansive definition of French citizenship that involved the extension of '*jus soli* to include second-generation immigrants'.[61] He goes on to say that this civic incorporation of immigrants was a political necessity in the context of the reforms regarding national military conscription, a move that would counter the controversy surrounding the exemption of second-generation immigrants.[62] Thus, the army began to be associated with the ideals and values of the Republic, with the reforms bringing about a powerful reinforcement of the assimilationist self-understanding that characterized French republicanism.

Certainly, the expansion of citizenship laws was conceived in a broader context than that of the military. In general terms, national unity and the formation of a national identity required the eradication of all sources of internal division. Thus, the civic incorporation of second-generation immigrants aimed to prevent the development of sub-national collective identities within the territorial limits of the nation but outside the

60   Weber, *Peasants into Frenchmen*, 292.
61   Brubaker, *Citizenship and Nationhood*, 93.
62   Ibid., 105.

social and political structures of mainstream society. In any case, Weber highlights the war with Prussia as a key moment in the development of the army as a vehicle for the consolidation of national identity, claiming that during this war 'the connection between local and national interests became more evident to large numbers of people'.[63] Ties between the army and *la patrie*, in terms of the development of national identity, were forged in the barracks, and the military became interwoven with the continuation and reinforcement of the republican myths. This process was greatly aided by educational propaganda and Weber claims that by the 1890s, 'there is persuasive evidence that the army was no longer "theirs" but "ours"'; that the army 'could become what its enthusiasts hoped for: the school of the fatherland'.[64] This idea of the army barracks as a means of schooling the conscripts in republican values and beliefs would develop as a practical reality. Mendras and Cole reveal that 'not only did the peasant learn how to wield arms, but he was also taught how the basic duties of being a citizen'.[65] Consequently, the image of the one and indivisible French Republic was ingrained in the popular imagination, becoming a permanent and central element of republican ideology.

Laïcité and the Place of the Secular State in the Republican Narrative

Alongside the development and elaboration of the values and ideas that emerged from the revolutionary period, the evolution of France was characterized by difficult relations between the Republic and the Church. Furet claims that the hostility of republicans towards religion, and more specifically the Catholic Church, was directly linked to 'la logique politique de lutte avec l'Ancien Régime'.[66] The inherent opposition between the faith-based belief system of the Church and the reason-based influence

---

63   Weber, *Peasants into Frenchmen*, 298.
64   Ibid.
65   Mendras and Cole, *Social Change in Modern France*, 52.
66   François Furet, *La Révolution* (Paris: Hachette, 1988), 2.

of the Enlightenment created a tangible antagonism between the clergy and the revolutionaries. In addition, the privileged position of the church under the *Ancien Régime* made it an obvious target for the supporters of the Revolution. The *Déclaration des Droits de l'Homme et du Citoyen* effectively constituted the first step in an extended process that would undermine the authority and influence of the church in the public arena, culminating in the secular state. In Article Ten, the Declaration proclaimed that 'nul ne doit être inquiété pour ses opinions, même religieuses', thus challenging the intellectual dominance of the Catholic Church in matters of spiritual belief and faith, and establishing the first guarantees regarding atheism and pluralism. Rémond describes 26 August 1789 as 'le moment où la laïcité a fait son entrée comme principe d'organisation de la société moderne'.[67] For the first time in France, and indeed Europe, there was a formal acknowledgement of the right of citizens to decide upon the nature of their personal religious beliefs. The formal declaration of liberty in terms of religious beliefs and opinions initiated a profound remodelling of society that has impacted upon social processes and structures up to the present day. The moral and intellectual dominance of the Church was challenged by revolutionaries influenced by the positivism inherited from the Enlightenment, resulting in a fundamental ideological opposition that polarized relations between the followers of the Church and the supporters of the Republic:

> La République est positiviste. Elle trouve en face d'elle une église qui condamne les idées nouvelles et les principes de la société moderne. Deux systèmes s'opposent terme à terme: la raison contre la foi [...] la science contre la superstition et l'obscurantisme. Le combat prend une dimension intellectuelle.[68]

In the context of national unity and the institutionalization of the fledgling Republic, this ideological opposition between Church and Republic had important implications for the continuation of the new order, especially given the development of the Church as a rallying point for those who opposed the Republic and desired a return to the *Ancien Régime*. In September 1791 the Convention declared 'l'an I non seulement de la Répub-

---

67   René Rémond, *L'invention de la laïcité. De 1789 à demain* (Paris: Bayard, 2005), 35.
68   Ibid., 46.

lique, mais d'un monde nouveau, sans Dieu', as republicans attempted to appropriate the concept of religion in order to both undermine the Church and strengthen the authority of the Republic.[69] Baubérot speaks of the development of a revolutionary religiosity where 'l'Etat-nation, la Constitution, la loi deviennent des "choses sacrées"'.[70] The religious cult was replaced by the republican cult, a development that aided the institutionalization of the Republic in ideological terms. In 1793, the Paris Commune celebrated the 'fête de la Liberté et de la Raison', ordering churches and temples to be closed. It was no longer necessary to be a 'fils de l'église catholique pour être un citoyen français jouissant de la plenitude des droits'.[71] Now the sermon was based on allegiance to the new order. The period around 1789 constituted the beginning of the process of separating the Church and the nation, the separation of national identity and religion, which, until that point, had progressed in union.[72] Of course, this is not to suggest that the Church became completely marginalized or sidelined. While the Church did lose a significant amount of its former power, especially in terms of property and assets, it remained a powerful force in French society.

The Church and the state reached a compromise under Napoleon in 1801 that recognized the Catholic religion as 'the religion of the "great majority" of French people'.[73] Moreover, the Church provided support for the restorations of 1815–1830, the July monarchy of 1830–1848 and for Napoleon III's Second Empire of 1852–1870.[74] However, Weber states that:

> In the nineteenth century, skepticism was increasing, just at the time when the Church's close association with the upper classes and their views became more evident. The Church no longer stood for the unity of all, but stood for the domination of one particular faction. Faith in the declining Church was linked to a political stance that was also declining; both lost from the connection.[75]

---

69 Sieffert, *Comment peut-on être (vraiment) républicain?*, 20.
70 Jean Baubérot, *Histoire de la laicité francaise* (Paris: PUF, 2000), 15.
71 Rémond, *L'invention de la laïcité*, 38.
72 Ibid.
73 Mendras and Cole, *Social Change in Modern France*, 58.
74 Ibid.
75 Weber, *Peasants into Frenchmen*, 360.

Thus the separation of Church and state that was initiated in 1789 progressed throughout the eighteenth century as republican ideology gained momentum to the detriment of religious orders. Little by little, progress towards the secular state was confirmed and the concept became intertwined with the ideological fabric of the republican narrative. The period between 1879 and 1883 was of particular importance as the secularization of the Republic was extended to incorporate certain aspects of the education system. At the beginning of the 1880s, Jules Ferry, in his role as Minister of Public Instruction, proclaimed that education in France would be free, *laïque* and compulsory. The significance of this move cannot be overstated given the position of the classroom as 'le terrain sur lequel se sont d'abord affrontées la philosophie libérale, inspiratrice de l'idée laïque, et l'Eglise catholique, se disputant le monopole de la formation des intelligences'.[76]

However, it was the law passed in 1905 that formally separated church and state, introducing the term 'laïcité' for the first time, which constituted the greatest step towards 'la France laïque'. In its first article, this law reaffirmed the duty of the Republic to 'assure la liberté de conscience'.[77] It was the second article that would redefine the relationship between church and state: 'La République ne reconnaît, ne salarie, ne subventionne aucun culte'.[78] The 1905 law removed all aspects of religion from the education system as well as the civic space; religious beliefs became confined to the private sphere, almost completely removed from the public domain. This distinction between the private life and the public arena was directly linked to the consolidation of national unity and the notion of the 'one and indivisible' Republic. The idea of the national community as the only legitimate unifying framework was reinforced and further embedded in the popular imagination, as the concept of *laïcité* took its place at the heart of the republican narrative. Formally established in the eyes of the law, from this point on the policy of *laïcité* would continue to consolidate its position as a

76   Rémond, *L'invention de la laïcité*, 47.
77   'Loi du 9 décembre 1905 relative à la séparation des Églises et de l'État', <http://www.assemblee-nationale.fr/histoire/eglise-etat/sommaire.asp#loi> accessed 2 September 2005.
78   Ibid.

cornerstone of French Republicanism. As the Republic and its supporting ideology continued to gain momentum, it sketched out 'ses représentations mentales, ses fondements philosophiques, ses références historiques, ses valeurs' with the passage of time.[79] And although the concept of the Republic was challenged at different periods by the intermittent restoration of monarchic and authoritarian regimes, it emerged strengthened by these challenges, developing an 'architecture subtile des valeurs' which formed the framework of the republican narrative.[80] The secular state and the idea of laïcité would come to form a central element of this framework, becoming inextricably linked with the concept of republicanism in the French context. Of course, the reconciliation of theory and practice in this area has always constituted a major challenge to those in power; in recent years, the continuous and often intense debate that has surrounded the question of laïcité, especially in the context of the evolution of the republican model of integration, is a testament to the importance attributed to this concept in relation to the republican tradition. Changes in migratory flux have had a significant impact on the secular state, bringing new challenges that have tested this central element of republican ideology.

A New Page in the Republican Narrative

Immigration and the Republic

This exploration of the republican model has identified and briefly examined the fundamental ideas and structures underlying the ideological construction and evolution of the modern French Republic, the social and political processes that have shaped French society since the revolutionary

---

79   Serge Berstein and Odile Rudelle, *Le Modèle républicain* (Paris: PUF, 1992), 7.
80   Paul Isoart and Christian Bidegavay, *Des Républiques francaises* (Paris: Economica, 1988), 22.

period. In the context of the current socio-cultural situation in the *ban-lieues*, an understanding of the nature of this evolution proves valuable in two respects. First, an awareness of the fundamental ideas underpinning French republicanism provides an ideological frame of reference within which contemporary social and cultural issues can be examined. Second, having broadly defined the characteristics of the republican model, it is now possible to assess the relevance of this model in the underprivileged suburbs, a process that will facilitate a deeper understanding of the causes behind the riots of 2005 and 2007. Before moving the analysis to the specific socio-cultural issues at stake in the *banlieues*, it is first necessary however to examine the republican model in the specific context of immigration, the consequences of which have emerged in recent years as perhaps the princi-pal threat, in terms of public and political perception, to the continuation of the French republican model. Silverman claims that immigration 'can represent both the liberal republic and the threat to the liberal republic; it is the embodiment of France's capacity for assimilation and proof of a break-down in assimilation; it is the embodiment of pluralism and proof of the impossibility of pluralism.'[81] An exploration of the relationship between French republicanism and the theme of immigration is also relevant as it incorporates the more specific questions of ethnicity and religion, topics that have provided major challenges for the republican model and that constituted salient political issues during the 2005 violence. These ques-tions of religion and ethnicity, introduced in this section, will be discussed in greater detail in the following chapter. Most importantly, the significant changes in migratory flux that have occurred in the latter part of the twen-tieth century have played a direct role in shaping and influencing the par-ticular situation in the suburbs – the *banlieues* have traditionally grouped together large numbers of immigrant populations and their descendants. Thus the suburbs have developed as a concentration of all the challenges, perceived or otherwise, brought to bear on the Republic as a result of issues stemming from immigration. This line of inquiry places the focus on what is termed 'the republican model of integration': an ideological and politi-

81   Silverman, *Deconstructing the Nation*, 15.

cal structure located within the broader context of French republicanism which has emerged in recent years as an independent area of political and academic interest as a result of changing attitudes towards immigration and the place of immigrants in French society.

Undoubtedly, immigration is a tangible social process that is inextricably linked with the progression and development of the modern French nation-state. Noiriel reveals that, alongside the United Sates and Canada, France is the industrialized country which owes the most to immigration.[82] Statistics show that 'one in every four French nationals has a parent or grandparent who is/was not French'.[83] In contemporary society, Weil affirms that questions of immigration and integration 'réveillent toujours de fortes passions [...] Elles touchent les citoyens au coeur de leurs valeurs les plus fortes et les plus contradictoires (l'identité nationale et le respect des droits de l'homme, par exemple)'.[84] However, despite the immense interest and debate that surrounds the subject of immigration and the concomitant theme of integration in contemporary French society, these issues did not play a prominent role in the affairs of the nation until the end of the 1960s and the beginning of the 1970s. For Hargreaves, the prolonged refusal to acknowledge the impact of immigration on the development of French society relates to the manner in which the concept of the Republic evolved: 'the central myths of national identity were [...] in place before the rise of large-scale immigration into France during the nineteenth century [...]. Entranced by the spell of those myths, historians in France paid little attention [...] to the contribution of immigrants to the national experience'.[85] Essentially, while in other nations, such as America, processes of immigration were inextricably linked with the foundation of the nation and intertwined with its progression and consolidation, France's national ideas and myths had already been cemented in the popular imagination by

82   Gérard Noiriel, *Etat, nation et immigration. Vers une histoire de pouvoir* (Paris: Gallimard, 2005), 102.

83   Silverman, *Deconstructing the Nation*, 10.

84   Patrck Weil, *La République et sa diversité. Immigration, intégration, discriminations* (Paris: Seuil, 2005), 7.

85   Hargreaves, *Multi-Ethnic France*, 14.

the time large-scale immigration occurred, situating immigration beyond
the perceived primary factors concerning the ideological structure of the
French republican model. It was not until the beginning of the 1970s that
the increasing salience of issues regarding immigration control and the
integration of immigrants propelled these questions into the academic
and political spotlight. Up to this point concern for immigration had been
confined 'in the main, to the specialized fields of demographic and tech-
nocratic planning, but it was now at the intersection of a far more diverse
disciplinary interest: that of sociology, geography, history, psychology,
ethnology, economics, law and others'.[86] Thus, perceptions of immigration
in mainstream society underwent a profound shift from an economic and
demographic perspective to an economic and socio-cultural one, a change
that was intimately linked to fluctuations in the prevalent migratory patterns and the changing status of immigrant workers in France, and one
that would have an enormous impact on the perceived role and place of
the immigrant in French society.

Rebuilding the Republic: Immigration and les Trente Glorieuses

In historical terms, France has maintained a strong tradition of immigration. Weil states that up until World War I a number of European countries
such as Belgium, Italy and Spain provided France with 'une immigration
de voisinage'; in the 1880s the immigrant population in France constituted
3 per cent of the total population.[87] It was in the years of the post-World
War period, however, that the phenomenon of immigration took on a
new scale and dimension in France. Industrialization, reconstruction and
demographic concerns constituted major factors inciting France to wel-
come immigrants. Demographic concerns arising from losses in the World
Wars gave a certain momentum to pro-immigration policies. In terms of
immigrant presence, Noiriel reveals that by the 1930s, in terms of percent-

---

86   Silverman, *Deconstructing the Nation*, 11.
87   Weil, *La République et sa diversité*, 14.

age of total population, immigrants in France represented a larger portion of the population than in the United States.[88] Naturally, migratory trends were constantly subject to prevailing economic conditions; during the economic crisis of the 1930s the French parliament, influenced by public opinion, passed the 1932 law permitting the government to impose quotas on foreign workers working in private enterprises within the industrial and commercial sectors. However, despite a drop in the influx of immigrants, industrial labour needs pushed the government to 'agir avec moderation, voire dans une autre direction' and levels of immigration remained above those recorded prior to World War I.[89]

Following the destruction of World War II, the situation underwent a profound change in official terms: the French government identified an urgent need for immigrant workers to participate in the national reconstruction. In the ensuing debate regarding the direction that immigration policy should take, two viewpoints dominated discussions. The economic perspective focused on the need to respond to the pressing labour shortages, while the demographic perspective looked towards permanent immigration to offset France's low population growth.[90] Discussion on the potential introduction of ethnic quotas, similar to those in place in the United States, also occupied a place in the debate, a product of the ever-dominant institutional concern relating to social cohesion and national unity. Although there was a widespread preference for European immigrants, proponents of the economic perspective were against the imposition of an 'ethnic hierarchy' that would give priority to Europeans but perhaps have a negative impact in terms of the nation's economic and industrial needs.[91] A compromise was reached with the 1945 government ordinance on immigration. At the heart of this ordinance was a formal acknowledgement that immigrants were not required to be employed in order to live in France. Moreover, it was officially accepted that an immigrant worker could be accompanied

---

88   Gérard Noiriel, *Le Creuset francais: histoire de l'immigration, XIXe–XXe siècles* (Paris: Seuil, 1988), 21.
89   Weil, *La République et sa diversité*, 14.
90   Hargreaves, *Multi-Ethnic France*, 19.
91   Ibid.

by his family when entering the country, or have them join him at a later date. This ordinance would shape French immigration policy for years to come as France was fixed 'comme pays d'immigration durable, de travailleurs mais aussi de familles'.[92] However it is important to note that even though this idea of long-term settlement was conceived only in relation to European immigration, the ordinance of 1945 did not set down any ethnic quotas, and in theory all ethnic groups were to be treated equally. Nonetheless, the desire to prioritize European immigration was evident. Erik Bleich states that 'the French state's organization of recruitment centres abroad [...] favoured the influx of migrants from Italy, Spain and Portugal over those from Turkey and North Africa.'[93]

Despite this officially unstated desire on the part of the French government to prioritize European immigration, the attribution of French citizenship to the population of the French colony of Algeria in 1946 represented a defining moment in the development of immigration in the French context since free circulation between these two territories was guaranteed, providing a lasting link between France and the Maghreb regions of Northern Africa. This move was compounded by the Evian Agreements of 1962 which implemented free circulation between France and Algeria following Algerian independence. In 1963, bilateral agreements were also signed with Morocco, among other nations, boosting the number of nationals from this country allowed into France.[94] As a result of these political developments, the boom in immigration that occurred during *les Trente Glorieuses* – the period of strong economic reconstruction, growth and prosperity that followed World War II and lasted until the early 1970s – went hand in hand with a massive influx of immigrants from the Maghreb regions. Hargreaves reveals, for example, that 'from a mere 22,000 in 1946, their numbers grew to 805,000 in 1982, making Algerians the largest national group among the foreign population in France.'[95]

92   Weil, *La République et sa diversité*, 15.
93   Erik Bleich, *Race Politics in Britain and France: Ideas and Policymaking since the 1960s* (Cambridge: Cambridge University Press, 2003), 116.
94   Silverman, *Deconstructing the Nation*, 43.
95   Hargreaves, *Multi-Ethnic France*, 21.

Although politicians recognized that immigration from Northern Africa was fulfilling a legitimate economic need, it is clear that those immigrants hailing from the Maghreb regions were not considered in the same light as immigrants originating in European countries. While the government rapidly facilitated family reunification for European immigrants, immigrants from the Maghreb regions were not treated in the same fashion. Weil reveals that in the 1950s, faced with increasing numbers of Algerian immigrants and a lack of housing for these workers, the government established hostels which were designed to discourage family reunification due to the incompatibility of this primitive form of housing with the needs of a family.[96] Essentially, immigrants from the Maghreb regions were viewed as temporary workers who would return to their homes once the economic and labour needs of French society had been met. Favell terms this aspect of French immigration 'insertion', given that the 'dominant logic of the state towards immigrants was centred [solely] on the idea of socio-economic *insertion*'.[97] The immigrant population were politically excluded from French society and socially disadvantaged due to their lack of citizenship. However, despite this position at the limits of society, Begag states that 'there came a time when, while the workers who had travelled to France on their own were still intent on their projected return, families began to arrive. This change was of great significance. It marked the beginning of real settlement, at any rate where children born in the receiving country were concerned'.[98] Thus the nature of immigration evolved from an 'economic immigration of manpower to a social immigration of dependants'.[99] This development marked the emergence of the theme of immigration as a social issue in the political sphere and, coupled with the economic downturn of the early 1970s, signalled a definitive shift in attitudes and perspectives regarding the place of immigrants in French society.

96　Patrick Weil, *La France et ses étrangers: l'aventure d'une politique de l'immigration, 1938–1991* (Paris: Calmann-Lévy, 1991), 60.

97　Adrian Favell, *Philosophies of Integration. Immigration and the Idea of Citizenship in France and Britain* (Basingstoke and New York: Palgrave, 2001), 46.

98　Azouz Begag, 'North African Immigrants in France: The Socio-Spatial Representation of "Here" and "There"', *Studies in European Culture and Society* (Loughborough: European Research Centre, 1988), 5.

99　Silverman, *Deconstructing the Nation*, 71.

The Immigrant as a Social Actor: Changing Perspectives on Immigration

Hargreaves states that 'by the end of the 1960s, the public authorities
were increasingly troubled by two main consequences of the laissez-faire
approach: their loss of control over the ethnic composition of the foreign
population and the appalling social conditions in which many immigrants
were living'.[100] The huge influx of immigrants to meet the labour demands
of *les Trente Glorieuses* had placed immense pressure on the social infrastructure of the nation. Thus, while the economy had expanded rapidly,
social conditions, especially in terms of housing, had progressed little.
These issues were compounded when family reunification accelerated and
further strain was placed on the system. In addition, the growing problem
of poor social conditions, especially with regard to housing, was the subject
of increased media attention in the early 1970s, transforming issues that had
previously been sidelined into salient political questions. Consequently,
the government acknowledged that the changes in migratory flux necessitated a new perspective on immigration, and the laissez-faire approach
of the past was replaced by a more interventionist policy. Similar to other
European countries, the approach of the government rested on two separate
policy strands: control and integration. With regard to gaining control of
immigration, the government of President Giscard d'Estaing 'temporarily'
suspended immigration in 1974. This political act was a direct response
to what had become the 'problem of immigration', a problem stemming
from the combination of a number of developments in the broader French
national context at the beginning of the 1970s: French internal migration
from rural areas to the cities; advances in industry; and a recent downturn
in the economy which resulted in rising unemployment. However, it is
important to note that underlying these economic motivating factors were
more profound concerns regarding ethnicity and social cohesion which
played a central role in directing the course of immigration policy. These
concerns were publicly expressed by high ranking officials such as Michel
Massenet, head of the Population and Migrations section at the Ministry of

100   Hargreaves, *Multi-Ethnic France*, 167.

Labour at the end of the 1960s: 'We hope that our society should contain no forms of segregation (even implicit), we should not underestimate the risk of seeing the appearance in our country of islands of people impermeable to the traditional processes of assimilation, which have, over the centuries, woven the unity of France from very diverse elements'.[101]

Essentially, this concern with questions regarding ethnicity reflected the construction of 'a new consensus on immigration [...] at the end of the 1960s and the beginning of the 1970s [...] At the heart of this consensus was a new racialization of the question of immigration, leading subsequently to the racialization of wider socio-economic and political questions'.[102] In practice, the 1974 ban did little to stem the flow of immigration due to the fact that the suspension was limited in a number of respects. First, given the position of France as a member of the European Community, EC nationals could not be denied entry. Second, the ban did not apply to asylum seekers who constituted a category apart ruled by international legal regulations. Certain categories of professionals were also exempt. In other words, the ban on immigration mainly targeted non-European immigration such as that originating in the Maghreb regions. Moreover, between 1977 and 1980, under the leadership of Giscard d'Estaing, the French government actively organized and facilitated the repatriation of immigrants, North Africans for the most part.[103] In this respect, Weil states that 'on visait le départ forcé de 100,000 étrangers par an [...] en majorité algériens, mais aussi marocains ou tunisiens'.[104] The political developments that took place around this time effectively illustrate the changing perspectives in relation to the theme of immigration, and, more particularly, immigration originating in Maghreb regions. It is interesting to note that these 'strong-arm tactics' employed by the government were counter-productive in terms of the government's aims.[105] Many Maghrebis feared losing access to the

---

101   Cited in Silverman, *Deconstructing the Nation*, 75.
102   Ibid. 71.
103   Thomas Janoski, *The Ironies of Citizenship: Naturalization and Integration in Industrialized Countries* (New York: Cambridge University Press, 2010), 84.
104   Weil, *La République et sa diversité*, 17.
105   Hargreaves, *Multi-Ethnic France*, 26.

French labour market if they returned home and thus decided to remain in France and have their families join them as part of the family reunification policy provisioned by the 1945 ordinance. Another area in which the ban on immigration had no effect was that of illegal immigration. Following the suspension, the immigrant population was progressively swollen by continuing illegal immigration.[106]

With regard to the government approach to the 'problem of immigration', Silverman makes it clear that both strands of this dual strategy were inextricably linked.[107] According to the official perspective, the successful integration of those immigrants residing legally in France could not be assured without first establishing firm control over further immigration. This achieved, it was then necessary to integrate those immigrants who were legally residing in France in order to ensure social cohesion. When the Left came to power in 1981, Mitterrand declared an amnesty for illegal immigrants. This amnesty regularized the situation of some 130,000 illegal immigrants. In relation to those immigrants already legally resident in France, many acquired citizenship and the associated full political participation through a process of naturalization requiring a formal request for citizenship after five years of residence in France. For legal immigrants of the second and third generations, citizenship was granted under Articles 44 and 23 of the *Code de la nationalité française* (Article 44 attributed citizenship automatically at the age of eighteen to second-generation immigrants who were born in France and had resided there since the age of thirteen, while Article 23 attributed citizenship at birth to third-generation immigrants born in France when at least one parent was also born in France).[108] It is worth noting that the Algerian situation required that citizenship law be interpreted in a slightly different manner. Given the colonial relationship between France and Algeria, Article 23 applied to second-generation immigrants in the Algerian context, given that persons born in Algeria

---

106   Ibid.
107   Silverman, *Deconstructing the Nation*, 83.
108   Brubaker, *Citizenship and Nationhood*, 140.

before its independence were technically born in France.[109] In any case, while formal possession or acquisition of citizenship did grant full political access to the immigrants concerned, for some populations of immigrant origin, citizenship would not prove sufficient to ensure complete acceptance in the social arena.

The Internal Outsider: Immigration as a Threat to National Unity

With the emergence, and subsequent growth, of the question of integration in the political sphere in the latter part of the 1970s and throughout the 1980s, the issue of immigration took on new proportions in the public domain. Discourse on integration provoked a renewal of the focus on ideas relating to the Republic and national identity, and, as a result, a change in perspective regarding the place of the immigrant in French society. It is important to note that the term 'integration' replaced that of 'assimilation' at the beginning of the 1980s due to the position of the latter, 'renvoyant à l'image, peu progressiste, de la France colonisatrice'.[110] A functionalist approach defines integration as the 'social, economic or political participation of people of minority origin without assuming that the end product of this process is, or necessarily should be, their assimilation into pre-existing French norms'.[111] However, Hargreaves reveals that in France there has been a tendency towards the 'normative equation of integration with assimilation' – that is, the eradication of all difference through total incorporation into French society, and most notably the abandoning of any minority cultural norms.[112] Paradoxically, as the idea of integration gained momentum in French society, so too did the idea of an inassimilable immigrant population. Powerful stereotypes became attached to the term 'immigration' in the popular imagination through a process that saw this

---

109   Ibid.
110   Michèle Tribalat, *Faire France. Une enquete sur les immigrés et leurs enfants* (Paris: La Découverte, 1995), 12.
111   Hargreaves, *Multi-ethnic France*, 36.
112   Ibid.

term being primarily associated with non-European workers. Silverman states that 'the reformulation of immigration [...] transformed the term "immigration" into a euphemism for non-Europeans (particularly North-Africans) and delegitimized it'.[113] The non-European immigrant population progressively came to be regarded as a threat to national unity and identity at a time when these themes were fast regaining popularity.[114]

Two significant and closely linked factors played an important role in this change in perceptions regarding immigrants. First, while non-European immigrants had formed an established part of immigration patterns in France for many years, their incorporation into French society, no matter how much it was desired by the immigrants themselves, was marked in a way that European immigration was not – the colour of their skin. Weil states that populations from Belgium, Italy, Spain, Russia, Germany and Portugal 'sont perçues comme s'étant intégrées dans la société française: au bout de deux générations, on pouvait difficilement distinguer dans la sphère publique le petit-fils [...] d'un immigrant de l'enfant originaire d'une famille depuis longtemps française'.[115] While European immigrants could not usually be physically distinguished from the *français de souche*, and thus could physically blend into the receiving society with relative ease in this respect, the skin-colour of non-European populations represented a permanent reminder of their status as immigrants. Consequently, when unfavourable economic conditions evoked public hostility towards immigrant populations, those immigrants marked by their somatic difference were immediately singled out. Moreover, the processes of family reunification begun under the 1945 ordinance resulted in a progressively deeper social penetration by these immigrants, and their descendants. Thus, while the ban on immigration was still in place, non-European immigrants appeared to be visibly multiplying in a context where ideas relating to the preservation of national unity and social cohesion were gaining pace. On its own, this issue does not appear to hold great significance; however when considered in conjunction with the second principal factor, it holds an added importance.

---

113   Silverman, *Deconstructing the Nation*, 73.
114   Ibid., 72.
115   Weil, *La République et sa diversité*, 48.

In historical terms, while the law of separation of 1905 established *laïcité* at the heart of the French Republic, this idea of the secular state was essentially superimposed on a society traditionally dominated by Christian religious beliefs, primarily Roman-Catholic. And while the secular state had originally placed the Church in firm opposition with the state and its representatives at a political level, the normally unobtrusive nature of the Roman-Catholic religion in terms of visibility in the public sphere meant that this separation placed little strain on the daily religious practices and demands associated with Catholicism. While the secular state did reduce the status and influence of the Catholic Church in the public sphere, Catholicism and *laïcité* coexisted comfortably in French society. However, with the influx of immigrants from non-European countries, particularly those from Northern Africa, the accepted coexistence of religion and state was challenged by the introduction to France of the Islamic religion, 'a religion which until their arrival had virtually no significant history within France'.[116] The beliefs associated with Islam made more physical demands on its followers, demands that were highly visible in the public sphere and that called into question the limits and boundaries of the secular state. Polygamy and the rules governing female modesty – most frequently manifested through the wearing of a headscarf – represented two of the most visible physical indications of the differences between the Islamic religion and French social structures and norms. Islam was thus viewed by many as incompatible with the republican model, fuelling the idea that immigrants originating in the Maghreb regions were inassimilable. The question of Islam will be addressed in the following chapter.

Politics Ethnicized: The Rise of the Front National

The question of integration, the (in)assimilability of immigrants, particularly those of North African origin, and the perceived threat to national cohesion, constructed a social setting that was ultimately hostile towards immigration and cultural difference. The development of this cultural,

116   Favell, *Philosophies of Integration*, 173.

social and political context cannot be understood unless considered in light of what Patrick Simon terms 'l'explosion politique du Front National' during the 1980s, because it was with the growth of the Front National on the political stage that the racialization or 'ethnicization' of the question of immigration was cemented, and indeed intensified, most notably in the political arena.[117] Hargreaves states that if ethnic politics is defined as 'political behaviour conditioned to a significant degree by conscious processes of ethnic differentiation', it was not until the 1970s 'that stirrings of this kind became apparent in mainstream party-political activities, and it is only since the early 1980s that they have played a sustained role in French national politics'.[118] Crucial here is the role played by mainstream parties in creating an environment that was favourable to the themes and agenda of the Front National. According to Hargreaves, the absence of the ethnic element in politics before the mid-1970s can be explained by three principal factors: 'the insulation of policy-making in the field of immigration from parliamentary debate, the largely non-interventionist role of the state prior to 1968 [...] and above all, the conditions of full employment and rapid economic growth which prevailed until the oil shocks of the 1970s'.[119] However, significant changes in these areas would facilitate the growth and development of ethnic politics.

In the area of policy-making, a series of legal rulings which occurred throughout the 1970s changed the structure of government action on immigration. 'Major immigration controls imposed by executive order [...] were declared to be unlawful, forcing the government to amend the measures and/or submit them to Parliament in the form of draft legislation open to analysis and argument from all sides of the political spectrum'.[120] For example, Lionel Stoléru, who was responsible for immigrant workers at governmental level, attempted to impose a three-year suspension of family

---

117   Patrick Simon, 'L'arbre du racisme et la foret des discriminations', in Nacira Guénif-Souilamas, ed., *La république mise à nu par son immigration* (Paris: La Fabrique, 2006), 160–177 (165).

118   Hargreaves, *Multi-ethnic France*, 170.

119   Ibid.

120   Ibid.

reunification in 1977.[121] Protests at this decision forced him to revise his position and the policy was altered to allow families to settle in France but not work there. Ultimately, however, judicial review found the policy to be untenable. In terms of state intervention, the government became more active not only in terms of the control of immigration, but with regard to the integration of those immigrants already settled in France. As has already been mentioned, this was particularly visible in the domain of social housing where increased media attention regarding the living conditions of immigrants spurred the government into action.[122] However, as more immigrants became 'greater consumers of other welfare services as a consequence of family settlement', members of the majority population began to resent the presence of immigrants in the face of rising unemployment.[123] In a climate of economic insecurity, immigrants began to be seen as competitors in terms of social and economic resources. Moreover, this state of affairs occurred at a time when unemployment was a pressing concern for the French public. The response of mainstream politicians targeted immigrant populations: 'Prime Minister Jacques Chirac and Labour Minister Michel Durafour both drew very public attention to the "paradox" that a country with two million immigrant workers had 90,000 unemployed'.[124] And it was within this context of increased hostility towards immigrants that Jean-Marie le Pen and the Front National (FN) garnered support and emerged as a visible force in the French political arena.

The FN had been founded by Jean-Marie Le Pen in 1972; between 1972 and 1982 the group barely registered on the electoral landscape. However, in the early 1980s, the anti-immigration stance and the idea of 'la préférence nationale' championed by the FN began to attract support among an uneasy electorate, support that was confirmed by the success of the party in both the 1983 municipal elections and the 1984 European

---

121   Peter Fysch and Jim Wolfreys, *The Politics of Racism in France* (Basingstoke: Palgrave Macmillan, 2003), 41.

122   This issue will be examined in detail in the following chapter in the context of the *politique de la ville* and the development of the HLM apartment blocks.

123   Hargreaves, *Multi-ethnic France*, 170.

124   Fysch and Wolfreys, *The Politics of Racism in France*, 40.

elections.[125] The major breakthrough of 1983 took place in Dreux, a small town near Paris. It was here, in a town 'which the FN had marked for cultivation with its socio-economic problems and immigrant population of over 20 per cent', that Le Pen's party marked a new stage in its political trajectory.[126] As a result of irregularities in the ballot taken at the municipal elections held in March of that year, and which the 'left had won by only eight votes', a municipal by-election was held in Dreux in September 1983.[127] In the first round of the election, the FN candidate, Jean-Pierre Stirbois, scored 16.72 per cent, and, in order to avoid a second defeat, an alliance was created between the centre-right Rassemblement pour la République (RPR), the Union pour la démocratie française (UDR) and the FN. The RPR-UDF-FN coalition won the second round with approximately 55 per cent of the vote, marking a huge success for the Front National.[128] The 'FN [...] now had a role in governing a town of some 35,000 inhabitants, with [three] FN colleagues becoming assistants to the neo-Gaullist mayor.[129] This administration replaced the Socialist-led one of Françoise Gaspard. The victory, combined with those at further by-elections in Aulnay-sous-bois and Le Pen's hometown, Morbihan, represented significant progress for the Front National as a political party. It is important to note that these unprecedented successes did not come about as a result of a change in the policies of the Front National. Rather, this success 'reflects [...] the growth of insecurity among a significant part of the electorate during a period of rising unemployment and a shift in the terms of political debate towards ethnic scapegoating'.[130] Bleich states that the Front National 'struck a chord with its themes of delinquency, criminality and immigration'.[131]

125   See Jane Freedman, *Immigration and Insecurity in France* (Aldershot: Ashgate, 2004), 144.
126   James Shields, *The Extreme Right in France: From Pétain to Le Pen* (Abingdon and New York: Routledge, 2007), 195.
127   Ibid.
128   Freedman, *Immigration and Insecurity in France*, 40.
129   Ibid.
130   Hargreaves, *Multi-ethnic France*, 173.
131   Bleich, *Race Politics in Britain and France*, 147.

The concept of 'national preference' was one of the Front National's primary political policies, the fundamental idea behind this policy being 'that in matters of employment, housing, education, and other state benefits, French and EU nationals should be given preference over others'.[132] Le Pen famously attempted to justify this policy on national television in 1984 when he explained that 'he prefers his daughters to his cousins, his cousins to his neighbours, his neighbours to people he doesn't know, and people he doesn't know to his enemies'.[133] Balibar confirms that in terms of the other political parties across the spectrum, this policy of national preference was 'politically, morally and philosophically difficult' to oppose.[134] There are two reasons for this difficulty. First, Freedman states that the concept of national preference can be described as a process of 'hierarchization' which could be interpreted as a mere extension of other policies already in place.[135] Freedman gives the example of employment in public services to illustrate this point, emphasizing that only EU citizens are eligible for employment in this sector. Consequently, it could be argued that the policy of the Front National was merely a localized adaptation of this framework. Second, and most significant, given the predominant concerns among the electorate regarding unemployment and social insecurity, the idea of national preference was a seductive one, appearing to offer reasonable and simple solutions. To those threatened with unemployment it appeared to be a protective policy rather than a racist strategy, and, as a result, the Front National succeeded in recasting the 'racist logic of absolute and national difference [...] in the euphemistic discourse of national preference'.[136]

Of course while the thinly veiled racist policies propagated by the Front National did gain certain support among the electorate, these policies did not go unopposed in the public sphere. A new form of mobilization against racism began to develop from the beginning of the 1980s, a

---

132 Freedman, *Immigration and Insecurity in France*, 144.
133 Ibid.
134 Etienne Balibar, 'De la preference nationale à l'invention de la politique: comment lutter contre le néofascisme', in Jean Viard, ed., *Aux sources du populisme nationaliste* (Paris: L'Aube, 1996), 197.
135 Freedman, *Immigration and Insecurity in France*, 145.
136 Ibid.

mobilization based on the marginalization and exclusion of young people of immigrant origins from French society. Members of the immigrant community decided that it was necessary to mobilize their own opposition to racism and discrimination since the state appeared unwilling to take up their cause. Indeed, the hardline approach to immigration adopted by mainstream parties served to compound the experience of discrimination and marginalization. The failure of Mitterrand, the Socialist Party presidential candidate, to fulfill his 1981 election promise to give immigrants the right to vote in local elections constitutes a prime example of the failure to oppose the hardline policies advocated by the extreme right. The announcement of this promise in August 1981, one of the one hundred and ten on Mitterrand's agenda, was met with hostility on the Right and mixed reactions on the Left, provoking Mitterrand to back down. In April 1985, 'le président de la République fait savoir qu'il reste favorable au droit de vote pour les immigrés, sachant pertinemment que la mesure n'est réalisable ni politiquement ni juridiquement'.[137] Freedman states:

> The fact that the mainstream political parties showed little inclination to resist the influence of the Front National as they became a force in French politics [...] confirmed to many that these politicians were not willing to sacrifice electoral popularity to defend the rights of immigrants or ethnic minorities against racism.[138]

Thus, young immigrants rallied themselves against institutional racism as well as racially motivated acts of violence. Fysh and Wolfreys reveal that during the 1980s, 'some 500 to 800 associations were founded every year by persons or groups of immigrant origins, with some 5,000 or so still in existence at the end of the decade'.[139] And it was in this context that the *beur* movement emerged. The word 'beur' referred to those youths of immigrant origin whose parents had immigrated to France from North Africa. A slang version of the word 'Arabe', the term was adopted by these youths as a means of expressing their identity. In 1983, following the electoral victory of the Front National, ten youths of Maghreb origins marched from Marseille to Paris to highlight the racism and discrimination suffered by

---

137   Weil, *Qu'est-ce qu'un francais?*, 171.
138   Freedman, *Immigration and Insecurity in France*, 156.
139   Fysh and Wolfreys, *The Politics of Racism in France*, 164.

beur youths. The march aroused enormous media attention and the youths were met in Paris by President Mitterrand, who promised to reform the 1972 anti-discrimination law, a promise that would remain unfulfilled. It was in this context that SOS-Racisme, a politically autonomous organization, formed around the theme of anti-racism in 1984. Hargreaves and McKinney affirm that '[c]ompared to groups that mobilized upon a Beur, Franco-Maghrebi [...] identity, the identity, message, and political strategy of SOS-Racisme were perfectly suited to gain broader popular and elite support'.[140] While the *beur* mobilization was limited to a particular community, 'SOS-Racisme was self-consciously pluricultural and directed its appeal to French youths of all origins'.[141] The slogan 'touche pas à mon pote' was representative of a broad commitment to anti-discrimination and the organization gained significant support. A key element in the success of the organization was the fact that whereas the 'Beurs rebuffed political overtures as cooption', SOS-Racisme was willing to work with the Socialist party and its leader, Harlem Désir, had close connections with the Socialists.[142] A rival group, France-Plus, was another manifestation of this mobilization in the public sphere. Unlike SOS-Racisme however, the aim of France-Plus was to encourage young people of immigrant origins to engage with the political process.[143] The emergence of these and similar action groups highlighted the sense of injustice among those of immigrant origins, faced with a political context that appeared to be moving progressively towards the extreme-right. However, despite the emergence and activities of anti-racist organizations and groups protesting at the alienation of immigrants in French society, the rise of the Front National had given the ethnicization of politics a powerful momentum.[144]

---

140 David Blatt, 'Immigrant Politics in a Republican Nation', in Alec Hargreaves and Mark McKinney, eds, *Post-colonial Cultures in France* (London: Routledge, 1997), 40–59 (45).
141 Ibid.
142 Andrew Geddes, *The Politics of Migration in Europe* (London: Sage, 2003), 69.
143 Ibid.
144 These protest groups encountered their own difficulties in terms of organization and political affiliations. For a detailed exploration of these issues see Fysh and Wolfreys, *The Politics of Racism in France*.

Limiting Nationality: Reforming the Code de la Nationalité Française

The success of the Front National had important and far-reaching consequences in terms of the ethnicization of politics in France. The anti-
immigration stance of the Front National effectively catapulted the theme
of national identity into the political limelight, and Hargreaves reveals that
'[r]esponding to this shift in the political agenda, the traditional parties of
both left and right organized major debates on the theme of French identity in the spring of 1985'.[145] Following this, in an attempt to reverse the
loss of voters to the Front National, the RPR and the UDF made reform
of the nationality code a key element of their shared campaign leading up
to the 1985 legislative elections.[146] The reform proposed by the traditional
right-wing was aimed at reforming, or indeed abolishing, Articles 23 and
44 of the French Nationality Code (CNF), a move which would end the
'automatic acquisition of French nationality by people of foreign origin'.[147]
This political standpoint was symbolic of the wider ethnicization of French
politics, and with the victory of the centre-right in the 1986 elections,
reform appeared to be inevitable.[148] The newly elected government, led
by Jacques Chirac, would introduce legislation to achieve the proposed
changes. However, the intended reforms encountered certain important
obstacles. In relation to Article 23, Hargreaves identifies two undesirable
consequences that would result from reform. First, if Article 23 was abolished, 'this would remove the simplest mechanism open to the mass of
French citizens for proving their nationality'.[149] As it stood, possession
of two birth certificates (that of the person proving their nationality and
that of one parent) showing that both births had taken place in France was
enough to prove that the person in question was French. The *Bureau de la
Nationalité* did not wish to see 'la remise en cause du double *jus soli*. Parce
que c'est un principe du droit français de la nationalité, jamais mis en cause

145   Hargreaves, *Multi-ethnic France*, 141.
146   Weil, *Qu'est-ce qu'un français?*, 170.
147   Hargreaves, *Multi-ethnic France*, 155.
148   Weil, *Qu'est-ce qu'un français?*, 171.
149   Hargreaves, *Multi-ethnic France*, 155.

depuis 1889, même sous Vichy.[150] Second, if the provisions of Article 23 were altered to exclude those originating in Algeria and other former French colonies, this would be 'tantamount to denying the historical legitimacy of French colonization'.[151] These factors effectively dissuaded the government from any attempts to reform Article 23; instead, efforts were directed towards Article 44. Chirac's government proposed a revision of Article 44 that would require a request for French nationality rather than automatic receipt. Moreover, the reformed Article 44 would require an oath of allegiance as well as excluding those with certain criminal convictions. Weil states that these conditions were particularly contentious since an oath of allegiance was not part of the republican tradition and the restriction based on convictions could stop a youth born in France accessing citizenship solely because of an infringement of the law.[152]

Protests against the proposed reforms were widespread on the political left among trade unions, church leaders and human rights organizations. The Socialist leader, François Mitterrand, made his opposition known at the Council of Ministers, where the text was adopted. Additionally, associations such as the Ligue des droits de l'homme and SOS-Racisme organized their own protests. Perhaps most significantly Albin Chalandon, the RPR Minister of Justice, refused to present the reforms to parliament.[153] Faced with huge opposition to the bill, Chirac backed down and decided to postpone it. This postponement was prolonged in 1987 when a special commission was set up to review the entire nationality code. Following this, Mitterrand won a second term in office and the centre-right lost their parliamentary majority and so it was not until the return of the right to power, five years later, that the question of the reform of the nationality code was brought up again. In this context, it is important to note that, while 'there was much opposition to the [1986] proposal by the Chirac government to modify the Code, there was a far wider consensus on the

---

150 Weil, *Qu'est-ce qu'un français?*, 171.
151 Hargreaves, *Multi-ethnic France*, 155.
152 Weil, *Qu'est-ce qu'un français?*, 173.
153 Ibid.

need to change the Code in some way'.[154] The report of the Long Commission, established in 1987 to review the nationality code, made it clear that reform was needed. Silverman states that this view was 'indicative of the way in which the contemporary construction of "the problem of immigration" had become legitimized as "common sense"'; there was general agreement that the Code was 'ill-suited to define nationality in the modern age'.[155] Thus in 1993, a modified proposal was brought before parliament and subsequently entered into legislation. The 1993 bill, put forward by the new Minister of Justice, Marceau Long, represented a victory for the right, the most important element of the bill being the requirement that children born in France of immigrant parents were required to request citizenship between the ages of sixteen and twenty-one.[156]

Thus the anti-immigrant sentiment that had progressively pervaded French society since the mid-1970s found concrete form in the political arena. The change to the nationality code confirmed the position of the 'problem' of immigration at the forefront of the concerns dominating the political sphere. Hargreaves states that the '1993 reform of the CNF was calculated to serve as a symbolic gesture of the government's intent to "do something" about immigration without fundamentally infringing the values associated with France's republican tradition'.[157] However, it cannot be denied that the fundamental principle of equality was in some way compromized by the 1993 reform. Weil sums up this compromise effectively in saying '[o]n demande plus, en 1993, au fils de Marocain, de Portugais ou de Turc que l'on n'a demandé au fils d'Italien, de Polonais ou d'apatride avant où après guerre, et l'on rompt ainsi avec une pratique de reconnaissance égalitaire qui avait un fondement profond'.[158] Hargreaves claims that had it not been for the rise of the Front National in the 1980s, 'it is doubtful whether the traditional centre-right parties would have implemented or even proposed the changes which were made in the CNF in 1993'.[159] It is clear that the success of the Front National was derived from

---

154   Silverman, *Deconstructing the Nation*, 145.
155   Ibid.
156   Weil, *Qu'est-ce qu'un français*, 176.
157   Hargreaves, *Multi-ethnic France*, 141.
158   Weil, *Qu'est-ce qu'un français*, 177.
159   Hargreaves, *Multi-ethnic France*, 161.

a more profound social malaise regarding the place of immigrants in society, a malaise that was at once rooted in concerns regarding ethnicity and national identity, and fears related to economic insecurity. Essentially, the reform of the nationality code crystallized the challenge to French republican values that widespread anti-immigrant sentiment had brought about. And although the 1993 reform was reversed five years later, when the left returned to power under the leadership of Lionel Jospin, the problem of immigration remained a salient political issue. The first-round victory of Le Pen in the 2002 Presidential elections is among the most recent illustrations of this fact.

The Eternal Outsider

In light of the issues introduced in this section, it is clear that the questions of ethnicity and religion have played a significant role in the general process that saw immigration move from having a positive effect on French economy and society, in terms of political and public perceptions, to being perceived as a threat to national unity and social cohesion. One example of this is a BVA poll carried out for *Paris-Match* in 1985 that found that two-thirds of those questioned felt that France was in danger of losing her national identity unless the foreign population was limited.[160] The rise of the Front National, campaigning on a platform of anti-immigration, brought this perceived threat to the political arena where immigration developed as a dominant concern among parties all across the political spectrum. Of course, in broader terms, the changes in perspectives on immigration and the place of immigrants in French society had an impact on more profound underlying issues such as the concept of citizenship. Historically fused, as illustrated by Brubakers, the notions of citizenship and belonging became disjointed as negative perceptions of immigrants, even those having acquired French citizenship, placed them beyond the traditional parameters of national belonging. Immigrants, and especially those of Maghreb origins, found themselves in a no-man's land at the outer reaches

---

160   Miriam Feldblum, *Reconstructing Citizenship: The Politics of Nationality Reform and Immigration in Contemporary France* (New York: SUNY Press, 1999), 45.

of the Republic – officially and legally citizens, but socially stigmatized and permanently viewed as outsiders. Ultimately, it is this position that constitutes the blind spot at the heart of French republicanism, a blind-spot that can be linked to the foundations of the Republic and the abstract nature of the *Déclaration des droits de l'homme et du citoyen*. Essentially, the paradox that saw different elements of society in revolutionary France struggle to be viewed as equal in the proclaimed home of equality, is the same paradox that has seen immigrants in the post-war epoch struggle to be accepted by a society of which they are legally and politically members, and to move past the label of 'outsider'. For, while the abstract nature of the *Déclaration* undoubtedly facilitated the development of this docu-ment as a universally applicable framework within which the democratic process could flourish, this same abstract nature meant that the principles of this ideological model were not always entirely grounded in concrete measures. In revolutionary France, the proclamation of universal equality was not enough to ensure its application to all parts of society. The same is true with regard to post-war immigration in France where the attribu-tion of citizenship has not translated into national belonging in a cultural sense. Jane Freedman draws on the work of Favell when she claims that 'the "myth" of Republican citizenship can be seen to have been mobilized as part of a "mystificatory discourse" to "sustain a political consensus that is less and less responsive to the social facts and demands of the situation"'.[161] This lacuna in the republican model has facilitated the racialization of the question of immigration in France in the post-war period. As a result, the French model of integration has been corroded from within due to the growth of racism and discrimination in French society. These issues have created a social context where the potential for social fragmentation is increased by internal processes that engender exclusion and alienation among immigrants and citizens of immigrant origins. Thus, the republican model is effectively undermined through a circular process that is rooted *within* the republican model rather than outside it.

---

161   Freedman, *Immigration and Insecurity in France*, 3.

This brief exploration of immigration and its place in the French republican narrative has served to give an insight into the changing place of immigration in French society in the post-war period, as well as introducing the dominant social attitudes, issues and perceptions impacting upon the lives of immigrants and their descendants living in France, particularly those originating in the countries of northern Africa. The chapter has not only examined the perceived challenges posed to the Republic in terms of integration and ongoing social cohesion, but has also introduced, in general terms, the more profound underlying issues at stake within the ideological parameters of the republican model, namely the discrimination and exclusion that threaten the continuation of the French social model. These issues all play a role in the social, cultural and economic situation in which citizens of immigrant origin, especially those of African origins, find themselves, and in the challenges faced by populations permanently marked by their different ethnic heritage. Having examined these issues in the more general national context, the next chapter will begin to focus on the specific context of the *quartiers sensibles*, where the effects of these developments are clearly visible. The effects of post-war immigration in France have directly influenced and shaped the social and economic environment of these areas, playing an important part in the creation and perpetuation of the *banlieues*.

In the Shadows of the Republic:
Social and Ethnic Issues in the *Quartiers Sensibles*

Since its foundation, the republican model has provided a social and political matrix within which French society has developed and progressed. As has been shown in previous chapters, this model has been moulded and shaped by numerous political events and debates since its conception in order to arrive at its present day state: an ideological entity representing the ideas and myths that are the very fabric of French society. Having explored the ideological construction of the Republic, I will now move the focus from the general to the specific, from a wide-ranging discourse exploring the founding principles of the Republic to a specific examination of those areas of relegation that exist at the limits of this political and social system. The general ideological context that has been established provides a frame of reference for an investigation into the development of the particular social, cultural and economic setting that has evolved in the *quartiers sensibles*. This chapter will thus begin to explore, in detail, the nature of the blind spot of French republicanism – that is, those areas demonstrating the gap that exists between the ideals of the Republic and the social application of those ideals. This lacuna separating principles and their application poses a threat to the continuation of the republican model; the socio-cultural situation that exists in the *quartiers sensibles* provides tangible evidence of its existence, and indeed growth, at the beginning of the twenty-first century. The *quartiers sensibles* serve to illustrate the limitations and failings of republicanism in France in terms of its social application.

The Origins of the Contemporary *Banlieues*

The Grands Ensembles

As mentioned in Chapter 2, the period of reconstruction and economic growth that followed World War II provoked an urgent need for workers in France. This need was answered in large part through immigration, and throughout the 1950s and 1960s foreign workers, a large proportion of whom travelled from the Maghreb regions of Northern Africa, came to work in France. However, while there was an abundance of work, the dramatic rise in population, especially the foreign population – the amount of foreigners living in France doubled between 1954 and 1975 – resulted in a severe housing crisis.[1] Annie Power reveals that by the mid-1950s there was an acute housing shortage, which meant that a large portion of the French population was living in inferior accommodation.[2] The state was forced to act and the 1951 law on housing law introduced new low cost housing measures in the form of the 'Habitations à Loyer Modéré' (HLM). The new term replaced the old 'Habitations à bon marché' and Jacques Barou states that the change was indicative of the wider scope that social housing would now assume.[3] The development of the HLMs involved the construction of large, purpose-built housing estates at the periphery of towns and cities.[4] The construction figures of the time reflect the enormity of this

---

1 James Hollifield, 'Immigration and Republicanism in France: The Hidden Consensus', in Wayne Cornelius, Philip Martin and James Hollifield, eds, *Controlling Immigration: A Global Perspective* (Stanford: Stanford University Press, 1994), 143–176 (151).

2 Annie Power, *Hovels to High Rise: State Housing in Europe since 1850* (London: Routledge, 1993), 40.

3 Jacques Barou, *La Place du Pauvre, Histoire et géographie sociale de l'habitat HLM* (Paris: L'Harmattan, 1992), 27. The *Habitations à bon marché* (HBM) had been established with the Bonnevay law of 1912, which allowed local authorities to create low-cost housing organizations. However the impact of these organizations was not significant and it was only with the introduction of the HLMs that the development of social housing progressed significantly.

4 Power, *Hovels to High Rise*, 44.

programme of social housing development: 316,564 apartments completed in 1960; 411,599 in 1965; and 456,274 in 1970.[5] The architecture of the HLMs was influenced by the modernist school of thought and especially by the style of the renowned Swiss architect, Le Corbusier, who placed emphasis on the 'efficiency' of buildings and prioritized geometric forms.[6] Le Corbusier attempted to reconcile man with the idea of the machine, a concept stemming from the unprecedented industrial growth that occurred in the post-war period, and concrete was the primary building material in many of his projects. As a result, the newly constructed HLMs took the form of enormous rectangular towers, often containing over a thousand apartments. From the point of view of housing authorities, Le Corbusier's design maximized size and functionality at low cost. One of the best-known examples of this style is the Quatre mille in the suburb of La Courneuve, the name a reference to the number of apartments contained in its eighteen stories. Thus France entered a period that would come to be known as 'les années béton'.[7] These huge apartment blocks, described as 'le plus grand ratage urbanistique français' by Ménanteau, were collectively christened 'les grands ensembles' in the context of the 1958 decree establishing the *Zones à urbaniser en priorité* (ZUP).[8] Essentially, the ZUP represented the political and administrative framework within which construction in the suburbs would be focused during *les Trente Glorieuses*.[9]

From Symbol of Progress to Point of Social Rupture

It is important to note that when the *grands ensembles* were first built, these enormous apartment blocks were hailed as the zenith of urban living, a tangible sign of urban and social progress. At the end of the 1950s and

5   Barou, *La Place du Pauvre*, 45.
6   See William Curtis, *Le Corbusier, Ideas and Forms* (London and New York: Phaidon, 2001); and Michael Miller, *The Representation of Place: Urban Planning and Protest in France and Great Britain, 1950–1980* (Aldershot: Ashgate, 2003).
7   See Michel Winock, *Chronique des années soixante* (Paris: Seuil, 1987).
8   Jean Ménanteau, *Les Banlieues* (Paris: Le Monde Editions, 1997), 54.
9   Ibid., 53.

throughout the 1960s, living in the *grands ensembles* was considered a step up on the housing ladder.[10] The *grands ensembles* represented modern living, an image that was compounded by the memory of the inferior housing of the early 1950s.[11] The newly constructed HLM apartments were comfortable and well-equipped and, as a result, attracted members of the middle classes as well as the members of lower classes suffering directly from the housing crisis. Pierre Merlin reveals that initially at least, the population of the *grands ensembles* was close to the national average in terms of revenue and socioprofessional makeup.[12] With the development of the *grands ensembles*, the state anticipated a mix of social classes, therefore the development of a context where social difference could be surmounted. The *grands ensembles* would take on an important social role as 'le support écologique de la culture de masse [...] et la genèse d'une autre société'.[13] However, this would not prove to be the case in reality. Grafmeyer and Joseph state that physical proximity did not offset social distance. On the contrary, 'la proximité physique n'exclut pas la distance sociale. Elle peut au contraire la révéler et la renforcer, en suscitant des tensions et des conflits bien différents, dans leur nature, des petites frictions observables dans la communauté villageoise'.[14] This observation proved to be correct: Jean-Claude Chamboredon and Madeleine Lemaire critiqued the illusion of a classless social context in an article published in the *Revue Française de Sociologie* in 1970.[15]

Chamboredon and Lemaire identified two principal categories of household occupying the *grands ensembles*. First, there were those households at the top of their housing ladder, glad to have finally secured accommodation that was sufficiently large and comfortable. For these families, the move to the HLMs represented the apex of their social progression; the standard of living was often significantly higher than in their previous

10　Jean-Marc Stébé, *La crise des banlieues* (Paris: PUF, 1999), 43.
11　Ibid.
12　Merlin, *Les banlieues*, 15.
13　René Kaës, *Vivre dans les grands ensembles* (Paris: Editions Ouvrières, 1963), 67.
14　Cited in Stébé, *La crise des banlieues*, 45.
15　Cited in Merlin, *Les Banlieues*, 15.

lodgings and provided a level of comfort that they could not otherwise afford. Second, there were households who were at the bottom of their housing ladder, families for whom the *grands ensembles* provided acceptable accommodation at a reasonable price, but who would move to superior accommodation as soon as they had the means to do so. These families were representative of the middle class that the social architects of the *grands ensembles* had hoped would fit seamlessly alongside members of the lower classes. However, this social bond failed to materialize as spatial proximity ultimately failed to reduce social distance. For middle class households, the experience of the *grands ensembles* allowed them a taste of modern comfort under the constraints of collective living.[16] However, as soon as these families could afford to progress on the housing ladder they left the *grands ensembles* in search of more comfortable and better-placed lodgings. The departing members of the middle class were then replaced by the poorest members of society, a large proportion of whom were immigrants. Jean Ménanteau effectively sums up the situation when he speaks of the flight of the middle class.[17]

Consequently, by the end of the 1970s, immigrants and French families facing financial hardship, or 'des Français en voie de désocialisation', constituted the majority of the population of the *grands ensembles*.[18] The disproportionate growth of the immigrant population taking up residence in the *grands ensembles* was particularly striking and David Lepoutre claims that certain suburban estates appeared to be spaces of relegation for immigrant households.[19] For his part, Silverstein states that 'in the most precarious *cités*, foreign nationals in general tend to be up to seven times more numerous than French citizens'.[20] This development in the socio-economic composition of the *grands ensembles*, combined with the economic downturn of the

---

16   Jacques Donzelot, *Quand la ville se défait* (Paris: Seuil, 2006), 49.
17   Ménanteau, *Les banlieues*, 60.
18   Body-Gendrot, *Sortir des banlieues*, 21.
19   David Lepoutre, *Coeur de Banlieue, Codes rites et langages* (Paris: Odile Jacob, 2001), 31.
20   Paul A. Silverstein, *Algeria in France: Transpolitics, Race and Nation* (Bloomington: Indiana University Press, 2004), 96.

1970s, represented a decisive shift that would have a profound impact on the evolution of the *grands ensembles* as areas of relegation and exclusion. Hargreaves reveals that 'until the late 1970s, [immigrants] were [...] more fully integrated into the world of work – in the simple sense of holding jobs of one kind or another – than the French nationals themselves.'[21] However, with the end of the period of sustained economic growth that constituted *les Trente glorieuses*, it was the immigrant population who suffered most from the economic fallout. The consequences, which became visible from the end of the 1970s, were far-reaching: 'In the industrial sector as a whole (including construction), foreigners represented two-fifths of the jobs lost between 1979 and 1982, though they accounted for only about a tenth of the total industrial labor force.'[22] The *grands ensembles*, with their significant immigrant population, became characterized by unemployment, creating a situation where processes of socio-economic relegation and exclusion gathered momentum. Stébé states that 'ceux qui avaient l'espoir de partir des cités n'en ont plus les moyens, et les nouveaux arrivants – immigrés ou français – sont pour une grande majorité dans une situation plus précaire encore que leurs prédécesseurs.'[23] The deteriorating economic climate and rapidly growing levels of unemployment placed the inhabitants of these suburban areas in an acute and prolonged state of economic insecurity.

Structural Isolation and Socio-cultural Exclusion in the Grands Ensembles

Alongside the social and economic changes taking place in the suburbs, the structure and physical form of the *grands ensembles* undoubtedly played a significant role in the evolution of the *banlieues* as a social habitat. The construction of these apartment blocks, upwards as opposed to outwards, posed a challenge to the traditional idea of the community. The street had always been a microcosm of urban society, a place of social interaction and

---

21   Hargreaves, *Multi-ethnic France*, 53.
22   Ibid.
23   Stébé, *La crise des banlieues*, 46.

development where adults could meet and children at play were easily supervised. However, while undoubtedly making great gains in terms of space and provision of accommodation, the high-rise apartment blocks destroyed this traditional role of the street. In this respect, the analysis of David Hargreaves relating to the effects of British high-rise apartment blocks on the traditional idea of the community can be applied to the French context:

> High-rise flats which replaced many slums [...] did not replicate the social structure or the physical structure of the streets which they supplanted. Young mothers and old people became socially dislocated and isolated, 'flat-bound' and so physically and socially separated. Children no longer played outside the open front door or round the corner, but in new public spaces where they were not known by passing adults and not seen by anxious parents.[24]

Thus, the *grands ensembles* brought about a fundamental change in the social processes at the heart of community life. The street no longer existed as an intermediary space between the public and the private, and the concrete corridors of the apartment blocks did not offer the same opportunity or scope for social interaction. The maze of corridors became a hostile place, populated by young people with nothing to do, and the idea of the community lost significance as families withdrew to the privacy of their apartment.

The size of the of the *grands ensembles*, combined with their location at the periphery of France's towns and cities, called for comprehensive new facilities, including transport infrastructure, schools, shops, health services and meeting places, to name but a few.[25] Unfortunately, an imprudent planning policy during the construction of the *grands ensembles* resulted in a severe lack of some of these necessary facilities and, as a result, the *grands ensembles* were not equipped to offer the high quality of life intended by those who conceived of the projects.[26] The *grands ensembles* had been built

---

24 David Hargreaves, *The Challenge for the Comprehensive School: Culture, Curriculum and Community* (London: Routledge, 1982), 31.

25 Power, *From Hovels to High Rise*, 50.

26 Ibid.

in response to a severe housing crisis, and facilities for young people in particular had not been given adequate consideration by planners. Consequently, the youth gathered in the parking lots, the corridors and the stairwells, and there was a marked increase in acts of delinquency committed by disenchanted young people frustrated with their situation. The feeling of isolation experienced by the residents of the *grands ensembles* was augmented by the geographical position of these apartment blocks, situated in development zones at the periphery of the town or city and effectively 'hemmed in' by large motorways and railway lines. And the proximity of these transport routes did not ensure a strong interaction with the town centre since the public transport network, upon which residents of these areas relied, did not develop at the same pace as construction work in the suburbs. Silverstein states that 'if the development of railroad lines [...] and their electrification after 1929 facilitated the integration and growth of urban peripheries, the current public transportation system has paradoxically maintained their social distance and exclusion'.[27] While the transport system in the centre of Paris progressed and developed, the suburban areas were faced with an acute lack of facilities – a 1990 INSEE report revealed that almost sixty percent of suburban municipalities still lacked their own train station.[28] Silverstein effectively highlights the contrast between the comprehensive transport network of the town centre and the sparse resources to be found in suburban areas:

> Paris is endowed with more than 240 *métro* stops on fifteen lines and an additional 12 [RER] stops on four lines, or more than three stations per square kilometer, with this density increasing as one moves toward the centre of the city [...] While the *métro* and RER lines extend into the proximate suburbs, they represent only about 120 stops for several thousand communes in Ile-de-France, with the further suburbs served, if at all, by local SNCF trains emerging from Paris's six stations.[29]

Essentially, as Wihtol de Wenden confirms, the *grands ensembles* were 'conçus pour une population équipée d'automobiles: les transports en commun sont souvent manquant dans ces quartiers qui ont poussé au

27   Silverstein, *Algeria in France*, 109.
28   Cited ibid., 110.
29   Ibid.

milieu des champs'.[30] However, Merlin reveals that a car was a luxury that many households could not afford: 15 per cent of suburban households had no form of motorized transport.[31] The bus service, often the only means of commuting to the town centre, was limited and, as a result, access to cultural events and activities taking place in the town was difficult if not impossible. Thus 'la localization périphérique des grands ensembles dans des zones résiduelles mal reliées au tissu urbain dynamique et inutilisables pour d'autres activités a eu pour conséquence leur marginalisation et leur exclusion tant sur le plan physique que symbolique', evoking frustration in the residents of the *grands ensembles*.[32] This frustration was compounded by an unavoidable dependence on the *centre-ville* that proved so difficult to access, due to the lack of facilities and services in the area in which they lived. In the *banlieues*, many of the retail outlets and amenities planned were never constructed.[33] The cause for this was clear: retailers had little desire to locate themselves in underprivileged areas where the local clientele had little purchasing power and there was little hope of drawing customers from other areas.[34]

Thus the *grands ensembles* progressively developed as a refuge for the underprivileged members of French society, and the utopian vision of the 1960s rapidly evaporated. Inhabitants of these areas became a marginalized population, occupying the fringes of urban society both physically and socially. The inhabitants of the *grands ensembles* were stigmatized by those inhabiting the town centre, a stigmatization that was compounded by virtue of its multidimensional nature. First, the *banlieusards* were stigmatized as a result of their position at the bottom of the socio-economic hierarchy, due to high levels of unemployment resulting from the economic stagnation that pervaded these areas. Henri Rey states that 'assignés au rôle d'accueil des usagers moins fortunés du parc locatif, les grands ensembles vieillissent

30   Sophie Body-Gendrot and Catherine Wihtol de Wenden, *Sortir des banlieues. Pour en finir avec la tyrannie des territoires* (Paris: Editions Autrement, 2007), 21.
31   Merlin, *Les banlieues*, 58.
32   Stébé, *La crise des banlieues*, 44.
33   Body Gendrot, *Sortir des banlieues*, 21.
34   Merlin, *Les banlieues*, 77.

mal. Les rares commerces ferment [ou] sont en difficulté.'[35] It is important to note that this precarious economic situation was amplified by the lack of adequate public transport facilities connecting these areas to the town centre, a reality which undoubtedly bore consequences for job prospects beyond the immediate locality. Silverstein and Tetreault describe a cyclical process whereby the stigmatization produced by a combination of geographical isolation, physical degeneration and inhabitants' impecuniosity made living in certain suburban areas an impediment to being hired for a job, thus reproducing the unemployment that formed a large part of the social stigmatization of the *grands ensembles* in the first place.[36] Second, the residents of the *grands ensembles* were stigmatized due to their deteriorating social status in the public sphere. Chapter 2 showed how public and political perceptions of immigrants underwent significant change as the situation of the immigrant workers changed and they became permanent members of the French social makeup. Public and political debate over immigration and the perceived threat to national identity developed in tandem with the economic crisis of the 1970s and the rise of the Front National in the 1980s, resulting in an image of immigrants as a destructive force at the heart of French society. The immigrant population was viewed as inassimilable, and thus a threat to social cohesion and the continuation of the Republic. These fears associated with the 'problem of immigration', and particularly immigration originating in Northern Africa, were projected onto the dense immigrant population of the *grands ensembles* and these areas came to be seen as a microcosm of all the challenges and problems facing contemporary French society.

François Dubet shows how perceptions relating to populations of immigrant origins compounded the stigmatization of a particular geographical area: 'La stigmatisation d'une cité se nourrit de la présence immigrée, rendue responsable de la dégradation: logements surpeuplés, difficultés de

35   Rey, *La peur des banlieues*, 45.
36   Paul Silverstein and Chantal Tetreault, 'Postcolonial Urban Apartheid', *Social Sciences Research Council: Riots in France* (2006) <http://riotsfrance.ssrc.org/Silverstein_Tetreault/> accessed 30 June 2007.

voisinage, inquiétudes face aux jeunes qui occupent les espaces publics'.[37] Inevitably, the physical drawbacks and limitations of their immediate environment, coupled with socio-economic difficulties and social exclusion, invoked a profound underlying frustration, or malaise, among the inhabitants of the underprivileged *grands ensembles*. According to Azouz Begag, 'il y a comme un constat communément accepté. Dans les espaces où les aménageurs ont cherché la cohabitation harmonieuse des différences, avec pour objectif un enrichissement mutuel, se sont accumulés handicaps et vulnérabilités, pour finalement faire surgir le spectacle du ghetto'.[38]

Islam and the Colour-Blind Republic

Beyond the socio-spatial segregation and far-reaching socio-economic problems contributing to the social relegation of the *banlieues*, many inhabitants of these areas were also subjected to a particular cultural stigma stemming not only from their status as immigrants (or as people of immigrant origins), but also from their affiliation (real or perceived) to the religion of Islam. Hargreaves states that with the ethnicization of politics that accompanied the growth of the Front National from the beginning of the 1980s, Islam and the threat of religious communitarianism formed an integral part of the construction that presented immigration as a threat to national unity and social cohesion. Before examining the nature of this religious stigmatization, it is important to emphasize that this phenomenon represents a relatively recent development in French society. Muslim immigrants have featured prominently in the total composition of French immigration throughout the post-war period. However, in terms of visibility in the public sphere (mosques, prayer rooms and associations), Muslims were ill-equipped and went largely unnoticed by mainstream society. In this respect, Hargreaves

---

37 François Dubet and Didier Lapeyronnie, *Les quartiers d'exil* (Paris: Seuil, 1992), 84.
38 Azouz Begag and Christian Delorme, *Quartiers Sensibles* (Paris: Editions du Seuil, 1994), 15.

reveals that, while Muslims constituted a large portion of immigration to France, they had little organization as a group until the mid-1970s.[39] As a result, the period saw high levels of tolerance with little recognition of religious needs.[40]

In the 1970s efforts were made by the state to accommodate the religious needs of Muslims following the large-scale reunification of immigrant families and the resultant growth in the Muslim demographic. Rey reveals that during the presidency of Giscard d'Estaing the authorities began to perceive religion as a means of promoting social order among immigrant populations and, as a result, devoted certain resources to establishing Islamic places of worship.[41] Inevitably, given the ever-dominant fundamental state policy of laïcité, the development of these facilities was dictated by a certain anonymity: Mosques were established in apartments and garage buildings, for example. However, this move by the government to support the creation of Muslim places of worship constituted an attempt to engage with the needs of the Muslim community and thus played a significant role in integrating this element of the population, and preventing the development of a religious-based communitarianism within French society. Silverstein claims that 'the state's implicit support of Islam amounted to a paternalistic strategy to gain subject loyalty and defuse potential immigrant labor unrest'.[42] As an organizational infrastructure emerged, Islam brought together immigrant workers of different nationalities. Moreover, Rey states that the penetration of the workplace represented only the first stage in the growth of Islam in French society, and the mid-1980s saw Islam play

---

39   Hargreaves, *Multi-ethnic France*, 106.
40   Jonathan Laurence and Justin Vaisse, *Integrationg Islam. Political and Religious Challenges in Contemporary France* (Washington, DC: Brookings Institution Press, 2006), 137.
41   Rey, *La peur des banlieues*, 58.
42   Silverstein, *Algeria in France*, 132. It is worth noting, however, that while this initiative was the first large-scale move towards supporting the religious needs of Muslims, it was not the first move towards establishing a framework of support for subscribers to the Islamic faith. Since as early as the 1950s, a small number of semi-public suburban factories had established on-site prayer-rooms for their Muslim workers.

an increasing role in the lives of young second-generation immigrants.[43] The Islamic community proved attractive to young people in the *banlieues* who had suffered discrimination due to their cultural origins and who were angered by their ongoing social relegation. Islam effectively filled the void left by failed attempts to establish a social movement that captured their hopes and desires, and offered a collective identity, shared values and a sense of community. During the 1980s, 'Islamic associations had become the main sites for local organizations and grassroots development in the *cités*, offering unemployed men and women jobs working in mosques [...] and even organizing summer camps in the provinces for *banlieue* youth.'[44]

This rise in the public visibility of Islam coincided with a number of international geopolitical events that had a far-reaching effect on the French perception of Islam. For his part, Hargreaves highlights the Iranian Revolution that brought the Ayatollah Khomeini to power in 1979. This event 'marked the onset of a more assertive Islamic dimension in international politics than had previously been apparent during the post-war period', and, coinciding with the increased visibility of Islam in France, resulted in the drawing of a 'blanket equation between "Muslims" and "fundamentalists"' in the popular imagination.[45] Moreover, this confusion equating Islam with extremism became greater still in the 1980s when terms such as 'Islamism' and 'Islam' became linked, and often confused, with fundamentalism in the popular imagination.

Essentially, generalized fears promoted a distorted view of Islam which aided in the construction of an interpretation that positioned Islam as a threat to the French Republic. Silverstein reveals how, throughout the 1990s, these fears were compounded by French news coverage of the Algerian civil war, which focused mainly on the activities of Islamic terrorists and the potential for radicalism to spread to France, linked with domestic concerns regarding the influence of Islamic associations in the *banlieues*.[46]

43   Rey, *La peur des banlieues*, 58.
44   Silverstein, *Algeria in France*, 133.
45   Hargreaves, *Multi-ethnic France*, 108.
46   Silverstein, *Algeria in France*, 133.

Two events in particular appeared to confirm these fears of the growth of a radical Islam within the Republic, strengthening the perceived link between Islam and terrorism. First, two young *beurs* from the Parisian suburb of La Courneuve were sentenced to death in Morocco in 1994 for their involvement in what was claimed to be an Islamist attack on a hotel in Marrakech. Second, two *banlieusards* from the suburb of Vaulx-en-Velin in Lyon were implicated in the 1995 bombings of Paris and Lyon, attributed to the *Groupe Islamique Armé* (GIA). In both cases, Rey states that the suburbs involved 'ne constituent des bases arrière d'un dispositif terroriste, mais l'exaspération et le désarroi qui ont gagné une frange de la jeunesse issue de l'immigration sont porteurs de dérives individuelles'.[47] However, these events evoked widespread fears of the threat of radical Islam to national unity and social cohesion, and 'la méconnaissance de l'Islam par la population française conduit à l'extrême simplification d'une réalité diverse et très éclatée'.[48]

Beyond the reductive association of Islam with religious extremism, one event seemed to crystallize the debate on the place of Islam in French society: *l'affaire du foulard*. The year of 1989 represented the first stage in this affair: three Muslim girls were excluded from a school in Creuil for wearing the Islamic headscarf, judged by the headmaster to be in contravention to the republican principle of *laïcité*. This incident provoked widespread debate as it seemed to touch at the heart of the issues at stake in the debate on integration. This event was constructed as 'an opposition between a principled, rights-based individualism and the *communautarisme* said to characterize both the Muslim's position and any compromising political stance which dealt with them as a distinct cultural group with political interests and claims'.[49] The suspension of the girls from school was later overturned by the Minister of Education, Lionel Jospin. The matter was referred to the *Conseil d'Etat* who ruled that the wearing of the headscarf did not contravene the laws on *laïcité*. However, Jospin's decision was 'lik-

---

47   Rey, *La peur des banlieues*, 61.
48   Ibid.
49   Favell, *Philosophies of Integration*, 175.

ened by a group of leading intellectuals – among them Régis Debray and Alain Finkielkraut – to Munich, a byword for the feckless appeasement of threatening foreign forces'.[50] This association implicitly highlighted the threat posed by Islam to the French Republic.

Inevitably, the Front National attempted to capitalize on the anti-immigrant sentiments evoked by *l'affaire du foulard*. In November 1989, the Front National candidate, Marie-France Stirbois, swept to victory in the first round of a legislative by-election held in Dreux, scene of the significant 1983 Front National victory. The victorious campaign was marked by its anti-Islamist dimension as the Front National evoked the spectre of communitarianism and the threat to national unity.[51] Stirbois went on to win the seat with over 60 per cent of the second-round vote, giving the FN a symbolic presence in the National Assembly.[52] The Headscarf Affair has resurfaced sporadically since the beginning of the 1990s, most recently in 2003 when President Chirac announced a new law banning the wearing of 'ostensible' religious symbols, including the Islamic *foulard*. This issue will be discussed at a later stage.

The importance of the 1989 incident, and subsequent related events, cannot be overrated in terms of the perception of Islam in mainstream French society. Rey claims that 'la vivacité des réactions à l'affaire du voile islamique révèle en tout cas la profondeur de la perturbation introduite par l'essor et la visibilité croissante de l'Islam'.[53] A 1989 IFOP opinion poll revealed the extent of the negative image of Islam amongst the French public: among non-Muslim French respondents, 71 per cent associated Islam with fanaticism and 76 per cent associated Islam with the oppression of women.[54] In general terms, the incident at the school in Creuil amplified the negative image of Islam in the popular imagination, which, coupled with the aforementioned international events, cemented the position of Islam as a perceived threat to French society and the national identity.

50   Hargreaves, *Multi-ethnic France*, 112.
51   Fysh and Wolfreys, *The Politics of Racism in France*, 46.
52   Shields, *The Extreme Right in France*, 237.
53   Rey, *La peur des banlieues*, 63.
54   Shields, *The Extreme Right in France*, 237.

In terms of the *banlieues* and the social exclusion of inhabitants, this brief exploration of the changing perceptions regarding Islam in French society has illustrated the processes by which French Muslims, and especially those living in the suburbs, have been progressively stigmatized due to their religious beliefs. The propagation of generalizations and the tendency to view the Muslim population through a 'monochromatic lens' has led to reductive interpretations linking Islam with terrorism, communitarianism and the fragmentation of the French Republic.[55] In the 'colour-blind' Republic that seeks to limit religious matters to the private sphere, the association of somatic difference, in the context of North African immigrants, with perceived or actual links to Islam has resulted in the construction of an additional stigma to be borne by those of immigrant origins. Olivier Roy affirms that 'it is presumed that European Muslims in general seek to undermine the European rule of law – and the separation of religion and state – in order to create a society apart from the mainstream.'[56] Essentially, Roy's analysis encapsulates the French situation. Moreover, the dynamic of fear that has resulted from these presumptions has been directed primarily towards the *banlieues* due to the high concentration of individuals of North African origins residing in these areas. The *banlieues* and their inhabitants have come to form the principal scapegoat of those who regard the grouping of followers of Islam as a threat in terms of identity fragmentation and the advancement of an Islam-based communitarianism.

Territories of Exclusion: Social Relegation and the Youth of the Suburbs

While the degenerating socio-economic, and indeed cultural, climate of the *banlieues* undoubtedly had a negative effect on the entire population of these areas, it was the youth who suffered most from this long-term accumulation of social and economic handicaps and discriminations. The generations of the 1980s and 1990s found themselves in an eminently different socio-economic position to their counterparts of the 1950s and

55   Laurence and Vaisse, *Integrating Islam*, 2.
56   Ibid.

1960s, who had benefited from the economic growth of that period. Marco Oberti states that for earlier generations, 'leurs conditions d'entrée dans la vie active, les possibilités d'accéder à des postes de cadre et de connaître une forte mobilité professionnelle au cours de leur carrière étaient bien plus favorables, à titre scolaire équivalent, voire inférieure.'[57] As industrial employment became less readily available, there was a rupture in the tradition of young people entering industry.[58] The established route of entering a trade following a period of training at professional training institutes disintegrated and those who were least qualified at the end of their education – whether with a diploma or without – were left unemployed. The impact of this form of social relegation was felt most by the youth of the *banlieues*, 'd'une part, parce qu'ils disposent de titres scolaires moins valorisés, et d'autre part, parce que les faibles ressources de leurs parents rendent cette période d'attente prolongée "galère" et peu comparable à celle des jeunes des milieux plus favorisés.'[59] The overall population of the *grands ensembles* was marked by a relatively high proportion of young people. In certain underprivileged suburbs over 32 per cent of inhabitants were under twenty years of age, compared to a national average of around 27 per cent. These areas were also characterized by large families: over 7 per cent of families numbered more than six people, compared to a national average of just over 3 per cent.[60] This demographic density served to amplify the socio-economic stagnation with large numbers of young people competing for fewer jobs. Consequently, a spiral of relegation and socio-economic exclusion rapidly gained momentum in the *banlieues* as the scale and extent of youth unemployment provoked a loss of hope for the future.[61] This situation explains further the growth in popularity of Islam among disillusioned young *banlieusards* throughout the 1980s.

---

57 Marco Oberti, 'Homogéniser ou différencier et spécialiser les contextes scolaires', in Hugues Lagrange and Marco Oberti, eds, *Emeutes urbaines et protestations. Une singularité française* (Paris: Presses des Sciences Po, 2006), 147–176 (150).

58 Rey, *La peur des banlieues*, 48.

59 Oberti, 'Homogéniser ou différencier et spécialiser les contextes scolaires', 150.

60 Stébé, *La crise des banlieues*, 53.

61 Rey, *La peur des banlieues*, 51.

Paradoxically, the school, traditionally a mechanism of assimilation, was another factor playing an important role in the exclusion of the *banlieues*. In 1987, Dubet wrote that 'l'école, plus que l'habitat, joue un rôle central dans l'apparition de la ségrégation'.[62] Essentially, Dubet argues that, for many, the institution of the school can no longer be identified with the Republic. Teachers are no longer identified with a collective mission of education, and have lost their role as an integral part of community life: 'Aujourd'hui, dans les quartiers "difficiles", il essaie de fuir en se logeant ailleurs ou en demandant sa mutation et ne soucie plus d'organiser la vie collective'.[63] In this context, schools are no longer the 'great engines of assimilation' in France.[64] Instead, these institutes of education have become a means of facilitating the demands of consumers and their desire to control the education of their children.[65] This form of consumerism has effectively resulted in a process of educational segregation that has played an important part in advancing the socio-cultural exclusion of the *banlieues*. In this respect, Yves Mény claims that parents identify 'good' secondary schools and then pursue location strategies to secure their children's entry.[66] Laurent Ott qualifies this observation when he reveals that, in the suburbs, 'une veritable tendance à la création des ghettos scolaires se développe: 10 per cent des collèges concentrent 40 per cent des élèves immigrés ou issus de l'immigration'.[67] Through this process of educational selectivity, schools in these underprivileged areas became an integral part of the underlying dynamic that saw the *banlieues* develop as areas of marginalization, stigmatized by the town centre.

62   Dubet and Lapeyronnie, *Les quartiers d'exil*, 84.
63   Dubet, *La galère: jeunes en survie?* (Paris: Fayard, 1987), 239.
64   Brubaker, *Citizenship and Nationhood*, 15.
65   Dubet, *La galère: jeunes en survie?*, 239.
66   Yves Mény, 'The Republic and its Territory: The Persistence and the Adaptation of Founding Myths', in Sudhir Hazareesingh, ed., *The Jacobin Legacy in Modern France: Essays in Honour of Vincent Wright* (Oxford: Oxford University Press, 2002), 183–195 (189).
67   Laurent Ott, 'Pourquoi ont-ils brûlé les écoles?', in Véronique Le Goaziou and Laurent Mucchielli, eds, *Quand les banlieues brûlent. Retour sur les émeutes de novembre 2005* (Paris: La Découverte, 2006), 120–138 (70).

Beyond the problems caused by its limitations and drawbacks, Dubet states that the school has also engendered problems through excess.[68] With the disintegration of traditional forms of socio-economic insertion associated with industrialization, the school has come to dominate the lives of the youth of society, in many cases playing the definitive role in shaping the quality of their future. Whereas before, educational failure or lack of formal qualifications could be offset by industrial insertion, with the significant drop in employment in the industrial sector, educational qualifications became increasingly important in order to secure employment and the concomitant potential for social mobility. Once again, this problem affected the youth of *banlieues* more than other areas of society, given the high proportion of immigrant children experiencing academic failure. Moreover, as the role of education evolved a destructive cyclical process took root: further qualifications became necessary to realize the same prospects of employment; however, the proliferation of diplomas led to a reduction in their value as a formal qualification. In any case, economically insecure households in the *banlieues* often did not have the financial means to provide for further education. The education system was viewed as 'favorable à ceux qui sont déjà favorisés', and thus the school system appeared unable to guarantee the equality that it proclaimed.[69]

Frustration, Anger and La Galère

With the physical, economic and social deterioration of the *banlieues* as a social habitat, it was inevitable that the degeneration of these areas would engender a sense of frustration in their inhabitants. The development of the suburbs as areas of exclusion and relegation, with limited potential for upward social mobility, had a demoralizing effect on the population. Faced with exclusion and failure, many of the youth of these areas were consumed by 'la galère'. Richard Derderian describes *la galère* as 'a highly volatile sense

---

68   Dubet, *La galère: jeunes en survie?*, 241.
69   Ibid., 241.

of detachment and frustration among suburban youth produced by an environment that excludes, alienates and stigmatizes'.[70] Essentially, *la galère* refers to the profound underlying malaise that developed as a consequence of the economic, cultural and social problems that progressed relatively unchecked in the *grands ensembles*. In his seminal work, *La galère: jeunes en survie*, Dubet identifies three stages in the processes of alienation and exclusion that lead to *la galère*.

Social disorganization constitutes the first stage in this dynamic that results from the 'décomposition du système d'action de la société industrielle, de la rupture d'un mode d'intégration populaire traditionnel'.[71] According to Dubet, the physical and social degradation of the local environment is tangible evidence of social disorganization to the young residents. This accumulation of handicaps results in a situation where 'tout est minable et dégradé. Les gens sont pauvres, il n'y a rien, les commerces sont absents, quant aux loisirs proposés, ils ne correspondent pas à ce qu'un jeune peut souhaiter'.[72] The 'pourriture' that characterizes this environment also comprises hostile social relations, as acts of delinquency (themselves often an expression of revolt by the young people against the accumulation of handicaps that dominate their social situation) become commonplace. Delinquency is accepted as a consequence of their situation and the young people accept it as such.

The second stage of *la galère* is exclusion. As well as being socially disorganized, the local environment is dominated by a feeling of exclusion. Dubet and Lapeyronnie state that this feeling of exclusion 'se manifeste avant tout par le thème de la réputation et du mépris'.[73] The *quartiers sensibles* are stigmatized by mainstream society due to their social and economic problems – academic failure, unemployment, concentration of pauperized immigrant populations – resulting in the construction of a reputation which itself reinforces the process of stigmatization. Moreover, the stigma

---

70   Richard Derderian, *North Africans in France: Becoming Visible* (New York: Palgrave Macmillan, 2004), 148.
71   Dubet, *La galère: jeunes en survie*, 66.
72   Ibid., 68.
73   Dubet and Lapeyronnie, *Les quartiers d'exil*, 114.

attached to the suburbs exerts a strong influence on daily life; a handicap in the search for employment, it also influences police-public relations. In this stage of exclusion, the response of those affected is not always the same and Dubet distinguishes two opposing reactions on the part of the young people concerned. In the first case, the experience of exclusion is treated as a permanent fixture of life in the suburbs by youths who feel powerless in the face of social processes that appear to be beyond their control. The trajectory of exclusion is thus accepted as unavoidable, and the youth, in this context, resign themselves to social alienation. Society is viewed as an immutable order and all the young person's energy is focused on survival in this harsh environment. It is important to note that beyond the overwhelming feeling of resignation in the face of processes and structures that cannot be controlled, exclusion can also be perceived as a direct result of personal failure. In this context, social actors may hold themselves responsible for their exclusion from society. This self-denigration compounds the feeling of exclusion as the individual lapses into a destructive spiral, often refusing to engage in new situations or projects that, for them, will only end in failure. In the second case, the experience of exclusion provokes a very different response, evoking a profound frustration in those affected. Here, refusal to accept social alienation pushes young people towards acts of violence and delinquency. In this instance, delinquency serves as a type of distorted conformism, whereby the authors attempt to circumvent the social and economic obstacles hindering their participation in mainstream society, albeit in an illicit manner. Dubet and Lapeyronnie confirm that this reaction often constitutes 'une stratégie d'intégration illégale, tout simplement parce que les voies de l'intégration légale sont fermées'.[74]

In Dubet's model, rage represents the final and most extreme stage of *la galère*. For Dubet, neither social disorganization nor exclusion alone are sufficient to explain the notion of *la galère*: 'un autre pôle déstabilise toutes les conduites et brise toutes les rationalités partielles, c'est la rage comme expression d'un sentiment de domination et pas seulement d'exclusion'.[75]

---

74   Dubet, *La galère, jeunes en survie*, 77.
75   Ibid., 80.

Essentially, this rage is directed against the feeling of domination experienced by many *banlieusards*. The anger of the *banlieues* is directed against those forces at the source of the discrimination and marginalization that pervade these areas. Inevitably then, this rage targets those figures of authority that represent social order and control – the police and other figures of authority, such as political figures and especially the government. For the inhabitants of the suburbs, these figures of authority represent the system that is the source of their exclusion. For Dubet, the rage that has become an integral element of the underprivileged suburbs represents the void left by the disintegration of the class-consciousness that was an integral part of the industrial period. This most explosive element of *la galère* expresses 'la haine de son propre milieu' in a context where traditional forums of expression have disintegrated, or where no other form of expression proves effective.[76] In terms of individual social interaction, this final stage of *la galère* can simply be viewed as the inevitable consequence of prolonged social, economic and cultural exclusion, the explosion of a continuously growing frustration at the injustices imposed by social relegation. Moreover, the anger of the young people creates a hostile environment that facilitates engagement in delinquent activities. However, while the rage of the *banlieues* is above all a generalized emotion resulting from the accumulation of social handicaps on the part of local residents, particularly the young people, Dubet and Lapeyronnie state that 'la rage s'incarne souvent contre un adversaire qui représente moins l'ordre que la violence et l'arbitraire: la police'.[77]

For the young people of the suburbs, the police embody all that is unacceptable in the system by which they are dominated. The police represent a tangible manifestation of the 'system' that excludes and alienates the youth of the suburbs and, consequently, relations between police and the youth of these areas are characterized by tension, distrust and violence. The forces of order are seen as corrupt and discriminatory in a Manichean opposition that places the youth of the *banlieues* firmly against the rep-

76   Ibid.
77   Dubet and Lapeyronnie, *Les quartiers d'exil*, 122.

resentatives of an unjust system that propagates social relegation in the suburbs. Relations between police and the young people of the suburbs form an integral element of the socio-cultural development of the *quartiers sensibles*, having a profound impact in terms of the potential integration of these areas into mainstream society.

In general terms, with the collective accumulation of feelings of frustration and rage experienced by many young *banlieusards*, it was perhaps inevitable that external expressions of *la galère* would take on a proportionate scale and intensity. From the beginning of the 1980s, certain underprivileged suburban areas were marked by incidents of large-scale urban violence, intense physical manifestations of *la galère* that resulted in significant destruction and confrontations with police. These events, which have erupted sporadically since the 1980s and reached unprecedented levels of destruction and violence in 2005, confirmed the position of the *banlieues* as areas of relegation, marginalized by mainstream society. Silverstein and Tetreault state that 'the violence associated with these clashes with police often exceeds the inter-personal, targeting those state and economic institutions (notably police stations, shopping malls, and municipal centers) symbolically associated by residents with their "exclusion"'.[78] Ironically, these episodes of violence, themselves the expression of the malaise of the *banlieues* and an attempt to denounce the exclusion and stigmatization to which the population of these areas is subjected, merely served to reinforce and augment the reputation of the suburbs, adding momentum to the spiral of relegation.

78   Silverstein and Tetreault, 'Postcolonial Urban apartheid', *Social Sciences Research Council: Riots in France* <http://riotsfrance.ssrc.org/Silverstein_Tetreault/> accessed 30 June 2007.

Policing the *Banlieues*

Law and Order at the Limits of the Republic

While this chapter has examined a number of the issues impacting on the socio-cultural context of the *quartiers sensibles*, there is one element of this situation that, perhaps above all else, has influenced, and continues to influence, the situation in the suburbs. The relationship between the police and the young people of the suburbs arguably represents one of the principle obstacles to the reconciliation of the suburbs with mainstream society. The question of policing in the suburbs plays an important part in developing an understanding of the socio-cultural situation in these areas, particularly the social trajectory that has resulted in the development of the *quartiers sensibles* as pockets of exclusion on the periphery of French society. The police force constitutes a primary actor in the practical relationship between the republican model and the *banlieues* for a number of reasons.

First, a causal link exists between the national police and the immediate cause of the riots in 2005 and 2007, given that, in both cases, members of the police were implicated in the deaths that were the catalysts of the violence. In isolation, this link would not appear to hold any exceptional significance. However, when placed in the broader historical context, this information forms part of a disturbing trend. In 1981, violent clashes between youths and the forces of order erupted in the Cité de la cayolle, a suburb of Marseille, following a police raid that left a number of women and children injured. The same year was marked by the violence and destruction of the *rodéos* at Les Minguettes, a suburb of Lyon, which a local resident and community activist attributed to continued police provocation.[79] The causal link between police and instances of urban violence assumes an

---

79   The term 'rodeo' was attributed by the media to the act of stealing a car, engaging police in a high-speed chase, and subsequently abandoning and burning the vehicle. Resident cited in Adil Jazouli, *Les Années banlieues* (Paris: Seuil, 1992), 21.

added significance here given that Mucchielli affirms that it was during the events of 1981 that the theme of urban disorder began to take root in the media, giving rise to two concepts that have come to dominate security-oriented discourse in contemporary French society: the idea of the malaise of the suburbs, and the association between delinquency and immigration.[80] In 1990, the police were again linked with the immediate cause of large-scale instances of urban violence following the events that unfolded in the Lyon suburb of Vaulx-en-Velin. The death of a twenty-one-year-old resident, Thomas Claudio, during the course of a police chase triggered several days of rioting and clashes between inhabitants of the area and police.[81] Silverstein and Tetreault highlight a number of similar events where the actions of police officers have played a decisive role in the immediate cause of instances of urban violance. In the suburb of Val-Fourré in 1991, for example, riots erupted following the death of Aïssa Ihich, eighteen, who asphyxiated after being denied his asthma medicine while in police custody.[82] More recently, in 1995, the death of Belkacem Belhabib, a young inhabitant of the Parisian suburb of Noisy-le-Grand, following a motorbike chase involving police, serves as a further example that confirms this pattern.[83] In his analysis of these outbreaks of urban violence which have erupted sporadically in French suburbs, Castel states that 'les contacts avec la police ont été à l'origine du déclenchement de toutes les violences urbaines que l'on a pu observer en France depuis l'été 1981'.[84] These events confirm the need to explore the role played by the relationship between police and the inhabitants of these areas in the construction of the socio-cultural landscape of the *quartiers sensibles*.

Second, the role played by police as representatives of the state's justice system is of paramount importance in the social development of the French

80 Laurent Mucchielli, *Violences et insécurité* (Paris: La Découverte, 2002), 13.

81 'La mort de Thomas Claudio à Vaulx-en-Velin: inculpation d'un policier et du pilote de la moto', *Le Monde* (9 February 1991).

82 Paul Silverstein and Chantal Tetreault, 'Postcolonial Urban Apartheid', <http://riotsfrance.ssrc.org/Silverstein_Tetreault/index.html#e9> accessed 10 July 2006.

83 'Noisy-le-Grand: un jeune écroué', *l'Humanité* (24 June 1995).

84 Robert Castel, *La discrimination négative* (Paris: Seuil, 2007), 42.

suburbs, because the conduct of individual police officers in these areas could potentially undermine the legitimacy of the entire justice system in the eyes of the inhabitants of the suburbs. In this respect, Klochars speaks of the importance of 'police discretion': 'A police officer or police agency may be said to exercise discretion whenever effective limits on his, her, or its power leave the officer or agency free to make choices among possible courses of action or inaction'.[85] Klochars states that police discretion is a necessary aspect of the practical operation of the police organization as the law cannot be written so as to anticipate every possible scenario.[86]

The idea of police discretion is particularly important in relation to the conduct of the officers who patrol the streets, constantly interacting with the general public. The personal discretion of officers in their dealings with the public may have a significant impact on public perception of the police as an organization. In describing this situation, Schneider cites Michael Lipsky: 'Police [...] "represent government to the people"; their actions influence citizens' perceptions of the state and their relationship to it'.[87] Nowhere is this more evident than in the French suburbs. Given the weight of authority and responsibility borne by the police as guardians of republican values, the officers policing the *quartiers sensibles* occupy an especially precarious position. In these areas where acute social and economic problems have engendered a certain loss of faith in the state and its institutions, the conduct of individual officers has the potential to undermine the legitimacy of the entire justice system. Reiss states that 'the capacity of the police to maintain legality in their relations with citizens depends to an important degree upon their ability to establish and maintain the legitimacy of their legal authority'.[88] In the context of the social integration of these areas into mainstream society, this potential becomes even more powerful because the conduct of individual officers can potentially undermine the validity of the republican model itself in the eyes of individuals who are already disillusioned with their social situation.

85   Carl B. Klockars, *The Idea of Police* (London: Sage, 1985), 93.
86   Ibid., 98.
87   Cathy Schneider, 'Police Power and Race Riots in Paris', in *Politics and Society*, 36 (2008), 133–159 (153).
88   Reiss, *The Police and the Public*, 2.

Third, as Mucchielli points out, the actual riots themselves consisted, for the most part, of direct and violent clashes between the youth of the suburbs and the forces of order: 'les deux catégories d'acteurs n'ayant aucun dialogue, aucune capacité de négociation, de régulation, de médiation; leurs relations étant enfermées dans les rapports de force, la provocation et la violence'.[89] Indeed, the events of both 2005 and 2007 were marked by the severity of the clashes between these young people and police officers.

A Relationship Defined by Conflict

In the *quartiers sensibles*, the relationship between police and residents is one built on mutual distrust, suspicion, and, above all, conflict. Marlière affirms that the youth of the *banlieues* regard the police as unjust and corrupt, 'en raison de la discrimination, de la stigmatisation et de la ségrégation dont ils sont constamment l'objet, notamment de la part de la police'.[90] For many youths in these areas, the police represent 'un outil de domination sociale et politique', a physical manifestation of the symbolic violence which dominates life in the *quartiers sensibles*.[91] Repeated identity checks, insults, provocation and constant suspicion have become part of the daily routine for the many of the young people who inhabit the suburbs. Kokoreff effectively encapsulates the situation in a description based on extensive fieldwork in Parisian suburbs:

> Dans la rue, le coté 'cow-boys' des brigades anticriminalité [...] qui, la nuit venue notamment, procèdent à des contrôles sans ménagement, arme au poing, plaquant sur le sol ou sur le capot des voitures les jeunes, les contrôles d'identité au faciès, leur répétition, le tutoiement systématique, le manque de respect de certains fonctionnaires à l'égard de ceux qui se retrouvent 'ethnicisés' (beurs, blacks) [...] autant de thèmes qui se prêtent à des variations sans fin.[92]

89   Laurent Mucchielli, 'Il faut changer la façon de "faire la police" dans les "quartiers sensibles"', 93.
90   Eric Marlière, 'La police et les jeunes de cité', in *Agora*, 39 (2006), 90–100 (92).
91   Eric Marlière, *Jeunes en cité: Diversité des trajectoires ou destin en commun?* (Paris: L'Harmattan, 2005), 238.
92   Kokoreff, *La Force des quartiers*, 145.

Kokoreff's description depicts a climate of extreme tension where young residents of the *banlieues* are placed in firm opposition to the forces of law and order. Based on this analysis, it is possible to identify two inter-related issues that cause the relations of conflict that exist between young people and the police. The first issue concerns practical policing and the *contrôle d'identité*, frequently cited by those denouncing police discrimination. The *contrôle d'identité* is the setting for the majority of the daily interactions between police and the young residents of the suburbs. Murray states that 'verbal interaction between the police and non-white youths is often initiated by the inevitable "show me your papers, please".[93] As such, this formal encounter plays an important role in the dynamic underlying police-public relations in these areas.

Drawing on the *Code de procédure pénale*, Jobard provides a definition of the *contrôle d'identité*: 'Les policiers peuvent, selon l'article 78.2 du Code de procédure pénale, "contrôler l'identité d'une personne, quel que soit son comportement". Le contrôle d'identité permet aux policiers de s'enquérir du statut de la personne contrôlée et, en premier lieu bien sur, de sa nationalité'.[94] Jobard goes on to reveal that this check may take place on the spot or at the police station, at the discretion of the officer involved'.[95] In theory, the *contrôle d'identité* offers police a legal means of rapidly identifying an individual and confirming their status in terms of nationality. However, Evelyne Sire-Marin affirms that:

> Les jeunes, objets de contrôles répétés, ont le sentiment que ceux-ci sont discriminatoires et que leur objet est autre que celui que la loi prévoit. Cela n'est pas entièrement faux, car de nombreux contrôles d'identité ne répondent pas aux critères légaux et sont en réalité un quadrillage policier de la population et l'affirmation d'une présence de surveillance et de contention des populations 'dangereuses'.[96]

93 Graham Murray, 'France: The Riots and the Republic', in *Race and Class*, 47 (2006), 26–45 (32).
94 Fabien Jobard, *Bavures policières? La force politique et ses usages* (Paris: La Découverte, 2002), 34.
95 Ibid., 55.
96 Evelyne Sire-Marin, 'Mortels contrôles d'identités', in Clémentine Autin, Stéphane Beaud, et al., eds, *Banlieue, lendemains de révolte* (Paris: La Dispute, 2006), 117–129 (118).

Essentially, in the suburbs, the *contrôle d'identité* has become a tool in the power struggle between the youth and the forces of order. Repeated identity checks have become a means of reinforcing police authority among the population of the suburbs. These encounters between young people and the police are often characterized by insults and violence as the police seek to impose their authority on the young people concerned.[97] Monjardet has identified this phenomenon as a fundamental problem facing policing at street-level. He states that police on duty in these areas, while technically adept, do not possess sufficient social skills or experience to manage daily public relations in these areas, leading officers to resort to 'outils dont ils disposent, pour l'essentiel le contrôle d'identité, c'est-à-dire des outils qui sont directement contre-productifs et qui augmentent [...] la tension au lieu de l'apaiser.'[98] This lack of social *savoir-faire* on the part of the police results in the creation of a vicious circle where imposing their authority is seen by police as the only way to 'save face' among the young people, while, at the same time, this imposition of authority often takes the form of repressive measures, such as repeated identity checks, which are resented by the victims and viewed as a form of harassment. Young people are humiliated by repeated identity checks that are carried out for no apparent reason: 'Souvent, en banlieue les BAC [Brigades Anti-criminalité] contrôlent l'identité de jeunes qu'elles connaissent sans qu'ils aient commis aucune infraction. Il arrive ainsi que la même personne soit contrôlée plusieurs fois par semaine par les mêmes policiers, ce qui provoque un agacement compréhensibles des jeunes.'[99] Of course, claims denouncing the abuse of the *contrôle d'identité* by police officers are extremely difficult to substantiate given that the aforementioned guidelines governing the *contrôle d'identité* in the *Code Pénal* are expansive.

---

97 See Marlière, *Jeunes en cité* and *La France nous a lâchés*; Kokoreff, *Sociologie des émeutes*; and Monjardet, *Ce que fait la police*. It is important to note that these encounters are not only characterized by provocations from the police; the youth of the suburbs also play a role in provoking police officers. This will be discussed when considering the point of view of police officers working in the *quartiers sensibles*.

98 Michel Kokoroff, 'La crise de l'institution policière ou comment y faire face? Entretien avec Dominique Monjardet', *Mouvements*, 44 (2006), 67–77 (70).

99 Sire-Marin, 'Mortels contrôles d'identités', 118.

The second issue raised by Kokoreff's description is one that extends beyond the technical parameters of the *contrôle d'identité*, and constitutes an integral element of the equation that has resulted in the progressive deterioration of police-public relations in the suburbs – the question of racism or discrimination based on ethnic origins. The question of racism is inextricably linked to the formal *contrôle d'identité* as the identity checks represent a frequently occurring context for the expression of discriminatory attitudes on the part of police officers.

A study published by Brouard and Tiberj in 2006 revealed that in certain suburbs people of immigrant origins have their papers checked twice as often as other residents.[100] In relation to police discrimination, Zaubermann and Lévy claim that 'even though [...] official French police policy rejects the classification of individuals on the basis of race, ethnicity or religion, the French police are highly cognizant of the ethnic tension that permeates their interactions with immigrant (and second-generation) youth'.[101] Zaubermann and Lévy, drawing on the work of a number or researchers, most notably Wieviorka, go on to reveal that '"pervasive racist discourse is a reality", and constitutes, for police officers, "an actual norm, extremely difficult to escape, not to speak of opposing, for a rank and file officer"'.[102] It is thus clear that discrimination is a salient issue in terms of policing the *banlieues*, an issue that significantly contributes to the ongoing tension between the forces of order and local youths. For his part, Kokoreff states that racist attitudes among police officers '[ajoutent] une dimension ethnique et raciale qui surdétermine les relations conflictuelles

---

100 See Sebastian Roché, *Le Frisson de l'émeute. Violences urbaines et banlieues* (Paris: Seuil, 2006), 104.
101 Renée Zaubermann and René Lévy, 'Police, Minorities, and the French Republican Ideal', *Criminology*, 41 (2003), 1065–1100 (1073).
102 Ibid. Research has shown that racist attitudes in the police are heavily influenced by the professional socialization of officers. Dominique Monjardet and Catherine Gorgeon, among others, have carried out research on this subject. See, for example, 'La socialisation professionnelle des policiers. Etude longitudinale de la 121è promotion des élèves gardiens de la paix' (Paris: IHESI, 1993).

entre jeunes "non-blanc" et policiers "blanc".[103] The result of this opposition is that systematic identity checks of the same groups, often combined with violence, humiliation, provocations and insults, are a regular occurrence and serve to undermine the legitimacy of the police.[104] Moreover, these encounters with racist attitudes accelerate the progression towards *la galère* as the youth of the suburbs, already faced with socio-economic insecurity, lose faith in a justice system whose values and principles appear to be scorned by its representatives. Mucchielli states that 'pour ces jeunes, les contrôles d'identité sont l'emblème et la confirmation quotidienne du racisme fondamental de la société française'.[105] In general terms the repetitive identity checks, insults, expressions of racism and widespread lack of respect on the part of the police 'have only served to further alienate and antagonize the very people whose assimilation the authorities claim to desire'.[106] In this context, the police have played a central role in augmenting the divide that separates the population of the *banlieues* from mainstream French society.

Suburbs of Fear: Police Perspectives

In attempting to understand the relations of conflict that exist between the youth of the suburbs and the forces of order, it is important to understand that there is, inevitably, a certain bilateral element to the relationship. Consequently, it is also necessary to consider the point of view of those police officers charged with policing the suburbs, a point of view that perceives the climate of tension that reigns in the *banlieues* from a very different perspective. Mouhanna states that 'the first element to notice is the fear police officers feel when they enter poor and violent areas. They are very reluctant to speak about this point, which undermines the brand image

---

103   Kokoreff, *Sociologie des émeutes*, 191.
104   Ibid.
105   Mucchielli, *Violences et insécurité*, 105.
106   Murray, 'France: The Riots and the Republic', 32.

of the cop. But in fact, they have to face severe blows to their integrity everyday.'[107] Clearly, there are a number of pressures and challenges associated with working as a police officer in the *quartiers sensibles*: 'Brutalement projetés dans l'univers des cités, les jeunes fonctionnaires sont confrontés à la violence sociale qui y règne, aux normes et aux codes qui y président, au désœuvrement et à la vitalité de leurs interlocuteurs.'[108] The response of police officers to these challenges is often an aggressive one as they seek to both hide their fear and impose their authority on the local population. Subject to the attacks of disillusioned and angry youths, many of the officers policing these areas experience 'le sentiment de participer à une "guérilla urbaine", voire à une "guerre".'[109] As a result, police-public relations in the *banlieues* constitute a destructive spiral where the young people feel persecuted by police, and police officers, fearful of the potential for violence, are quick to resort to more forceful methods. Furthermore, excessive use of force nourishes the sense of injustice felt by the young people and ultimately serves to reinforce the cycle.[110]

It is thus clear that both young people and police officers play a role in the conflict and tension that dominates police-public relations in the suburbs. However, it is also clear that the actions of the police in these areas have a decisive impact on the trajectory of police-public relations, due to their role as the guardians of law and order and the representatives of justice. Discriminatory practices and attitudes have undermined the legitimacy of the police in the *banlieues* where they are no longer seen to represent justice. In the context of the shared experiences of discrimination and violence, Tribalat has suggested that groups of youths of immigrant origin potentially see the police as a rival gang, a racist force.[111] This is perhaps a somewhat reductive interpretation that labels all police as corrupt

---

107 Christian Mouhanna, 'Young People and Police Officers in French Poor Suburbs: The Social Construction of a Conflict', in Przemyslaw Piotrowski, ed., *Understanding Problems of Social Pathology* (Amsterdam: Rodopi, 2006), 118.
108 Kokoreff, *Sociologie des émeutes*, 186.
109 Ibid.
110 Zauberman and Lévy, 'Police, Minorities, and the French Republican Ideal', 1072.
111 Roché, *Le frisson de l'émeute*, 110.

and discriminatory; nonetheless, it effectively illustrates the destructive potential of police discrimination, reversing the role of police officers and positing the representatives of justice as a racist gang. Moreover, the spiral of conflict is influenced heavily by the fact that many police officers have little knowledge of the neighbourhoods in which they are stationed, are culturally distant from the inhabitants and have little knowledge of how to deal with them.[112] This situation highlights a closely linked issue at the heart of the police organization – institutional organization.

In terms of institutional organization, the police force constitutes a state-controlled and primarily centralized institution. Decisions regarding the allocation of means, the size of patrols and the destination of newly commissioned officers are all made at state level. This structural formation has had an impact on police-public relations in urban areas, and particularly in the *quartiers sensibles*, due to the 'development of a centralized management and administrative model that was impervious to local needs and the variety of public demands'.[113] The centralized hierarchy of control ensures that 'police officials are not accountable to anyone but the central administration, and they are evaluated on the basis of their ability to act in conformity with the expectations of the latter and to implement the directions specified uniformly for the entire country'.[114]

However, this rigid structure makes no provision for the social and cultural differences that exist from one locality to the next and, as a result, city police forces have become cut off from the local community as they seek to implement a generic, state-wide policy. In other words, performance criteria are not adapted to the individual needs and demands of specific areas. Potential officers are recruited nationally rather than locally, and assigned to posts according to the centrally identified policing needs of specific localities. This process results in a situation whereby officers are placed in cities of which they have no knowledge. It is in this context that

---

112 Zauberman and Lévy, 'Police, Minorities, and the French Republican Ideal', 1073.
113 Dominique Monjardet, 'Police and the Public', in *European Journal on Criminal Policy and Research*, 8 (2000), 353–378 (355).
114 Zauberman and Lévy, 'Police, Minorities, and the French Republican Ideal', 1082.

Monjardet asserts that the generalized mobility of police personnel resulting from state-control over the police force has had a negative effect on
the situation in the problem suburbs: 'ce n'est plus le mari de la concierge
qui devient sergent de ville à Paris et qui police son territoire natif, c'est
le petit jeune de Saint-Malo qu'on envoie dans la banlieue parisienne à la
sortie de l'école et qui est complètement paumé'.[115]

   Above all, it is clear that police activity at ground level is causing significant social friction in these areas and, as a result, the tension between
the forces of law and order and the population of the suburbs has reached
unprecedented heights. The police have lost the faith and the respect of the
residents in these areas, especially the younger inhabitants, and a destructive power struggle has gained momentum at the expense of the concept of
justice. On a larger scale, the French justice system, bastion of republican
ideals, has been undermined by the loss of faith in the representatives of
authority. Ironically, the forces of order have played a central role in the
production of violence in the *banlieues* through the discriminatory actions
that have isolated them from the population of these areas.

Managing the *Quartiers Sensibles*

La Politique de la Ville

Since their conception in the 1950s, the evolution of the *grands ensembles*
has seen these peripheral urban spaces undergo profound change, from
their position as areas symbolic of modernity and urban progress to areas

115   Kokoroff, 'La crise de l'institution policière ou comment y faire face? Entretien avec
      Dominique Monjardet', 72. This 'generalized mobility' resulting from the decision
      to bring the national police under state control in the 1940s was initially intended
      as a positive development. Stationing officers away from their home or natal regions
      was seen as a move to combat corruption within the force, a preventative measure
      that would reduce the possibility of family or social links influencing the decisions
      or actions carried out by police officers during the course of their duty.

synonymous with marginalization and exclusion. Having discussed the physical and socio-economic evolution of the *banlieues*, as well as the impact of these developments on the local population, especially the youth demographic, I will now explore the response of the state to this spiral of social and economic degeneration. In this respect, the *politique de la ville* has constituted the blueprint for urban policy in France for almost three decades, a product of the efforts of the state to manage the problems and difficulties engendered by urban development.

It was only at the beginning of the 1970s that the government began to take notice of the growing problems caused by the physical, social and economic deterioration of certain *grand ensembles*. The authorities realized that a number of issues needed to be addressed, including social relations, crime and delinquency, and, as a result, a number of initiatives were launched with the goal of improving the social dynamic of these areas. To this end, the 1973 directive signed by Olivier Guichard, Minister of Territorial Development and Public Works, limited the potential size of new constructions to 2000 apartments. This was quickly followed by the creation of the *Habitat et vie sociale* (HVS) committee, charged with the rehabilitation of the *grands ensembles* through funding provided by the state. This initiative, put in place during the presidency of Giscard d'Estaing, was transformed into an inter-ministerial body in 1977 and became responsible for coordinating the actions of the different ministers concerned. In response to the steady rise in crime and delinquency in areas surrounding the *grands ensembles*, the *Comité d'études sur la violence, la criminalité et la délinquance* was established in 1976 under the auspices of the Ministry of Justice and presided over by the then Minister of Justice, Alain Peyrefitte. The report resulting from the work of this committee highlighted 'les dysfonctionnements inhérents aux groupes d'habitat collectif et insiste sur la nécessité d'une prévention active.'[116] The following year, in 1977, the Secretary of State for Housing, Jacques Barrot, implemented the first *plan banlieue*. This plan, working in tandem with the HVS committee, envisaged a synergy between the State, local collectives and housing organizations, and aimed at restorative projects that would encompass housing, public

116 Merlin, *Les banlieues*, 79.

spaces and amenities. In the period 1977–1980, fifty-three separate sites formed the focus of studies carried out under this plan.[117] Essentially, these initial steps taken by the state constituted the forerunners of the policy drive against exclusion and marginalization in underprivileged areas.

Despite these preliminary attempts to reverse the spiral of social deterioration that was fast gaining momentum in the suburbs, Rey reveals that in 1981 the question of the *banlieues* did not figure among the priorities of the new Socialist government.[118] However, the need for a coherent policy to deal effectively with the problems faced by inhabitants of the *grands ensembles* gradually became clear. This need was crystallized by the events that unfolded in the Lyon suburb of Les Minguettes in 1981. The widely televised *rodeos* and instances of violence involving local youths acted as a catalyst for a range of government measures aimed at tackling the problems in certain suburban areas. Following the events at Les Minguettes, the socialist Prime Minister, Pierre Mauroy, announced the creation of the *Commission nationale pour le développement social des quartiers* (CNDSQ), intended to tackle social issues relating to the *banlieues*.[119] In 1983, the president of the CNDSQ, Hubert Dubedout, published a report entitled 'Ensemble refaire la ville' which would serve as a reference text for the nascent *politique de la ville*.[120] In this report, Dubedout acknowledged the failure of the *grands ensembles* to fulfill the utopian, class-bridging role envisaged by their architects, and emphasized the need for a concerted effort to rebuild these areas, both socially and physically. The report highlighted the importance of participation on the part of inhabitants, who, together with the state and local authorities, would reinvigorate these areas: 'Cet "ensemble" qui doit refaire la ville, les auteurs du rapport Dubedout le conçoivent comme le produit surtout d'une mobilisation locale des quartiers appelés à s'investir dans la réhabilitation de leurs cités [...] les élus locaux sont invités à travailler de concert avec les services de l'Etat pour réaliser cette dynamique'.[121]

---

117   Ibid.
118   Rey, *La peur des banlieues*, 81.
119   Body-Gendrot, *Sortir des banlieues*, 50.
120   Ibid.
121   Donzelot, *Quand la ville se défait*, 61.

In general terms, the policies implemented by the government in the early 1980s as part of the *politique de la ville* incorporated four main areas: 'l'habitat, l'insertion dans le marché du travail, l'éducation et la prévention'.[122] In relation to the urban environment of the *grands ensembles*, the tentative steps taken by the HVS were augmented by the launch of the *Banlieue 89* programme in 1983, which was introduced by President Mitterrand and directed by two renowned architects, Roland Castro and Michel Cantal Dupart. This programme refocused attention on improving the physical and aesthetic aspects of the *banlieues*, the architects claiming that inhabitants of the suburbs had a 'right to beauty'.[123] The programme attempted to improve the quality of life in the *grands ensembles* through rehabilitating buildings and managing public spaces, with state-financed support (in the form of the *Fonds social urbain*) for projects linked to the *Banlieue 89* programme reaching some 226 million francs between 1983 and 1989.[124] However, the results of this programme were superficial for the most part. In a retrospective analysis of the achievements of the *Banlieue 89* programme, Roland Castro states that while 'des sommes d'argent considérables sont gâchées en peinturlurage – peut-on croire que des peintres soient en mesure de rattraper des erreurs structurelles profondes? – quand rien n'est envisagé pour embellir et désenclaver les logements [...] c'est donc aux plus modestes que l'on fait payer les erreurs politiques et urbaines d'une autre époque'.[125] Moreover, Castro identifies one of the primary underlying problems affecting the rehabilitation of the *grands ensembles*: 'ces réhabilitations ne modifient en rien l'absence de sentiment d'appartenance à une communauté humaine, mais confirment aux habitants, s'il était nécessaire, qu'ils vivent dans des territoires marginaux'.[126] In a climate of growing social and economic exclusion, fundamental sociostructural problems regarding the place of the (mainly immigrant) population of the *grands ensembles* in

122 Body-Gendrot, *Sortir des banlieues*, 49.
123 See Merlin, *Les banlieues*, 80.
124 Délégation Interministérielle à la Ville, 'Les Politiques de la ville depuis 1977: Chronologie des dispositifs', <http://i.ville.gouv.fr/reference/134> accessed 12 August 2007.
125 Roland Castro, *Faut-il passer la banlieue au kärcher?* (Paris: l'Archipel, 2007), 42.
126 Ibid., 43.

French society could not be glossed over with superficial physical improvements to the rapidly deteriorating apartment blocks.

With regard to young people and employment, the Schwarz Report commissioned in 1981 by Prime Minister Mauroy detailed the difficulties facing young people in terms of their social and professional insertion. This report 's'accompagne de la création des premières missions locales destinées à lutter contre leur taux de chômage. Des travaux d'utilité collective et des stages sont lancés en direction des 16–20 ans'.[127] The recommendations of the Schwarz Report were complemented by moves to improve levels of education in the *grands ensembles*. The Minister for Education, Alain Savary, announced the creation of the *Zones d'éducation prioritaires* (ZEP) in 1982. The ZEPs aimed to provide additional resources and attract the best teachers to schools in underprivileged areas.[128] In theory, this would reduce regional inequalities in terms of education and, consequently, improve the career opportunities of the young people inhabiting the *grands ensembles*. Although this programme did go some way towards reducing the gap in quality of education existing between the *banlieues* and other areas, the programme was limited in its achievements. The offer of additional means was offset by the threat of insecurity associated with the *banlieues*: a combination of the acts of violence and delinquency actually taking place, and the previously discussed weight and impact of the resultant reputation in furthering the negative image of these areas in the popular imagination, thus propagating the stigma associated with inhabitants.

Alongside the various programmes put in place to target the physical and social deterioration of the *grands ensembles*, the actions of the government in the context of the *politique de la ville* included a number of measures aimed at reversing the rapid growth of crime and delinquency among young people. Following the publication of the Bonnemaison report in 1982, communal (CCPD) and departmental (CDPD) councils for the prevention of delinquency were established under the national umbrella organization: the *Conseil national de prévention de la délinquance* (CNPD).[129]

---

127 Body-Gendrot, *Sortie des banlieues*, 50.
128 Merlin, *Les banlieues*, 86.
129 The Bonnemaison report was commissioned by the *Commission des maires pour la sécurité* in 1982.

The CNPD facilitated an agreement on cooperation between politicians, police, social workers and local associations. It was agreed that tackling delinquency should not be considered the sole preserve of the police, and that a balance between prevention and repression of delinquency should be established.[130] Body-Gendrot reveals that at this early stage of the *politique de la ville*, repression was not regarded as a priority by the left-wing government. Rather, 'le gouvernement de gauche, soutenu par des maires, suppose que l'insécurité des habitants disparaîtra quand le "lien social" (expression référant à la confiance partagée) sera raffermi et la croissance économique de retour'.[131] Terms such as 'échange d'expériences' and 'participation des habitants' were central to a more general process of decentralization that gave more power to local actors in an attempt to ensure social cohesion through a rebuilding of confidence.[132]

For his part, Donzelot states that the 1980s represented 'une nouvelle forme de gouvernement, celle du contrat', as the state attempted to achieve results through the empowerment of local administrative bodies.[133] In spite of this, the early years of the *politique de la ville* did not bring about a significant reversal of the trend of social and economic relegation. This failure to resolve the problems facing the *grands ensembles* can be attributed in large part to the fundamental structural flaw at the heart of the state's response. Essentially, policies that emphasized the need for an active participation on the part of inhabitants relied heavily on preconceived ideas of citizenship and national unity, concepts at the heart of the republican tradition: 'la citoyenneté n'est pas un des aspects de la politique de la ville. Elle est son principe fondateur, son objectif'.[134] However, changing perceptions regarding immigrants and the place of populations of immigrant origins in French society, discussed in Chapter 2, had challenged and undermined

130 Merlin, *Les banlieues*, 86.
131 Body-Gendrot, *Sortir des banlies*, 51.
132 See Rey, *La peur des banlieues*, 89. For a more detailed account of the processes of decentralization that ocurred in the early 1980s see Sylvie Tissot, *L'Etat et les quartiers* (Paris: Seuil, 2007).
133 Donzelot, *Quand la ville se défait*, 99.
134 Cited in Emmanuelle Deschamps, *Le droit public et la ségrégation urbaine (1942–1997)* (Paris: LGDJ, 1998).

these traditional cornerstones of French republicanism. Consequently, while a proliferation of studies and reports appeared in relation to the socio-economic and physical problems of the *banlieues*, the underlying problems regarding the new challenges to the ideas of identity and belonging were left unaddressed.

Towards a Politics of Failure?

The defeat of the Left in the municipal elections of 1983, combined with the unexpected success of the Front National, had important consequences for the *politique de la ville*. This political development displayed, among other things, a generalized lack of faith in the policies set in place by the left in the context of the *politique de la ville*. Three years later, the right returned to government following victory in the 1986 legislative elections, marking the beginning of the first period of cohabitation of the Fifth Republic. Rey claims that with the change in power 'un nouveau credo guide l'action des dirigeants: le libéralisme'.[135] The governmental programme revolved around efforts to 'réduire drastiquement le poids de l'Etat et le nombre des emplois publics, faire baisser la pression fiscale, tout en renforçant les fonctions régaliennes, le rôle et les moyens de la police'.[136] Inevitably, such an approach was in contrast to that undertaken by the Socialists in the preceding years and, consequently, a number of projects initiated by the Socialists appeared to be under threat. However, despite a reduction in state funding, the survival of localized projects was guaranteed 'en raison des compétences entérinés par des lois de décentralisation de 1982 et 1983'.[137] For the architects of these measures that were threatened by the right-wing government, this period of reduced funding was used to streamline and reinforce structural coordination.

135   Rey, *La peur des banlieues*, 102.
136   Ibid.
137   Body-Gendrot, *Sortir des banlieues*, 53.

Following the re-election of President Mitterrand in 1988 and the return of a left-wing majority to the Assembly, it was decided to establish an administrative body that would fuse the three primary approaches of the government. The *Délégation interministérielle à la ville* (DIV) combined the approach 'des projets architecturaux, celle du logement et du cadre de vie, et celle de la prévention de la délinquance'.[138] Yet, the violence that unfolded in the suburb of Vaulx-en-Velin in 1990 was a clear sign of a fragmented society, and highlighted the fact that, despite the implementation of numerous government policies, a divide continued to separate the town centre from the *quartiers sensibles*. The Lyon suburb experienced riots and destruction following the controversial death of a 'jeune motard [...] poliomyélitique handicapé aux jambes, cadet d'une famille de neuf enfants d'origine italienne'.[139] This violence was an undeniable indication of the gap separating the suburbs from mainstream society. Moreover, it is important to note that the violence that took place in Vaulx-en-Velin occurred in an area where apartment blocks had recently been renovated, proof of the failure of superficial policies in the face of more profound structural issues.[140] Vaulx-en-Velin had been lauded as a successful example of urban policy since the mid-1980s. Consequently, the violence in Vaulx-en-Velin was seen as a challenge to urban policy in more general terms.[141] In the wake of the events at Vaulx-en-Velin, President Mitterrand announced the need to 'concentrer les efforts de l'Etat sur les quatre cents quartiers pour prévenir les drames dont Vaulx-en-Velin a été le théâtre; veiller à organiser la diversité en termes de populations et de services, faire participer les habitants [...] à la renaissance des cités et à la citoyenneté'.[142] It is worth noting at this point that, by calling for the population of the *banlieues* to actively participate in terms of citizenship, Mitterrand illustrated, once again, the paradox that

138   Ibid., 55.
139   'Incendies, pillages et affrontements dans la banlieue lyonnaise. La mort d'un jeune motard provoque une émeute à Vaulx-en-Velin', *Le Monde* (9 October 1990).
140   'L'émeute de Vaulx-en-Velin', *Le Monde* (9 October 1990).
141   Mustafa Dikeç, *Badlands of the Republic: Space, Politics and Urban Policy* (Oxford: Blackwell, 2007), 72.
142   Body-Gendrot, *Sortie des banlieues*, 56.

had developed in relation to the place of the *banlieues* in French society. In other words, Mitterrand inadvertently drew attention to the failure of the state to correctly interpret the role of cultural difference as one of the primary factors influencing the exclusion and relegation of the *banlieues*.

The ethnicization of politics from the beginning of the 1980s had seen issues of ethnicity and integration take their place at the heart of political debate; however, little was done to address the racial and ethnic discrimination suffered by inhabitants of the *banlieues*.[143] The threat to French society in terms of cultural difference was not associated with mainstream society; rather, it was seen to be stemming from the potential for communitarianism among populations of immigrant origins inhabiting the suburbs. In December 1990, as a response to the violence of Vaulx-en-Velin, a governmental seminar on the *politique de la ville* identified five priorities in relation to the progression and successful development of the *politique de la ville*: 'lutter contre la ségrégation et développer les solidarités intercommunales; améliorer l'efficacité de la politique de la ville et en faire un enjeu majeur du renouveau du service public; les jeunes de la ville; vie sociale, prévention de la délinquance et sécurité; emploi, formation, vie économique'.[144] In line with these priorities, a multitude of administrative organisms, government bills and urban projects were put in place throughout the 1990s in an attempt to integrate the *banlieues* into mainstream French society. At government level, it was recognized that further coordination was needed if the *politique de la ville* was to succeed and, in December 1990, Michel Delabarre was nominated as the first Minister of State responsible for the *politique de la ville*. In this role, Delabarre was required to set out the concrete measures that this public policy would adopt.[145] This was followed, in January 1991, by the establishment of thirteen sub-prefects responsible for leading and coordinating these national projects at the local level.

143   Although the *Haut Conseil à l'Intégration* was set up in 1989, the goals of this organization were primarily research oriented and it held little political weight.
144   Délégation Interministérielle à la Ville, 'Les Politiques de la ville depuis 1977: Chronologie des dispositifs', <http://i.ville.gouv.fr/reference/134> accessed 12 August 2007.
145   Tissot, *L'Etat et les quartiers*, 189.

In terms of urban development projects, the first *Grands projets urbains* (GPU) were set in motion in July 1991, followed by the *Programme 50 Quartiers* in 1992. Both of these programmes aimed to rehabilitate problematic urban areas, such as Clichy-Montfermeil, Mantes la Jolie and Aulnay sous Bois, through rebuilding social relations and renovating physical structures. By the end of the 1990s, the GPUs, already numbering around fifty separate sites, 'deviendront les grands projets de ville (GPV) marquant une volonté d'intervention physique, économique et sociale de la puissance publique sur les territories sensibles'.[146] The *Plan de relance pour la ville*, launched in 1993, represented yet another attempt to reverse the social relegation of the *banlieues*. This project constituted an emergency plan that directed some five billion francs towards improving public services, amenities and infrastructure in the suburbs. These development programmes and other strands of urban policy linked to the *politique de la ville* were structurally supported by a number of new laws passed by the state. Body-Gendrot gives three examples of new laws designed to give shape to the future of French urban policy. The 'loi Besson' came into force on the 31 May 1990 and forced departments to draw up a plan of action with regard to the provision of housing for underprivileged inhabitants of the department.[147] The 'loi sur la solidarité financière' passed on 13 May 1991 was aimed at reinforcing financial solidarity and improving the quality of life in under-resourced urban communities.[148] These were followed by the 'loi d'orientation pour la ville' (LOV) in July 1991.

Essentially, the LOV set out the principles of a 'new' urbanism: 'Elle détaille les moyens de la politique de la ville qui vont enrichir le code de l'urbanisme et celui de la construction et de l'habitat. Il s'agit "pour les collectivités locales d'offrir des conditions de vie et d'habitat qui favorisent la cohésion sociale et permettent d'éviter les phénomènes de ségrégation"'.[149]

---

146 Body-Gendrot, *Sortir des banlieues*, 57.
147 Ibid.
148 Délégation Interministérielle à la Ville, 'Les Politiques de la ville depuis 1977: Chronologie des dispositifs', <http://i.ville.gouv.fr/reference/134> accessed 12 August 2007.
149 Body-Gendrot, *Sortir des banlieues*, 57.

This law was particularly important in terms of countering the process of segregation that had taken root in the suburbs. In particular, this law aimed to force communes located in urban agglomerations with more than 200,000 inhabitants to provide 20 per cent social housing.[150] This was intended to prevent 'further concentration of social housing in agglomerations that already had a high proportion of it, and to achieve "social mixity" in agglomerations that did not have much social housing.[151] Another important development was the creation of the *Zones urbaine sensible* (ZUS) and the *Zones de redynamisation urbaine* (ZRU), established by the 'Loi d'orientation pour l'aménagement et le développement du territoire' (LOADT) in 1995. Making particular reference to the twin problems of physical deterioration and socio-economic difficulty, Article 42 of the LOADT stated that:

> Les zones urbaines sensibles sont caractérisées par la présence de grands ensembles ou de quartiers d'habitat dégradés et par un déséquilibre accentué entre l'habitat et l'emploi. Elles comprennent les zones de redynamisation urbaine confrontées à des difficultés particulières et correspondant [à certains] quartiers [...] dans les communes éligibles à la dotation de solidarité urbaine.[152]

However, while these new laws were evidence of the state's commitment to the *politique de la ville*, and undoubtedly had the potential to provide a framework of legal support for the rehabilitation of the *banlieues*, the heavy bureaucratic system prevented any major advancement. The LOV, for example, met with resistance from agglomerations who were opposed to providing social housing. In this respect, the *Conseil économique et social* stated that 'the law did not push hard enough in terms of solidarity between communes', but 'simply expect[ed] that each commune [would] accept and organize the mixity of populations.'[153]

---

150   Dikec, *Badlands of the Republic*, 77.
151   Ibid.
152   See Article 42, Loi d'orientation pour l'aménagement et le développement du territoire (LOADT) <http://www2.urbanisme.equipement.gouv.fr/cdu/accueil/histoire/loiloadt.htm> accessed 23 March 2007.
153   Ibid., 77.

Influencing Urban Policy: The Rise of Insecurity

The 1990s saw a change in direction in terms of the policies implemented in the context of the *politique de la ville*. Body-Gendrot states that 'au cour des années ponctuées par des désordres dans les banlieues et par la montée en puissance des victimes, le sentiment d'insécurité épargne peu de catégories sociales'.[154] The heavily mediatized instances of violence that occurred in the suburbs throughout the 1990s contributed to a growth in the idea of 'insecurity', an idea that was progressively and almost exclusively associated with the *banlieues*. Statistical records of the strong growth in crime and delinquency supported the propagation of this theme in the popular imagination.[155] Tissot reveals that 'les émeutes, progressivement détachées de leurs événements déclencheurs, sont rapportées au problème général des "banlieues" ou des "quartiers sensibles", décrit comme un problème social nouveau'.[156] Inevitably, this growth in insecurity impacted upon the elaboration of the *politique de la ville*. The 'circulaire du 19 mai 1994 relative à la politique de prévention de la délinquance et de lutte contre l'insécurité en milieu urbain' emphasized the role of the prevention of crime and delinquency in the *politique de la ville*.[157] In 1996, the *Pacte de relance pour la ville* was launched; it was intended to reinvigorate economic action, with tax concessions for businesses locating in areas designated as 'sensible'.[158] However, while emphasis was placed on the creation of jobs in underprivileged areas, public security was also identified as one of its primary goals. Under the plan, '4,000 new police officers would be assigned to communes with "difficult neighbourhoods"'.[159]

154   Body-Gendrot, *Sortir des banlieues*, 60.
155   Ibid., 61.
156   Tissot, *L'Etat et les quartiers*, 19.
157   Délégation Interministérielle à la Ville, 'Les Politiques de la ville depuis 1977: Chronologie des dispositifs', <http://i.ville.gouv.fr/reference/134> accessed 12 August 2007.
158   Ibid.
159   Dikeç, *Badlands of the Republic*, 98.

Beyond these measures, the Villepinte Conference of October 1997, which took place five months after the Socialists came to power, marked an important moment in the growth of insecurity in French politics – the acquiescence of the left to the rhetoric of insecurity. For Mucchielli, this conference represented the 'tournant symbolique' affected by the political left who would embrace the theme of insecurity from that point on.[160] Villepinte provided a forum for the expression of a new, more security-oriented policy by the socialist government of the time, led by Lionel Jospin. In relation to this new orientation of the socialist government, Mucchielli writes that 'l'opposition idéologique traditionnelle entre la droite et la gauche sur la politique criminelle va en partie s'effacer', and claims that this was the culmination of several years of internal ideological maturation within the Socialist party.[161] In this respect, Dikeç reveals that the municipal elections of 1995 contributed to this major turn by the Socialists. In these elections, the right had gained ground with a campaign that prioritized the question of insecurity.[162] The success of the Front National also played a significant role in these developments: the party obtained 30 per cent of the votes in a context of high unemployment and rising levels of crime and delinquency.[163] More specifically, Shields reveals that the party's lists 'exceeded the 10 per cent threshold in 116 of the 226 towns of over 30,000 inhabitants (compared with fewer than half that number in 1989), including eighteen towns of over 100,000. This guaranteed the party's presence in many run-off ballots and its representation on numerous town and city councils'.[164]

The gains of the Front National reflected the growth of insecurity among the general public. Thus, in terms of the political left, it is clear that the growing preoccupation with insecurity in the public and political spheres had a significant impact on the policy direction of the Socialists.

160   Mucchielli, *Violences et insécurité*, 30.
161   Ibid., 31.
162   Dikeç, *Badlands of the Republic*, 107.
163   Jacques de Maillard, 'The Governance of Safety in France: Is There Anybody in Charge?', *Theoretical Criminology*, 9 (2005), 325–343 (329).
164   Shields, *The Extreme Right in France*, 259.

This impact was crystallized by the Villepinte conference. At this conference – 'Des villes sûres pour des citoyens libres' – the Minister of the Interior, Jean-Pierre Chevènement, engaged fully with the theme of insecurity. In his opening address, Chevènement claimed: 'il y a aujourd'hui deux menaces auxquelles la République doit faire face: le chômage et l'insécurité'.[165] Chevènement went on to launch the *Contrats locaux de sécurité* (CLS), a 'local security diagnostic' that would assess insecurity in sensitive areas.[166] At the end of the conference, the threat of insecurity evoked by Chevènement was reinforced by Prime Minister Jospin in his closing speech: 'il faut donner la priorité à la sécurité quotidienne des français'.[167] The speech of the Minister took its place in the more general rhetoric of insecurity that was developing as a central societal and political concern as he succumbed to emotive evocations of the 'frontière de la délinquence', the 'petits groupes menaçants, mendiants agressifs, dégradations diverses de l'espace public'.[168] The new direction of the left, embracing the theme of insecurity as a primary political concern, was confirmed by the closing remarks of Prime Minister Jospin where he spoke of the intention of the government to respond to the issue of insecurity. Jospin confirmed that 'après l'emploi, la sécurité est, en effet, l'une des préoccupations essentielles des français'.[169] In terms of the government response to the growth of insecurity, Jospin went on to state that 'il appartient à l'Etat d'assurer la sécurité de nos concitoyens. A cette fin, il lui revient d'organiser le service public de la sécurité [...] de telle sorte que la réponse apportée soit la plus efficace'.[170] For Mucchielli, this change in policy direction effected by the left, which had traditionally highlighted the

---

165 Jean-Pierre Chevènement, 'Discours d'ouverture de Jean-Pierre Chevènement, minister de l'intérieur', in *Des villes sures pour des citoyens libres. Les actes du colloque* (Paris: Ministre de l'Intérieur, Service de l'information et des relations publiques, 1997), 13.

166 Dikeç, *Badlands of the Republic*, 107.

167 Lionel Jospin, 'Le discourse de clôture de Lionel Jospin, Premier ministre', in *Des villes sures pour des citoyens libres. Les actes du colloque* (Paris: Ministre de l'Intérieur, Service de l'information et des relations publiques, 1997), 88.

168 Ibid., 8.

169 Ibid., 88.

170 Ibid., 90.

importance of the broader social contexts related to crime and delinquency, constituted a defining moment in the development of police discourse on urban violence and the suburbs: 'la nouvelle orientation du gouvernement Jospin depuis 1997 a donc libéré un discours de type néosécuritaire qui s'affirme désormais publiquement'.[171] The Villepinte conference, followed by the transformation, in 1999, of the *Conseils communaux de prévention de la délinquance* (CCPD) into the *Conseils communaux de prévention et sécurité* (CCPS), served as a sure indication that 'la gauche a compris que les préoccupations sécuritaires renforcées par l'impact des médias allaient devenir une priorité pour les parties politiques'.[172]

Zauberman and Lévy reveal that, in recent years, 'the public debate on crime and safety in France has increasingly focused on "visible minorities", especially North Africans and Black African youth, who have come to be seen as a major cause of delinquency, interpersonal violence, and urban disturbances'.[173] The growth of this type of discourse has been further aided by the emergence and growth of the Front National on the political stage. Chapter 2 revealed how the Front National developed as a player in the political stakes throughout the 1980s, campaigning on a strong anti-immigrant platform and effectively engendering the ethnicization of the French political scene. This anti-immigrant position was compounded throughout the 1990s by an emphasis on insecurity, as the Front National attempted to capitalize on the sporadic instances of large-scale urban violence occurring in the *banlieues*. The success of the Front National in garnering support through this discourse, which linked immigration, insecurity and a threat to national unity, was most evident during the 2002 presidential elections. Throughout 2001, in the run up to the 2002 elections, the Front National promoted a programme that posited immigration as 'a mortal threat to civil peace in France'.[174] This situation was intensified by the priority given to security issues by the other candidates, namely the Socialist candidate,

---

171   Mucchielli, *Violences et insécurité*, 43.
172   Ibid., 64.
173   Zauberman and Lévy, 'Police, Minorities, and the French Republican Ideal', 1065.
174   Shields, *The Extreme Right in France*, 312.

Lionel Jospin, and the RPR candidate, Jacques Chirac. Jospin, 'playing to middle-class fears, claimed he had been naïve about crime and now supported zero impunity policing.'[175] The year had seen a 10 per cent increase in recorded crime and the government's record on law and order was under scrutiny.[176] However, Jospin's move to embrace zero-tolerance did him no favours, simply serving to legitimize the discourse of the far right.[177]

In the first round of the 2002 elections, Le Pen caused widespread political shock in overtaking the Socialist candidate and progressing to the second round. This success represented the first time a candidate of the extreme right wing had progressed to the second round of the presidential elections, a fact that highlights not only the achievements of the Front National as a political party, but also the degree to which the linked themes of immigration and insecurity had progressed as salient issues in both the public and political spheres. In this respect, Shields claims that 'in the aftermath of the attacks of 11 September 2001 on the World Trade Centre in New York [...] equations between *insécurité*, illegal immigration and Islamic fundamentalism found a louder resonance.'[178] Ultimately, Chirac was elected as President; however his 'new cabinet reflected the harsh punitive policing tone of the campaign.'[179]

Since 2002 and the return to power of the right, the *politique de la ville* has incorporated a firm emphasis on the repression of crime and delinquency in the *quartiers sensibles*. While further measures aimed at combating high levels of unemployment and rehabilitating the structural deterioration of the *grands ensembles* have been introduced – such as the 2002 operation *Talent des cites*, which granted the sum of 5,000 euros to thirty-eight separate enterprises and associations originating in the *banlieues*, and the 2003 'loi Borloo', aimed at improving social housing conditions in the suburbs – the attention given to rectifying social issues in the *banlieues* has been matched, if not outweighed, by the focus on security. The 'Perben laws' provide a

---

175 Schneider, 'Police Power and Race Riots in Paris', 147.
176 Shields, *The Extreme Right in France*, 282.
177 Schneider, 'Police Power and Race Riots in Paris', 147.
178 Shields, *The Extreme Right in France*, 284.
179 Schneider, 'Police Power and Race Riots in Paris', 147.

good example of this focus. The first Perben law of 2002 strengthened penal responses to acts of minor delinquency, while the 2004 law 'increased police custody to four days, and extended the scope of the notion of "organized gang"'.[180] These developments were accompanied by the 2003 'loi pour la sécurité intérieur', a law that 'renforce les moyens juridiques de la police judiciaire par l'extension de la compétence territoriale des officiers de police judiciaire, incrimine un certain nombre de comportements qui troublent au quotidien la sécurité et la tranquillité des personnes (racolage, mendicité agressive, rassemblements dans les halls d'immeubles...)'.[181] Paradoxically, while these measures have indeed given the forces of order additional tools to aid their task, the increase in police powers has, to a certain extent, only inflamed the situation in these areas.

For almost thirty years, the *politique de la ville* has constituted a maze of policies, programmes and actors, with responsibility being shared widely between a significant number of bureaucratic units. This has resulted in several problematic issues. First, despite attempts to coordinate the direction of the *politique de la ville*, the involvement of numerous administrative organisms has represented an ever-present obstacle to the successful co-ordination of policy matters. The fragmented system of management has itself offered considerable resistance to a concerted approach to the issues at stake. Second, the progress and development of the *politique de la ville* has been continuously overshadowed by inter-organizational competition.[182] Changes in government and the hierarchy of power, coupled with the dynamic that has seen the creation and mutation of committees or departments constantly reproduced, have inevitably produced a competitive environment where committees find themselves vying for state funding and prominence. Moreover, the frequent changes in bureaucratic makeup have resulted in a climate of disjointed and incomplete policies. Since departments were dissolved only to be reformed in a new context and with new

180   Dikeç, *Badlands of the Republic*, 119.
181   Délégation Interministérielle à la Ville, 'Les Politiques de la ville depuis 1977: Chronologie des dispositifs', <http://i.ville.gouv.fr/reference/134> accessed 12 August 2007.
182   See Tissot, *l'Etat et les quartiers*.

responsibilities, the responsibility for individual policies inevitably became detached from its original point of contact, as the actors involved were assigned new priorities that took precedence over former duties.

Since the beginning of the 1980s, the proliferation of government policies designed to facilitate the integration of the *banlieues* has resulted in a bureaucratic web of policies that, ultimately, has failed to reverse the double dynamic of exclusion and relegation in the suburbs. It cannot be denied that the various policies, laws and administrative bodies that have directed the *politique de la ville* for almost thirty years have enabled a certain improvement in standards of education in the suburbs, and made funds available for the rehabilitation of the physical environment of these areas. However, it is also clear that, in more general terms, the *politique de la ville* has failed. In 2004, the report of the newly established *Observatoire national des zones urbaines sensibles* indicated the existence of more than one hundred *Zones urbaines sensibles* (ZUS) across the nation, and effectively highlighted the failure of the *politique de la ville* to bridge the divide separating the *banlieues* from the rest of society. The report stated:

> L'observation des ZUS met en évidence l'accumulation des problèmes sociaux et urbains auxquels sont confrontés ces territoires. En matière d'emploi, de développement économique, de logement, de réussite scolaire ou d'insécurité les écarts demeurent importants entre l'ensemble des ZUS et le reste du territoire national.[183]

The violent events of 2005 and 2007 represented a further and more emphatic indication of the failure of the *politique de la ville* and the growth of the divide that continues to separate the *banlieues* from mainstream society. This violence represented a physical expression of the frustration and anger experienced by the marginalized populations of these areas who, beyond the discrimination of which they are victims, have no faith in governmental policies that do not appear to effect any tangible change in their situation.

---

183 Service communication de la Délégation interministérielle à la ville, 'Observatoire national des zones urbaines sensibles. Rapport 2004' (2004) <http://www.ville. gouv.fr/pdf/editions/observatoire-rapport-2004.pdf> accessed 16 July 2006.

Progressive Exclusion versus Changing Identities

A Loss of Faith in the System

Since the early 1970s, the end of *les Trente Glorieuses*, the *quartiers sensibles* have come to represent a concentration of all the problems affecting French society. A downward spiral of relegation has gathered pace in the suburbs leaving inhabitants socially marginalized and in an economically precarious position. Previous chapters have shown how the dynamic of these areas has resulted in high levels of unemployment, limited academic achievement and, for the *banlieusards*, a deeply rooted frustration with their social situation. The youth in particular have been adversely affected by the emergence of the *quartiers sensibles*. Many young people, overcome by *la galère*, have been placed on a destructive social trajectory that has found physical expression in the sporadic episodes of violence that have occurred in the *quartiers sensibles* since the beginning of the 1980s. In recent years this destructive pattern has intensified as negative factors have continued to influence the situation in the suburbs. In terms of education, Oberti states that the school 'reste l'institution par laquelle tout est possible mais qui, de l'autre, exclut, dévalorise et parfois humilie'.[184] In this context, the democratization of the education system has in itself caused problems: 'bénéficiant des effets de la démocratisation scolaire, ils aspirent à un autre statut que celui de leurs parents, tout en étant marginalisés par rapport à la culture scolaire'.[185] In contemporary French society the ideal of the school as a means of securing upward social mobility, as the path towards social progression, is firmly anchored in the popular imagination. As a result, the middle classes direct all their energy towards maximizing

---

184 Oberti, 'Homogénéiser ou différencier et spécialiser les contextes scolaires?', 147.
185 Michel Kokoreff, *La force des quartiers* (Paris: Payot, 2003), 120. See also Stéphane Beaud and Michel Pialoux, *Retour sur la condition ouvrière* (Paris: Fayard, 1999).

the academic opportunities available to their children.[186] However, in the *quartiers sensibles*, while many young people may have the same aspirations as the middle classes, structural constraints often make the realization of these aspirations impossible.

Castel claims that 'l'école continue à prétendre fonctionner sur le principe républicain de légalité des chances et de la promotion par le mérite, mais elle s'avère incapable d'assurer la parité des groupes sociaux pour parvenir effectivement à réaliser cet idéal'.[187] This analysis supports the empirically based interpretation of the education system expounded by Bourdieu, based on research carried out in the 1960s and 1970s. In 1964, Bourdieu and Passeron carried out research that showed that questions of class and gender continued to have a significant impact on levels of academic success.[188] Bourdieu and Passeron went on to claim that 'the low-objective chances of lower-class children entering higher education were internalized into their habitus, into an implicit sense of what did or did not constitute an objectively possible future, at once a subjective disposition and a "class ethos" which encouraged such children to rule out university as a practical possibility'.[189]

The theoretical position and arguments set out in 1964 in *Les héritiers: Les étudiants et la culture* were clarified and elaborated upon in *La reproduction: éléments pour une théorie du système d'enseignement*, published in 1970. In this study Bourdieu and Passeron acknowledged that opportunities of access to higher education rose throughout the 1960s. However, they go on to state that 'if "democratization is taken to mean what it always implicitly suggests, namely the process of equalization of educational opportunities for children from the different social categories [...] then the empirically ascertained increases in the chances of all catego-

---

186 Robert Castel, *La discrimination négative. Citoyens ou indigènes?* (Paris: Seuil, 2007), 51.
187 Ibid.
188 Jeremy Lane, *Pierre Bourdieu: A Critical Introduction* (London: Pluto Press, 2000), 61.
189 Ibid.

ries does not in itself constitute a sign of "democratization".[190] Essentially, Bourdieu and Passeron argued that it was the more privileged classes who had benefited most from the 'democratization' of education. The authors spoke of an *upward translation* of the structure of the educational chances of the different social classes'.[191] In other words:

> [W]here in 1961–62 the possibility of the son of an industrialist reaching university had been 'a probable future', by 1965–66 it had become 'a banal future'. [...] The rise in the chances of the son of a manual worker from 1.5 to 3.9 in a hundred over the same period, however, had not been enough to modify the image of higher education as an unlikely, if not 'unreasonable' future.[192]

Through their specific research into higher education, Bourdieu and Passeron gave an insight into the broader structural disadvantages facing underprivileged members of society in terms of equal access to the education system. Moreover, this research also emphasized that 'equality in the chances of university entrance still only very partially expresses the socially conditioned educational inequalities'.[193] The distinctions and inequalities in operation outside the education system, or at least at the point of entry, were also replicated within it. As new categories of students entered higher education there was a structural shift: middle class students opted for courses in medicine and law which held more prestige than those courses in the faculties of science or arts.[194] Bourdieu and Passeron claimed that 'the lower a student's social origin, the more his access to higher education had to be paid for by a *restriction on choice*, even to the extent of the more or less compulsory *relegation* of the least favored categories into Arts or Science'.[195] This led the authors to conclude that any improvements to access for working-class children to education were offset by internal structural processes of relegation.

190 Pierre Bourdieu and Jean-Claude Passeron, *Reproduction in Education, Society and Culture*, trans. R. Nice (London: Sage, 1996), 224.
191 Ibid.
192 Lane, *Pierre Bourdieu*, 62.
193 Bourdieu and Passeron, *Reproduction in Education*, 228.
194 Lane, *Pierre Bourdieu*, 63.
195 Bourdieu and Passeron, *Reproduction in Education*, 229.

In addition to these fundamental structural disadvantages, Oberti identifies another flaw in the education system that contributes, to a certain extent, to the propagation of this structural inequality. Oberti states that 'c'est l'une des impasses de la politique scolaire dans ces quartiers que de se limiter à son seul domaine de compétence alors que les dynamiques sociales en jeu nécessiteraient d'agir sur le logement, l'emploi, la famille, le rapport à la culture etc.'.[196] The *politique de la ville* has attempted to do this, facilitating collaborations between organizations and empowering local actors in the hope of creating a broader collaborative effort to target social development. However, these efforts have effectively been obstructed by the school as an institution: 'traditionnellement très attachée à son indépendance et à situation de monopole légitime de la fonction éducative, l'institution scolaire dans son ensemble s'est d'autant plus repliée sur elle-même qu'elle est sentie de plus en plus menacée par la dégradation, la dureté et l'étrangeté de son environnement immédiat'.[197] Schools have proven reluctant to engage with other organizations in terms of collaborating to bring about a more productive social environment for young people. This situation has contributed to the educational inequality that exists in the *banlieues*.

The *carte scolaire* represents another element of the educational framework with the potential to contribute to segregation and exclusion within the education system, augmenting the social problems facing the residents of the *banlieues*. The *carte scolaire* defines the catchment area for a particular school and, while this structure is primarily viewed as an effective means of regulating the distribution of students, it also aims to ensure social mixity. Meuret emphasizes the positive elements of this system which, in general terms, attempts to ensure equality through a uniform system of matching students with schools, thus upholding the ideal of equality that is at the heart of republican values in France: 'those who administer the *carte scolaire* operate with the conviction that parents who try to avoid a given school

---

196 Oberti, 'Homogénéiser ou différencier et spécialiser les contextes scolaires?', 153.
197 Ibid.

are pursuing their own interest at the expense of the common good'.[198] Moreover, Meuret claims that there is evidence to support the argument that mixing students of different levels of academic ability actually improves the effectiveness of the entire system.[199]

However, Oberti finds the *carte scolaire* problematic in terms of social segregation: 'Bien évidement, [la mixité sociale] se trouve largement compromise par la différenciation sociale et ethnique de l'espace urbain qui se traduit aux deux extrêmes par une forte homogenéité'.[200] In this sense, the *carte scolaire*, despite its goal of social mixity, simply serves to reinforce the social categories and hierarchies that exist in urban areas.[201] Additionally, this form of segregation is directly related to another, more localized form of segregation within schools. Maurin reveals that the social composition of a classroom, and indeed a school, is almost a mirror image of that of the local community.[202] Thus, the social disadvantages that dominate the locality are reflected in the classroom. Maurin writes, for example:

> La proportion d'enfants de classe modeste (ouvriers ou chômeurs) varie ainsi de 1 à 3 entre les 10 pour cent de collèges les moins populaires et les 10 pour cent de collèges les plus populaires: ils représentent 20 pour cent des effectifs dans le premier cas, et 70 pour cent dans le second. De même dans les 10 pour cent de collèges les plus populaires, 1 élève sur 6 environ (soit 4 à 5 par classe) est très en retard (au moins deux ans de retard) alors que cette proportion est résiduelle (inférieure à 1 pour cent) dans les collèges les plus bourgeois.[203]

This segregation between establishments effectively propagates the social divide separating the suburbs from mainstream society through the very institution that traditionally constituted a means of unifying the nation.

---

198   Denis Meuret, 'School Choice and Its Regulation in France', in Patrick Wolf and Stephen Macedo, eds, *Educating Citizens: International Perspectives on Civic Values and School Choice* (Washington, DC: Brookings Institution Press, 2004), 238–267 (256).
199   Ibid.
200   Oberti, 'Homogénéiser ou différencier et spécialiser les contextes scolaires?', 158.
201   Ibid.
202   Eric Maurin, *Le ghetto français* (Paris: Seuil, 2004), 36.
203   Ibid.

Through processes that result in social segregation and exclusion, many young people rapidly lose faith and become frustrated with a system that appears to offer opportunities only to those who are already in an economically and socially favorable position. Hope is replaced by resentment from an early age as prospects of financial success in a society of consumption appear slim. Kokoreff states that 'on ne sera pas surpris que ces carrières scolaires façonnent l'expérience sociale', and undoubtedly the dynamic that sees many young *banlieusards* lose faith in the education system has important consequences in terms of their progression towards delinquent activity.[204] According to Oberti, 'quand la distance avec l'école devient trop grande, une autre type de socialisation s'impose et le risque d'un basculement dans la délinquance devient plus fort'.[205]

Employment is another area, directly linked to education, where circumstances for the residents of the suburbs have worsened in recent years, significantly contributing to the frustration and anger of inhabitants. In the period 1990–1999, for example, unemployment in the *Zones urbaines sensibles* rose from 19 per cent to 25.4 per cent, more than double the national average.[206] More importantly, in terms of the socio-economic situation of the youth of the suburbs, Kokoreff reveals that 'la part des chômeurs âgés de 15 à 24 ans a explosé, passant dans cette même période de 28.5 pour cent à 39.5 pour cent; et ce, alors même que la proportion de jeunes poursuivant leurs études a augmenté entre 1990 et 1999'.[207] Furthermore, high levels of unemployment are compounded by discrimination on the part of employers. French employment law prohibits discrimination: the 'loi du 16 novembre 2001 relative à la lutte contre les discriminations' forbids discrimination on grounds of appearance or family name, for example.[208] Nonetheless, these laws, difficult to enforce, have failed to protect the population of the *banlieues* from being discriminated against when seeking employment. Weil illustrates this fact by drawing on a study carried out by

204   Kokoreff, *La force des quartiers*, 123.
205   Oberti, 'Homogénéiser ou différencier et spécialiser les contextes scolaires?', 152.
206   Kokoreff, *Sociologie des émeutes*, 152.
207   Ibid.
208   Castel, *La discrimination négative*, 46.

Jean-François Amadieu of the *Observatoire des discriminations*, based at the Université de Paris 1, in 2004.[209] This study tested the reaction of various employers to different CVs sent in response to a total of 258 positions on offer. 'Ce testing a permis de montrer que le "référent" (homme, résident à Paris, blanc de peau) était convoqué à 75 entretiens, tandis que le même homme résidant au Val Fourré à Mantes-la-Jolie n'est plus convoqué qu'à 45 entretiens, 14 s'il a un nom et un prénom maghrébin, 5 seulement s'il est handicapé.'[210]

When considering the question of employment in the *quartiers sensibles* it is also necessary to take into account the situation of those inhabitants who are employed, as employment is not necessarily a guarantee of financial security. In other words, unemployment figures alone do not reveal the full extent of the precarious socio-economic situation that dominates life in the *banlieues*. Kokoreff demonstrates this by highlighting the fact that 'trois quarts des allocataires de la CAF perçoivent une aide au logement dans les ZUS, contre un peu plus de la moitié de l'ensemble des allocataires de France métropolitaine.'[211] Ultimately, while economic insecurity has affected a significant portion of the population of the *banlieues* since the 1970s, this situation has deteriorated in recent years, leaving these individuals in a prolonged state of socio-economic relegation from which there appears to be little hope of breaking free. This situation is compounded by ethno-racial discrimination in terms of securing employment, a form of discrimination that undermines the ideals and values of the French Republic in the eyes of the inhabitants of the suburbs. The failure of the authorities to resolve these problems has led to a loss of faith in the French social system. Consequently, young people in the *quartiers sensibles* continue to fall victim to *la galère* and, as a result, often become involved in acts of delinquency and violence which, in turn, make the possibility of upward social mobility through conventional means ever more remote.

---

209 Weil, *La république et sa diversité*, 78.
210 Ibid.
211 Kokoreff, *Sociologie des émeutes*, 155. The CAF, or *Caisses d'Allocations Familiales*, provide housing benefits among other forms of social benefits.

Perceptions of Islam in a Post-9/11 Society

The chapter has already touched upon the question of Islam and the emergence of a particular cultural stigma that developed since the beginning of the 1980s, namely a connection between the generalized categories of immigration, Islam and fundamentalism in the popular imagination. The growth of reductive interpretations linking Islam with the threat of terrorism has particularly affected the *banlieues*, due to a concentration in these areas of populations of North African immigrant origins. The *banlieues* have become a scapegoat for those who perceive Islam as a threat to republican unity. In post 9/11 society, an alarmist discourse has renewed and consolidated national attention around the perceived threat of Islam to national unity. The work of Jocelyne Cesari is particularly informative in this respect. Cesari states that 'in France of the 1990s, anti-Islamic statements were almost exclusively the prerogative of the far right. Today, however, intellectuals, journalists, writers and artists unashamedly express their aversion to Islam'.[212] Robert Redeker, for example, wrote that 'haine et violence habitant le livre dans lequel tout musulman est éduqué, le Coran. Comme aux temps de la guerre froide, violence et intimidation sont les voies utilisées par une idéologie à vocation hégémonique, l'Islam, pour poser sa chape de plomb sur le monde'.[213] The French author Michel Houllebecq stated that 'Islam is definitely the most f***** up of all the religions', in a 2001 interview with the magazine *Lire*.[214] Moreover, 'that same year (on 24 October), the founder of the newspaper *Le Point* publicly declared himself an "Islamophobe", calling Islam an "inanity of various archaisms"'.[215]

---

212   Jocelyne Cesari, 'Islam, Secularism and Multiculturalism After 9/11: A Transatlantic Comparison', in Jocelyne Cesari and Sean McLoughlin, eds, *European Muslims and the Secular State* (Aldershot: Ashgate, 2005), 39–54 (45).

213   Cited in Sylvain Brouard and Vincent Tiberj, 'Enquêter sur la religion: curiosité malsaine ou nécessité scientifique?', *Mouvements* (2007) <http://www.mouvements.info/spip.php?article226> accessed 12 February 2008.

214   Cited in Cesari, 'Islam, Secularism and Multiculturalism After 9/11', 45.

215   Ibid.

Cesari goes on to claim that since 9/11, 'the crucial division is no longer between foreign politicized and radical Islam and individual Muslims; now, the main distinction is between "good" and "bad" Muslims: in other words those Muslims who accept the norms and political values of western societies and those who reject them.'[216] Inevitably, this Manichean division and the manner in which it is imposed – often based on perception rather than facts – poses significant problems in terms of social acceptance and integration. Cesari highlights the fundamental problem here: 'In some cases, the mere fact of being religiously observant may be sufficient to put one in the category of being a "bad" Muslim, as religious observance is associated, increasingly, with radicalism.'[217] Islam has come to be perceived as 'the religion of fanaticism, of "ayatollahs", of intolerance, of an impossible adjustment to modernity, to democracy and most of all to the secular French model.'[218]

Undoubtedly, the events of September 2001 have had a far-reaching impact in terms of the opposition to the increased visibility of Islam in French society. Bowen confirms that the attacks 'did lead the mass media to train their lenses once again on possible internal threats attributable to Islam.'[219] As a result, Cesari reveals that 'resistance to the increased visibility of Islamic symbols is on the rise due to a logic that automatically associates the practice of Islam with "fundamentalism" and thus a potential transition to terrorist activity or the support of terrorist activity.'[220] This resistance could be seen clearly in 2003 with the reprise of the debate surrounding the 1989 Headscarf Affair. The announcement by President Chirac of the new law banning conspicuous signs of religious affiliation ('those which lead to the wearer being immediately perceived and recognized by his or her religious affiliation') signaled a new stage in the Headscarf Affair

---

216 Ibid.
217 Ibid.
218 Fahrad Khosrokhavar, *L'islam des prisons* (Paris: Balland, 2004), 14.
219 John Bowen, *Why the French Don't Like Headscarves: Islam, the State and Public Space* (Princeton: Princeton University Press, 2007), 93.
220 Cesari, 'Islam, Secularism and Multiculturalism After 9/11', 46.

begun in 1989.[221] Chirac's motives for implementing a ban on headscarves were clearly influenced, to a certain extent, by the anti-Islamic sentiment stemming from the events of 9/11, especially in light of the fact that 'the number of girls wearing headscarves in state schools had never been large and was at its lowest for many years in 2003'.[222] The President appeared to view the Islamic headscarf as a potential threat to national cohesion at a time of heightened fears regarding the place of Islam in French society.

Since 2001, negative perceptions of Islam have increased in French society. Islam is now firmly associated with fundamentalism and terrorism in the popular imagination. This semantic development has led to the stigmatization of French Muslims. Furthermore, the heightened insecurity in relation to Islam has affected not only practicing Muslims but also those perceived to be Muslim. In other words, the link between Islam and North African countries has led to the construction of an associative web that brings together Islam, fanaticism and populations that are somatically identifiable as being of North African origin in the popular imagination. The Republic has thus become colour-sensitive rather than colour-blind. As previously mentioned, the dynamic of fear that has gained momentum at the heart of French society as a result has been directed primarily towards the *banlieues*. Many residents of these areas have found themselves increasingly stigmatized due to their immigrant origins and their real or perceived link to the Islamic religion. The interpretations of the 2005 urban violence in French suburbs offer a case in point of this situation. Rik Coolsaet states that 'almost immediately after the first riots broke out, speculation arose about manipulation by Islamist radicals. Even after the French *Renseignements Généraux* confirmed that the involvement of Islamists was nil, some media continued to refer to the rioters as "Muslim", thus obfuscating the social and political causes driving these events'.[223]

---

221 The new law was formally passed by a majority of members of the Assembly in February 2004.

222 Hargreaves, *Multi-ethnic France*, 113.

223 Rik Coolsaet and Tanguy Struye de Swielande, 'Zeitgeist and (De-)Radicalization', in Rik Coolsaet, ed., *Jihadi Terrorism and the Radicalization Challenge in Europe* (Aldershot: Ashgate, 2008), 155–181 (155).

In terms of the integration of the *banlieues* into mainstream society, the propagation of such stereotypes has contributed significantly to the growth in the social divide separating these areas from the rest of French society. However, the great irony of the stereotypes attributed to the suburbs lies in the fact that these representations have been formed from a distorted view of the *banlieues*, one that does not reflect the reality of the situation. Oussama Cherribi speaks of a tendency on the part of the media and the dominant population 'to stereotype immigrants from Islamic countries as a group having a religious identity that is more important than their various ethnic identities'.[224] In the French context, however, and particularly that of the *banlieues*, this statement touches at the heart of a fundamental paradox regarding the question of identity that lies beneath popular discourse on integration.

Developing a New Identity: Socio-cultural Evolution in the Suburbs

The question of identity is an integral element of the socio-cultural situation in the *quartiers sensibles*. Issues relating to the identity of the inhabitants of these areas, combined with the dominant social and economic problems, form the basis for a paradigm of exclusion that constitutes the primary obstacle to the successful integration of these areas. Since the 1970s and the 'flight' of the middle classes, the *banlieues* have been associated with immigration in the popular imagination. The previously discussed rise in the visibility of Islam in French society since the beginning of the 1980s has cemented this link, while adding a religious dimension that has evoked fear in an increasingly security-oriented society. Consequently, in the wake of the 2005 violence, as well as the aftershock of 2007, it is perhaps unsurprising that the interpretations articulated by various social commentators blamed the immigrant population of the suburbs. Indeed

---

224 Oussama Cherribi, 'The Growing Islamization of Europe', in John Esposito and François Burgat, eds, *Modernising Islam: Religion in the Public Sphere in Europe and the Middle East* (London: Hurst, 2003), 193–214 (210).

Ulrike Schuerkens states that 'French commentators have described this societal crisis as the attack of a post-colonial proletariat and of the "enemies of our world"'.[225]

Some commentators directly attributed the riots to immigrants; Philip Jenkins spoke specifically of the 'riots by Arab and African youths', for example.[226] In the discourse of others, the link was implied. Hélène Carrère d'Encausse, permanent secretary of the *Académie française*, blamed polygamy for the violence, stating that 'ces gens viennent directement de leurs villages africains. Or la ville de Paris et les autres villes d'Europe ne sont pas des villages africains'.[227] The idea of polygamy – and the concomitant link with immigration – was also 'reprise à leur compte par le ministre délégué à l'Emploi, Gérard Larcher et le président du groupe UMP à l'Assemblée nationale, Bernard Accoyer'.[228] However, to blame the 'immigrant' population for these episodes of violence is a simplistic and reductive interpretation that fails to take into consideration the mutations and developments that have occurred in the identity of the population of these areas with the passing of generations.

To discuss the issue of identity is undoubtedly a difficult task, given the complex and multifaceted nature of the subject. Identity is a fluid concept, constantly changing and evolving due to its position at the point of intersection of an incalculable number of cultural, social and political influences, to name but a few. In *Multi-Ethnic France*, Hargreaves provides a particularly insightful analysis of the question of identity in the context of immigrants in France. Hargreaves states that 'if we define identity as the pattern of meaning and value by which a person structures his or her life, it is clear that this involves a dynamic process rather than an immutable condition'.[229]

225 Ulrike Schuerkens, 'France', in Anna Triandafyllidou and Ruby Gropas, eds, *European Immigration: A Sourcebook* (Aldershot: Ashgate, 2007), 113–126 (124).

226 Philip Jenkins, *God's Continent: Christianity, Islam and Europe's Religious Crisis* (Oxford: Oxford University Press, 2007), 152.

227 Cited in Gérard Mauger, *L'émeute de novembre 2005: une révolte protopolitique* (Broissieux: Editions du Croquant, 2006), 94.

228 Ibid., 95.

229 Hargreaves, *Multi-ethnic France*, 82.

With regard to the *banlieues* and national identity, the question of identity becomes even more complex due to two additional elements: the history of immigration in these areas and the resultant impact of this history; and the marginalized position of inhabitants who find themselves socially and culturally excluded from the *centre-ville* due to their ethnic origins. Hargreaves writes that 'the most potent forms of ethnic identification have generally been those associated with nationhood' and essentially, this statement provides the key to understanding the developments in terms of identity and belonging that have taken place in the *banlieues* since the huge influx of immigrant workers in the 1960s.[230] However, in order to analyse the evolution of identity, it is necessary to make a distinction between the first generation of immigrants who flocked to France during *les Trente Glorieuses*, and the descendants of these immigrants, the majority of whom were born and raised in France. This distinction is necessary because the experience of those immigrants who arrived in France from foreign countries, particularly from former colonies, is eminently different from that of their descendants.

Hargreaves claims that 'socio-cultural ties based on collective origins distinct from those of other groups are the foundation of ethnic identities', and this fundamental idea explains, in large part, the challenges that faced those 'first generation' immigrants that became a permanent element of the French demographic landscape throughout the post-war period of economic growth.[231] Effectively, due to their status as immigrants from another country, products of a different social background with its own dominant cultural codes and practices, as well as a unique cultural heritage, these people experienced a certain duality in terms of identity. On one hand, they were natives of another country where they had become imbued with the cultural codes and practices of the dominant society. On the other hand, they were residents in a new social context and thus inevitably became acculturated, to a certain extent, to the dominant codes of this setting. In this context, it is useful to consider the theory of 'primordial attachments' introduced by Shils in 1957, and further developed by Geertz in the early

230   Ibid., 140.
231   Ibid., 82.

1960s.[232] Geertz described a primordial attachment as 'one that stems from [...] the assumed givens of social existence: immediate contiguity and live connection mainly, but beyond them the giveness that stems from being born into a particular religious community, speaking a particular language [...] and following particular social practices.'[233] Essentially, 'primordialist theorists of ethnicity highlight shared kin, territory, language, religion, and traditions as the factors that often give people a sense of intense solidarity, passion, sacredness, and loyalty to one another.'[234] Hargreaves identifies three senses in which the idea of primordial attachments is appropriate:

> First, the cultural codes on which ethnic identities are built tend to be of a funda-
> mental nature, setting a general framework of meaning within which particular acts
> are constructed [...] Second, cultural codes of this kind are usually [...] learnt at an
> early age, and in this sense enjoy ontological primacy. Thirdly, they are by the same
> token associated with deep-seated affective ties which may make them difficult to
> dislodge or replace.[235]

However, while the notion of primordial attachments is useful in the contexts described by Hargreaves, since it highlights the importance of those socio-cultural ties developed to the dominant society during the formative years of a person and progressively reinforced after, it is problematic in the sense that it 'refute[s] the idea that identity is changeable, rational, or calculated.'[236] In this respect, proponents of rational choice theory, a concept rooted in the notion of instrumentalism, propose a conflicting understanding of identity.[237] According to Philip Yang, rational choice

---

232 Gloria Totoricagüena, *Basque Diaspora: Migration and Transnational Identity* (Reno: University of Nevada Press, 2005), 105.

233 Cited in John Rex, 'The Theory of Identity', in Harry Goulbourne, ed., *Race and Ethnicity: Critical Concepts in Sociology* (London: Routledge, 2001), 232–252 (237).

234 Ibid., 106.

235 Hargreaves, *Multi-ethnic France*, 82.

236 Totoricagüena, *Basque Identity*, 107.

237 For a definition and description of instrumentalism see Matthew Hoddie, *Ethnic Realignments: A Comparative Study of Government Influences on Identity* (Lanham, MD: Lexington Books, 2005), 3.

theory argues that 'people act to promote their socio-economic positions by minimizing the costs of, and maximizing the potential of, their actions. In terms of ethnic identity, rational choice theory maintains that ethnic affiliation is based on the rational calculation of the costs and benefits of ethnic association'.[238] In the French context, this implies that the prospect of improving their socio-economic position through employment in France motivated immigrants to acculturate, engaging with many of the cultural codes and practices dominant in French society, while at the same time maintaining a certain attachment to their ethnic origins. Ultimately, the socio-cultural situation of immigrants incorporates an element of conflict, as the immigrant social actor attempts to reconcile the cultural codes, practices and heritage inherited from the native society with those presented by the new host society. It is in this sense that it becomes possible to speak of a duality in terms of identity, the internal struggle to unite past and present socio-cultural experiences.

Forging a New Identity: The Youth of Immigrant Origin

While 'first generation' immigrants undoubtedly experienced this identity conflict directly – that is, the conflicting emotions resulting from the experience of uprooting from the native culture and entering a new social context – subsequent generations did not, and indeed could not, experience this conflict directly since they were born and raised in the receiving society: France. Rather, the children of immigrants experienced this conflict indirectly through the influence of their parents, as their parents tried to 'ensure that the cultural codes inherited from the country of origin are sustained by the younger generation'.[239] Hargreaves states that these young people were encouraged to educate themselves as a means of securing upward social mobility, and 'as they pass through the educational

238 Philip Yang, *Ethnic Studies: Issues and Approaches* (New York: SUNY Press, 2000), 47.
239 Hargreaves, *Multi-ethnic France*, 83.

system and mix with children from the majority population, immigrant-born youngsters tend to internalize the cultural codes of the dominant population not simply as a means to an end but as desirable objects in their own right'.[240] Consequently, though elements of their ancestral ethnic origins persist, most notably in terms of somatic difference and religious heritage, from the point of view of the descendants of those populations who migrated to France and established themselves as permanent residents (with many acquiring citizenship), 'France is their most immediate point of reference'.[241] It is worth noting that 'there is ample evidence to show that religious belief and observance are far weaker among the descendants of immigrants than among first-generation Muslims in France', a fact that counters claims of religious communitarianism and the growth of a subversive Islam. Brouard and Tiberj support this statement with conclusions drawn from 'l'enquête RAPFI [Rapport au politique des français issus de l'immigration]', a survey carried out in 2005 under the auspices of the *Centre de recherche politique de Sciences Po*. The survey was based on a representative sample of French citizens of African and Turkish origins, and explored questions of religion and values among these populations of immigrant origins. This study found that 'parmi les nouveaux Français interrogés seuls 59 pour cent d'entre eux se déclarent musulman, soit une proportion proche de celle des catholiques dans l'électorat en général, et compte dans leurs rangs 20 [pour cent] de "sans religion"'.[242] Crucially, the survey found that 'le phénomène général de sécularisation s'opère également parmi les nouveaux Français. L'athéisme progresse en effet avec l'ancienneté de l'implantation en France puisqu'on compte 14 pour cent de sans religion parmi les immigrés naturalisés, 22 pour cent dans la première génération née en France et 39 pour cent dans la seconde génération'.[243] These results

---

240 Ibid.
241 Jane Hiddleston, *Reinventing Community: Identity and Difference in Late Twentieth-Century French Philosophy and Literature* (Oxford: Legenda, 2005), 177.
242 Sylvain Brouard and Vincent Tiberj, 'Enquêter sur la religion: curiosité malsaine ou nécessité scientifique?', *Mouvements* (2007) <http://www.mouvements.info/spip.php?article226> accessed 12 February 2008.
243 Ibid.

confirm the decline in religious adherence among descendants of Muslim immigrants, thus negating the notion of a threat to national unity posed by the spread of Islamic communitarianism in France.

For these subsequent generations, whose social and cultural experiences have derived, for the most part, from French society, links to their ancestral country were and continue to be experienced predominantly through the lived experiences of their parents and grandparents. However, the distance, both physical and in terms of social experiences, from these ancestral societies has undermined attempts to propagate minority cultural codes and practices in the midst of the dominant socio-cultural setting. Hiddleston sums up the situation in her description of the children of North African immigrants born in France: 'unlike their parents, they themselves have not emigrated but were born in France. Though frequently spoken of as immigrants, they are not immigrants at all and they have experienced no such displacement or uprooting'.[244] The generational gap separating the youth of the *banlieues* from their immigrant origins constitutes two or three and, in some cases, even four generations. The young *banlieusards* are, for the most part, French citizens, and identify with the dominant French socio-cultural context. This is especially the case in terms of self-perception; these young people may be of immigrant origin but they define themselves as French citizens.

The paradox then is clear. Previous chapters have illustrated how the historical development of the *banlieues* has engendered a powerful link in the popular imagination that associates immigration with the suburbs. Since the 1980s, a religious element has been added to this link, with negative representations of Islam being projected onto the inhabitants of these areas. Consequently, the inhabitants of the *banlieues* have been socially marginalized due to the construction of damaging stereotypes stemming from real or perceived ethnic difference. Profound changes in the socio-cultural situation in the suburbs, in terms of identity and belonging, have gone unnoticed as negative representations have persisted, reinforced by episodes of violence that have been interpreted as a rejection of French

244 Hiddleston, *Reinventing Community*, 177.

society and culture. Ironically, these instances of violence, while undoubtedly strongly influenced by the socio-economic and socio-structural deterioration in these areas, are, in reality, a product of the refusal of mainstream French society to accept the inhabitants of these areas as equal members of society. In this respect, it is worth considering the analysis put forward by Castel in *La discrimination négative*. Paradoxically, Castel claims that the youth of the suburbs, are 'ni dedans, ni dehors'.[245] Castel argues that on one hand, 'ces jeunes ne sont pas exclus parce qu'ils partagent un grand nombre de pratiques et d'aspirations communes à leur classe d'âge, et que beaucoup d'entre eux bénéficient en principe de droits qui sont ceux de la citoyenneté française'.[246] In terms of culture, Castel states that 'ces jeunes de cité ne sont pas non plus exclus au sens où ils seraient coupés de la culture française dominante. En dépit d'un certain bi-culturalisme hérité de leur milieu familial, leur culture de base est massivement française'.[247] However, while the youth of immigrant origins residing in the *quartiers sensibles* are not in this sense situated outside of French society, neither are they 'dedans'. According to Castel, 'ils ne sont pas non plus *dedans* puisqu'ils n'y occupent aucune place reconnue et beaucoup d'entre eux ne paraissent pas susceptibles de pouvoir s'en ménager une [...] Leur exil est un exil intérieur qui les conduit à vivre en négatif, sous la forme de promesses non tenues, leur rapport aux opportunités et aux valeurs qu'est censée incarner la société française'.[248]

The youth of the *quartiers sensibles* experience what may be described as a detached citizenship. Legitimate members of French society from a political and cultural point of view, especially in their own eyes, these young people have the potential to make a positive contribution to French society. However, while the changing socio-cultural situation of the *banlieues* has confirmed the dominant identity of recent generations as French – that is, as legitimate political members of the French state sharing the same

245 Castel, *La discrimination négative*, 27.
246 Ibid.
247 Ibid., 36.
248 Ibid., 38.

social and cultural codes and practices as the dominant community – this identity has not been accepted by mainstream society where the youth of immigrant origin are still very much seen as the 'other'. The young people of the suburbs regard themselves as French; however, they are not afforded complete access to French society. In the public sphere, a potent conflict places the French identity of the young *banlieusards* in opposition with the imagined immigrant identity superimposed upon these youths by social commentators. The young people find themselves in the blind spot of French republicanism, inhabiting areas to which the fundamental values and principles of the Republic do not extend. This dynamic has resulted in the growth of a deep-rooted malaise among the population of the suburbs. Despair and frustration have taken hold of *inhabitants*, particularly the young people, as a result of exclusionary processes. In the suburbs, the youth have been placed on a destructive trajectory that continues to gain momentum. Inevitably, this situation has contributed to the progressive growth of a widespread *galère*. In these areas where dialogue has failed, young inhabitants perceive violence as the only means of drawing attention to their situation. The events of 2005 and 2007 constituted the physical manifestation of this underlying malaise, a culmination of all the social and economic problems facing the youth of the suburbs. The scale and intensity of these violent events bear testament to the increasing intensity of the *galère* that is provoking reactions among young people against the unjust system that dominates life in the *quartiers sensibles*.

Villiers-le-Bel: Profile of a *Quartier Sensible*

The majority of the book to this point has approached the issues at stake from a theoretical perspective, drawing on the work of historians and sociologists in order to establish the necessary historical and ideological context within which the events of 2005 and 2007 must be understood. This approach has provided a valuable insight into the socio-cultural situation that exists in the suburbs. However, any attempt to develop an understanding of life in these areas, and, consequently, to elucidate the causes and motivations underlying the riots, cannot rely on theory alone. In order to gain a comprehensive understanding of the complex cultural, economic and social processes at play in these areas, it is necessary to go beyond a normative approach and gain empirically based knowledge of the practical social dynamic that dominates life in the *banlieues*. In light of this fact, my analysis will now focus on a case study of Villiers-le-Bel, a suburb that witnessed significant violence and destruction during the events of both 2005 and 2007.

The choice of Villiers-le-Bel as the object of this case-study stems from a number of significant factors. First, as will be shown, the commune of Villiers-le-Bel shares many of the features that characterize the *quartiers sensibles*, such as a high percentage of young people, high levels of unemployment, and low levels of educational achievement, to name but a few. It has been shown in previous chapters how these issues all impact upon the trajectory of local youths and play a significant role in the rise of urban violence and delinquency. Second, Villiers-le-Bel experienced violence and destruction during the events of 2005. This is perhaps unsurprising, given the geographical proximity of this commune to the source of the unrest, Clichy-sous-Bois. Paradoxically however, while the violence progressed in scale and amplitude in suburban communities across the nation over the course of the three weeks, Villiers-le-Bel did not experience the levels of destruction recorded further afield, despite being situated at such a short distance from the source of the riots. Consequently, while the primary aim of this study is to discern the causes of the violence, another pertinent question is also raised: Why did the violence in Villiers-le-Bel remain somewhat muted in comparison to that of other suburban communities? This question has important implications in terms of preventing and managing urban violence. Third, although the violence and destruction recorded in Villiers-le-Bel in 2005 did not match the levels recorded elsewhere, in 2007 Villiers-le-Bel was the site of two nights of rioting that reached unprecedented levels in terms of intensity. As has been shown in Chapter 1, the disorder of 2007 crossed a threshold in terms of urban violence with youths firing shots at police, which left a significant number of officers injured. This development again raises interesting questions. For example, why did the violence of 2007 reach such levels of intensity and, on a larger scale, what does this reveal about the state of urban violence in the *quartiers sensible* in more general terms? The combination of these factors makes Villiers-le-Bel a unique and interesting field of study, with clear potential to produce qualitative research data that will contribute to current research on French urban violence.

Exploring Villiers-le-Bel

Profile of a Quartier Sensible

The suburban commune of Villiers-le-Bel, part of the ninety-fifth *département* of Val d'Oise, is located eighteen kilometres north of Paris. Since the beginning of the nineteenth century, the commune has experienced significant urban development that has radically changed the landscape of the area. Alongside the old village of Villiers-le-Bel, whose existence predates the 1789 French Revolution, the inter-World War period saw the rapid development of *lotissements pavillonnaires* in the eastern sector of the commune as Paris strove to respond to the growing demand for housing. These estates were often privately developed with little control in terms of planning and, as a result, developed in a haphazard manner with little consideration for collective facilities and amenities. Additionally, the estates required a lot of physical space and the development of transport links to the city was a costly affair. At this time, the estates catered primarily for workers who commuted to Paris on a daily basis. The development of these *lotissements* was followed, from the beginning of the 1950s, by the development of a number of *grands ensembles*. As explained in Chapter 3, a severe demand for housing in France erupted during the post-World War II period, a demand that was more acute in the Paris area, and which resulted in the development of large-scale housing projects in many of the city's suburbs. In this respect, the developmental trajectory of Villiers-le-Bel was no different than many other Parisian suburbs, and in 1955 the *Société Centrale Immobilière de la Caisse des Dépots et Consignations* (SCIC) began work on the development known as Les Carreaux in the eastern sector of the commune. The architects of the project initially envisaged the construction of 1,000 dwellings; however, this figure would eventually rise to 1,675.[1] The *grands ensembles* of Puits-la-Marlière (hereafter PLM), la Cerisaie and Derrière-les-Murs-de-Monseigneur (hereafter DLM), all located in the western sector of the old village, followed from the early 1960s.[2] After an initial period of euphoria surrounding the construction of low-cost dwellings housing all the basic conveniences, such as electricity, running water and indoor toilets, the *grands ensembles* underwent a prolonged period of progressive physical deterioration. Following the creation of the *Zones urbaine sensible* (ZUS) and the *Zones de redynamisation urbaine* (ZRU), established by the 'Loi d'orientation pour l'aménagement et le développement du territoire' (LOADT) in 1995, Les Carreaux, PLM and DLM were all designated as both ZUS and ZRU, a clear indication of the physical and social degradation of these areas.

---

1   Communauté d'agglomération Val de France Villiers-le-Bel, *Les Carreaux, 1955–1963: Naissance d'un grand ensemble en banlieue parisienne* (Paris: Communauté d'agglomération Val de France Villiers-le-Bel, 2006), 14.

2   Ibid.

In terms of geographical layout, Villiers-le-Bel is somewhat fragmented, with the town divided into two main sectors. The bulk of the town's commercial enterprises are to be found in the south-east of the commune, in the area adjoining neighbourhoods of Gonesse and Arnouville-lès-Gonesse, while the administrative centre is located in the north-west of the commune, in the old village of Villiers-le-Bel. These two sectors are linked by one principal east-west traffic artery. This urban fragmentation is significant because the administrative centre is disconnected from the commercial centre, challenging the traditional idea of a unified centre and resulting in a 'tissu urbain hétérogène, sans répérage, sans centralité forte'.[3] Moreover, a significant portion of the population of Villiers-le-Bel, including residents of the *Zone d'aménagement concerté* (ZAC) and one of the ZUS, inhabit the north-western sector and are thus isolated to a certain extent from the commercial centre of the town.

On a larger scale, Villiers-le-Bel represents just one of many communes in the east of the department of Val d'Oise. In 1997, the *Communauté de Communes Val de France* was established by the local authorities of Villiers-le-Bel and Sarcelles. Since 2000, this intercommunity organization, aiming to combat processes of segregation and exclusion, has been extended to incorporate seven communes in the east of the department of Val d'Oise.[4] This organization's report and plan (2000–2006) stated that 'on a [...] aujourd'hui un patchwork de quartiers [...] souvent enclavés et sans liens entre eux. Le secteur souffre d'une absence de lisibilité de la trame urbaine accentuée par une forte présence des infrastructures EDF, TGV Nord, échangeurs autoroutiers [...] et emprises autoroutières'.[5] In other words, despite the presence of a number of significant infrastructural developments, the communes concerned have limited access to these transport routes. Moreover, in terms of the immediate locality of Villiers-le-Bel, the transport infrastructure is also somewhat limited. Internally, the different

---

3   'Contrat de ville du Secteur Est du Val d'Oise – Convention Cadre' (2000) <http://i. ville.gouv.fr/reference/328> accessed 12 May 2008, 10.
4   Ibid., 3.
5   Ibid., 10.

areas of the commune are serviced by four bus routes. Buses connecting the old village to the commercial area typically run at twenty- to thirty-minute intervals. Villiers-le-Bel is linked to Paris by the RER D train line, which terminates in the north-Paris suburb of Creil. It is worth noting that the train station servicing local residents, while located next to the commercial area of the commune, is not within the administrative boundaries of Villiers-le-Bel, but, rather, is located in the adjoining commune of Arnouville-lès-Gonesse. Trains typically run at thirty to forty minute intervals with the journey lasting twenty minutes on average. Given that almost 30 per cent of households do not own a car (this percentage increased slightly between 1999 and 2005), public transport constitutes the principal form of transport.[6] Residents inhabiting the ZUS in the old village are at a significant disadvantage in terms of access to the city of Paris, with an overall journey time of at least forty minutes to reach the Gare du Nord alone. In terms of cost, the transport system is expensive, particularly for those who are unemployed, and this situation undoubtedly contributes to the geographical exclusion of inhabitants from the centre of Paris. In general terms, the limitations of the infrastructure have important implications with regard to those seeking employment, given the travel time, distance and expense involved, and goes some way to explaining the high levels of unemployment that dominate the commune.

In aesthetic terms, Villiers-le-Bel constitutes an extremely diverse urban landscape. It is important to consider the visual aspect of the commune since the physical environment of an area gives an immediate and often significant insight into the social environment of the local population. The commercial sector of Villiers-le-Bel, while small, has a well-kept and aesthetically pleasing appearance. The streets are clean and the various shops – a number of which specialize in African food and goods – are complemented by cafés and restaurants. Busy at weekends, the area is also reasonably populated on weekdays. Residential properties in the immediate

6   INSEE, 'Chiffres clés issus des enquêtes annuelles de recensement de 2004 à 2007' (2008) <http://www.insee.fr/fr/ppp/bases-de-donnees/recensement/resultats/chiffres-cles/n2/n2_95680.pdf> accessed 12 January 2009.

surroundings are also well-kept and recently painted. The overall impression given by the area is a far cry from the 'zones de non-droit' presented by the media during and after the urban violence of 2005 and 2007, and challenges the visual stereotypes associated with the *banlieues*. The old village, in the western sector of the commune, houses the architecturally impressive town hall and the local church, an example of Gothic architecture dating from the eighteenth century and classed as a historical monument. Similar to the commercial area, the immediate surroundings of the administrative centre are neat and well-preserved. However, the estates forming part of the ZUS and ZRU, situated less than a ten-minute walk from both the commercial and administrative centres, represent an entirely different side of Villiers-le-Bel. Les Carreaux, PLM, DLM and the estate of la Cerisaie all share similar characteristics. These areas are dominated by HLM apartment blocks. The buildings themselves are, for the most part, in various stages of degradation. Burnt-out apartments can be seen in several buildings, notably in DLM. The majority of entrance-halls are unlit and many have no doors or broken windows. These hallways provide a meeting place for groups of young people during the day or in the evening, after the *Maison de quartier* closes. The young people also frequent the labyrinth of basement corridors that pass among the very foundations of the HLM apartment blocks. According to interviewees, these corridors are especially popular in autumn and winter, when the young people of the locality seek shelter from the rain and the cold. When I visited PLM in summer 2009, the local bus stop was surrounded by shattered glass, its windows having been broken at some point. The shards of glass remained on the ground around the stop for a number of weeks. The few cafés to be found in the shadows of the HLMs have damaged fronts and graffiti sprayed on their walls. Effectively, these estates present a depressing and intimidating image; the hostile urban environment is completely at odds with the impression created by the commercial centre.

Sociodemographic Environment

The commune of Villiers-le-Bel has a population of just over 27,000. This population of Villiers-le-Bel is characterized by a high proportion of young people: 23 per cent under the age of fourteen; 46 per cent in the under-twenty-nine age bracket.[7] Consequently, social issues such as youth unemployment, academic failure, and urban violence and delinquency evidently have a potentially greater impact on Villiers-le-Bel than in other areas. It is important to note that 56 per cent of the overall population reside in areas designated as ZUS, areas in which a large portion of the commune's social housing is located (over half of all housing in Villiers-le-Bel is social housing).[8] The foreign population residing in Villiers-le-Bel is also significant; foreign nationals make up over 20 per cent of the population of the commune.[9] This figure rises to 25 per cent in the specific context of the ZUS. The concentration of foreigners residing in the ZUS of Villiers-le-Bel is greater than the departmental average; in the Val d'Oise department the average percentage of foreigners residing in the ZUS rests at 21 per cent.[10] Moreover, this figure does not include the significant amount of foreigners who have acquired French nationality. Thus, despite the lack of statistics relating to the population of foreign origin discussed in Chapter 3, it is clear that the population of Villers-le-Bel incorporates a significant population of immigrant origin. In terms of households, the commune incorporates a substantial number of large families, with almost 10 per cent of families

---

7   INSEE, 'Villiers-le-Bel: Chiffres clés' (2010) <http://www.statistiques-locales. insee.fr/FICHES/DL/DEP/95/COM/DL_COM95680.pdf> accessed 27 August 2010.

8   Délégation Interministérielle à la Ville, Système d'Information Géographique, 'Commune Villiers-le-Bel', <http://sig.ville.gouv.fr/Synthese/95680> accessed 8 June 2010.

9   Ibid. It should be noted that more recent figures relating to the percentage of foreign nationals residing in Villiers-le-Bel were not available at the time of writing. However, while the figures given are dated, they give an indication of the strong presence of populations of immigrant origins in the commune.

10   Ibid.

having at least four children.[11] The proportion of monoparental families residing in Villiers-le-Bel is also significant. In 2007, for example, the average number of monoparental families in the commune was 22 per cent – this compared with an average of 18.8 per cent in 1999.[12] These factors, combined with rising levels of unemployment, have increased the proportion of the local population facing economic hardship and social difficulties. Furthermore, the rise in monoparental families has contributed to the erosion of the traditional family unit and its associated support structure.

In relation to employment, research has shown that 56 per cent of revenues in Villiers-le-Bel are exempt from tax, being below the minimum threshold of taxable income.[13] In an interview in 2009, Marion Petit-Jean, the then Deputy Mayor responsible for the *politique de la ville* and issues regarding discrimination, revealed that 'ça fait huit ans qu'on n'a pas augmenté les impôts locaux' because the local population already faces financial difficulty.[14] This fact, considered alongside the high levels of unemployment in the commune, indicates a challenging socio-economic environment.

In Villiers-le-Bel, approximately 19 per cent of the population is unemployed, a figure which rests well above the national average of approximately 10 per cent.[15] Moreover, the percentage of those unemployed rises to 21.3 per cent in the specific context of the ZUS in Villiers-le-Bel, highlighting the status of these areas as pockets of socio-economic relegation. These high levels of unemployment have resulted in a significant reliance on social benefits such as the *Revenu de solidarité active* (RSA). The RSA represents the

---

11   INSEE, 'Villiers-le-Bel: Chiffres clés' (2010) <http://www.statistiques-locales.insee.fr/FICHES/DL/DEP/95/COM/DL_COM95680.pdf> accessed 27 August 2010.

12   Délégation Interministérielle à la Ville, Système d'Information Géographique, 'Commune Villiers-le-Bel', <http://sig.ville.gouv.fr/Synthese/95680> accessed 8 June 2010.

13   Ibid.

14   Interview with Marion Petit Jean, Adjointe au maire chargée de la politique de la ville et de la lutte contre les discriminations (24 November 2008).

15   INSEE, 'Taux de chômage' (2010) <http://www.insee.fr/fr/themes/info-rapide.asp?id=14> accessed 3 February 2011.

latest incarnation of the *Revenu minimum d'insertion* (RMI), an allowance first introduced in 1988 to support the poorest members of society. As of 1 January 2011, the RSA rests at 466.99 euro per person per month or 700.49 euro per couple per month.[16] The figure increases by 136.36 euro per child for the first two children and then rises to 181.85 euro for each additional child. The number of inhabitants receiving the RSA in Villiers-le-Bel rose from 586 in 1996 to 977 in 2006. By 2007 this figure was at 1,100. This dramatic increase is yet another indication of the difficult socio-economic situation facing certain members of the population in the commune and hints at a deteriorating economic climate. Perhaps most significant in the context of this research on the subject of urban violence is the percentage of the youth population who are unemployed: approximately 25 per cent of young people between the ages of fifteen and twenty-four.[17] This economic stagnation is compounded by the demographic density of young residents which sees large numbers of youths competing for relatively few jobs. The high levels of unemployment place young residents of the area in a financially difficult situation, and can lead to a loss of hope for the future and a growing sense of frustration. It has been shown in Chapter 3 how socio-economic factors play an important role in the onset of the profound malaise that constitutes *la galère*. Dubet illustrates how unemployment, along with other social and cultural factors, can evoke a feeling of exclusion on the part of the young person, which, in turn, leads to an ever-increasing discontentment relating to their socio-economic situation. In this instance, the refusal to accept the social alienation brought on by their socio-economic exclusion, coupled with the desire to conform to social norms, can push the youth of the suburbs towards acts of crime and delinquency, such as theft. Dubet and Lapeyronnie regard this development as an illegal means of conforming to socio-economic norms, since unemployment blocks pursuit of the legal route.

16   Service-Public.fr, 'Calcul du montant du revenu de solidarité active (RSA)', <http://vosdroits.service-public.fr/particuliers/F502.xhtml> accessed 12 February 2011.
17   INSEE, 'Villiers-le-Bel: Chiffres clés' (2010) <http://www.statistiques-locales.insee.fr/FICHES/DL/DEP/95/COM/DL_COM95680.pdf> accessed 27 August 2010.

The problems relating to unemployment in Villiers-le-Bel are exacerbated by poor levels of academic development. Only 14 per cent of those over the age of fifteen have obtained a qualification beyond the baccalauréat or the brevet professional, while over 32 per cent of the same demographic do not possess any diploma.[18] These statistics indicate a high level of academic failure throughout the commune. Rey highlights the implications of academic failure in terms of the search for employment:

> [L]es jeunes les moins qualifiés au terme de leur scolarité, conduite ou non jusqu'à l'obtention d'un diplôme, n'ont le choix qu'entre le chômage, le passage dans la série de dispositifs, prévus à leurs intention et dont les maîtres mots sont stage et formation, ou des emplois précaires dans les services et dans les sociétés de travail temporaire.[19]

The figures relating to education are important in the context of research published by the Canadian Organization for Economic Co-operation and Development, which concludes that 'young adults with low levels of education have a significantly lower employment rate than other twenty- to twenty-four-year-old non-students who have gained educational credentials either at the upper secondary and non-tertiary level or at the tertiary level'.[20] To summarize, academic development in Villiers-le-Bel is characterized by a high failure rate, which, in turn, has a significant impact on the prospects of employment available to young people residing in the area.

Problems regarding unemployment and academic failure have an important impact on the population of Villiers-le-Bel, and on the young people especially. Socio-economically excluded, these young people find themselves at the margins of French society. Naturally this has a certain impact on the issue of political participation. Over half of those young people interviewed (both formally and informally) in the course of this case study confessed that they did not vote regularly. For these young people, participation in the electoral process is often seen as a waste of time: 'Nous, on vote pas [reference to an immediate peer group of about 10 youths].

18   Ibid.
19   Rey, *La peur des banlieues*, 48.
20   'From education to work: a difficult transition for young adults with low levels of education', Report by the Organization for Economic Co-operation and Development, Canadian Policy Research Network (OECD, 2005), 45.

Ça ne vaut pas la peine...rien ne change, tu vois?'.[21] Young *banlieusards* feel that the political establishment does not listen to their voices; at the same time it is important to note that there was a marked increase in voter registrations before the 2007 presidential election. In national terms, the rise in voter registrations in the *banlieues* during this electoral period has been documented.[22] In the case of Villiers-le-Bel, the *Directeur de cabinet* of the Mairie confirmed that there was an increase of about 2000 registrations in the run-up to the election, a significant rise in a community of 27,000.[23] Could this boost to electoral lists be explained by the anti-Sarkozy sentiment that remained in many *banlieues* long after the violent events of 2005 and 2007 themselves had ended? Kokoreff explores this question in *Sociologie des émeutes*. However, in his analysis he concludes that a boost in electoral registrations usually accompanies presidential elections and that there is not enough evidence to suggest that the 2005 riots provoked a surge of young people to vote in the following presidential election. Following the 2007 presidential election, the *Mairie* of Villiers-le-Bel confirmed that 'le nombre d'inscrits sur les listes électorales reste stable. Ni les événements nationaux de 2005, ni ceux locaux de 2007 n'ont eu d'incidence sur le nombre d'inscrits'.[24] In other words, the riots of 2005 and 2007 did not appear to produce any significant mobilization in Villiers-le-Bel in terms of conventional political engagement. Thus it would appear that a significant portion of the young people of Villiers-le-Bel remain disillusioned with a political system that does not appear to answer their needs. One young person, Driss, summed up the situation: 'la plupart [des jeunes] ils diront "nique sa mère à...aux politiques"'.[25]

---

21 Interview with Nassim, twenty-year-old French citizen of North African origins, unemployed (23 June 2009).

22 See Stéphane Jugnot, 'La participation éléctorale en 2007' (INSEE, Division Enquêtes et études démographiques) <http://www.insee.fr/fr/themes/document. asp?ref_id=ip1169> accessed 20 August 2009; and Kokoreff, *Sociologie des émeutes*, 129–133.

23 Carrier, Nicolas (ncarrier@ville-Villiers-le-Bel.fr), "Chercheur de Londres", email to Matthew Moran (m.moran@ucl.ac.uk), 30 November 2009.

24 Ibid.

25 Interview with Driss, twenty-one-year-old French citizen of North African origins, unemployed (22 April 2009).

Facilities and Amenities

In terms of facilities and amenities, Villiers-le-Bel is relatively well-equipped, possessing a large number of educational, sports and cultural facilities. Regarding educational facilities, there are eleven primary schools, three *collèges* (lower secondary school) attended by 1,680 students, and one *Lycée Professionnel* (upper secondary school). The commune also houses an *Institut de Métiers de l'Artisanat*. This institute, opened in 2003, offers apprenticeships in hospitality, the food industry, the car industry and the retail industry.[26] The courses offered lead to a variety of state-recognized diplomas. The institute is located near the ZUS of Derrière-les-Murs and Puits-la-Marlière and most of the attending students live in these areas. It is worth noting, however, that the courses offered all lead to qualifications pertaining to the lower end of the tertiary sector. There are no courses that serve as a gateway to studies leading to higher-end professions such as medicine or law. Moreover, as discussed in Chapter 3, the evolution of education has resulted in a devaluation of qualifications. In other words, as education has become more widespread, further qualifications have become necessary in order to realize the same prospects of employment. Consequently, while the benefits of this institute are clear, the base-level qualification or two-year diploma offered to students there is not enough to ensure long-term employment in an increasingly competitive job market.

Villiers-le-Bel is equipped with a number of cultural and youth-oriented resources. The commune houses, four *Maisons de quartier* or community centres, are managed by social workers on a daily basis and offer a range of community-based services designed to aid the local population. *Maison Salvador Allende* and *Maison Camille Claudel* are located in the north-western sector, near the ZUS of DLM and PLM, while *Maison Jacques Brel* and *Maison Boris Vian* are situated in the south-eastern sector. *Maison Boris Vian* is located in the ZUS of Les Carreaux. Some of the social and cultural activities on offer include educational support (in the form of supervised study) for young people between the ages of six and seventeen,

---

26   Institut des Métiers de l'Artisanat, <http://www.ima95.fr/html/ima/formation-remuneree-val-oise.php> accessed 12 July 2009.

as well as theatre and music events for local youths. The community centre also plays an important role in linking the commune's elected officials to the local population. Approximately every month, the *Maison de quartier* provides a forum for the *Conseil de quartier*: a meeting between local youths, parents, adults, social workers and elected officials. These meetings allow the residents to have an input into the organization of activities at their local community centre, and also provide an opportunity to discuss various issues with the elected officials. In terms of the disadvantaged youth of Villiers-le-Bel, the community centre represents an important means of combating the negative aspects of *la galère* and, consequently, has important implications regarding the prevention of delinquency. These organizations provide local youths with an alternative space to gather and meet their peers under the supervision of qualified social workers. In the community centre, social workers can also dialogue with young people who exist outside conventional strands of development such as the school.

Although the role played by the community centre in the community is a significant one, there are limitations to these organizations in terms of the support offered to young people. For example, the opening hours of these centres do not normally extend beyond 6.30pm. Consequently, the support structure offered by the social workers in charge of these centres is absent during the hours when, arguably, it is needed most: during the hours of darkness, when acts of delinquency and violence are more likely to take place. At this time, youths with no supervised place to 'hang out' together, and no desire to go home, are more likely to engage in acts of delinquency. During both the 2005 and 2007 riots, the majority of the violence and destruction occurred after darkness had fallen. It must be noted that exceptions to normal working hours were made by social workers based in Villiers-le-Bel for a number of nights during the events of 2005 and 2007. At these times of large-scale violence and destruction, social workers maintained a visible presence on the streets of the commune as they attempted to calm young people and prevent violence. This phenomenon had important implications for the violence and its progression. This issue will be examined in more detail at a later stage. In general terms, however, the community centre and its workforce are not generally available to youths after 6.30pm Beyond the *Maison de quartier*, the commune also houses three libraries, one sportsground and five sports halls. Unfortunately, some of these facilities are lacking in equipment and are in need of repair. The equipment in the sports hall at la Cerisaie, for example, is damaged and requires replacement, while the building itself requires structural repairs.

In terms of local associations, the commune is very active, with over one hundred sports, social and cultural associations recognized by the town hall. These associations incorporate a wide range of activities and groups, from the *locataires du PLM*, an association bringing together residents of the ZUS Puits-la-Marlière, to IMAJ (*Initiatives Multiples d'Action auprès des Jeunes*), an association targeting social issues facing underprivileged young people. Many of the associations, including IMAJ, play an important and visible role in the community, organizing discussion groups and training, for example. These associations may apply for funding at the level of the commune and at the level of the department. In the case of Villiers-le-Bel, the local authorities of have donated a significant amount to the needs of associations. In 2006, for example, the town hall gave over 650,000 euro in subsidies to registered associations, a figure increased from 480,000 euro in 2006.[27]

Crime and Delinquency

With regard to crime and delinquency, the majority of statistics available relate to the broader departmental level rather than that of the commune. Nonetheless, this information gives an insight into the dominant patterns that exist throughout the department and provides a general frame of reference within which Villiers-le-Bel can be placed. In general terms, the number of delinquent acts recorded at the level of the department of Val d'Oise between 1999 and 2006 has been consistently higher than the figure for the greater Ile-de-France region. However, in recent years this gap has narrowed, with the department as a whole recording a drop in levels of delinquency. Figures published by the *Préfecture du Val d'Oise* reveal that

27   Ville de Villiers-le-Bel, 'Textes officiels', <http://www.ville-Villiers-le-Bel.fr/la-Mairie/textes-officiels/> accessed 5 July 2010.

there has been an average drop of almost 1 per cent in 'délinquance générale' since 1997.[28] This figure incorporates a decrease of almost 14 per cent since 2002, undoubtedly linked to the implementation of a zero-tolerance approach to delinquency implemented by Sarkozy upon his promotion to the post of Minister of the Interior.

With regard to Villiers-le-Bel, recorded levels of delinquency are similar to neighbouring communes in the department. A report published by the *Préfecture du Val d'Oise* in 2008 reveals that in terms of 'délinquance générale', 2,180 acts of delinquency were recorded in Villiers-le-Bel in 2007, compared with 4,782 acts in Sarcelles; 2,381 in Pontoise; 2,267 in Goussainville, and 3,090 in Garges-lès-Gonesse. In all of these cases, the statistics showed a slight drop in violations recorded in 2008. (In the case of Villiers-le-Bel, this drop was of the nature of 1 per cent.)[29] It is important to note that the decrease in levels of delinquency throughout the department has been accompanied by a steady increase in personnel among the forces of law and order.[30] Despite the fact that general levels of crime and delinquency have fallen in the Val d'Oise, there has been an increase in instances of collective violence against the forces of law and order. Statistics show that, at the level of the department, 'violences collectives à l'encontre des services de sécurité, de secours et de santé' rose by 53 per cent between 2007 and 2008.[31] This pattern indicates that, while the zero-tolerance policy implemented by Sarkozy during his time as Minister of the Interior has resulted in an increased number of arrests (the number of arrests has risen by 53 per cent since 2001) and convictions (there is now a 32 per cent case success rate compared with a 22 per cent rate in 2001), this development has been accompanied by a deterioration in police-public relations.[32] As the evidence in the following sections will show, this situation has played an important role in the development of large-scale instances of urban violence.

28 Préfecture du Val d'Oise, *Les chiffres de la délinquance dans le Val d'Oise*, 'Lutte contre la délinquance: bilan pour 2010' <http://www.val-doise.pref.gouv.fr/media/media4016720.pdf> accessed 5 December 2010.

29 Ibid., 1.

30 Ibid., 13.

31 Ibid., 12.

32 Ibid., 5.

Community Solidarity and Urban Development

This introduction to the social, cultural and economic environment of Villiers-le-Bel has highlighted the position of the commune as a *quartier sensible*. Villiers-le-Bel shares many of the characteristics facing under-privileged French *banlieues*: high levels of unemployment, educational failure and physical degradation, to name but a few. However, given the tendency of the media to prioritize sensational and often negative events such as instances of urban violence, it is equally important to highlight the positive aspects of the commune. This is important for two reasons. First, given the omnipotence of the media in contemporary society, as well as the tendency of the media to gravitate towards sensationalist material, the dramatic images of rioting are often the images that define the *banlieues* in the popular imagination. Chapter 1 discussed the role of the media in constructing the 'reality' of the suburbs in the social and political spheres. The images published and broadcast by the media frequently support and further the stereotypical idea of the *banlieues* as areas where even the police fear to go. However, this is a reductive stereotype that presents a limited insight into a multifaceted socio-cultural environment. Second, the inhab-itants of suburban communities such as Villiers-le-Bel often share a strong sense of community, a solidarity that stems from the shared experience of social and economic hardship. This solidarity is rarely seen by those living outside the community, submerged as it is under the plethora of violent images circulated by the media. Nonetheless, the importance of this com-munal bond should not be underestimated in terms of its potential role in the constructive development of the *quartiers sensibles*.

At the immediate level of the youth of the commune, social work-ers provide assistance and advice to young people at the aforementioned *Maison de quartier*. In this setting, young people can discuss problems (such as those relating to education, employment, discrimination) with qualified professionals. Participant observation at these community centres provided a comprehensive insight into the relationship between social workers and the local youths. In all of the cases observed, interactions between social workers and local youths were characterized by a high level of respect; the respect of the adult for the young person concerned and the respect of the young person for the experience and authority of the adult. The social workers know the area, many having grown up or resided in the locality, and, as a result, have a profound knowledge of the issues affecting the youth of the commune. These adults settle disputes among the young people, provide advice and listen to what they have to say. One youth interviewed summed up the general opinion among local teenagers regarding the social workers who manage the community centre and interact with the young people on a daily basis. He affirmed that the social worker is 'quelqu'un qui a le respect des jeunes, il donne des conseils [...] il veut nous aider'.[33] Moreover, the majority of social workers encountered by the researcher in Villiers-le-Bel displayed an obvious commitment to and passion for their work, and indeed their role, in the community. This commitment was evident from the beginning of the field-work undertaken by the researcher. For example, initial access to the research setting was marked by a certain distrust on the part of some social workers, who are aware of the stigma imposed on the suburbs by the media as 'no-go areas'. Persistent negative media coverage following instances of urban violence has eroded trust in journalists and interview-access was limited until trust was established. This also occurred at the administrative level of the commune.

The parents of the young people of Villiers-le-Bel represent another important aspect of the community solidarity that is to be found in the commune. A number of initiatives have been established by social workers to provide a support to parents in the community. Supervised study classes, for example, offer support to young people whose parents may be constrained by their work schedule or who may not have the necessary education to fill this role. Regarding the issue of urban violence, meetings for parents opposed to youth violence in the commune have encouraged dialogue between parents from different backgrounds, and engendered a feeling of solidarity among parents in similar situations. For instance, a meeting between parents living in the different areas of the commune's ZUS, held on 22 November 2008 in one of the community centres, brought together over thirty parents to discuss various issues relating to youth violence,

---

33   Interview with Wilfred, twenty-two years old (28 November 2008).

including the role of parents in preventing such occurrences. Parents who attended the meeting expressed a strong desire to work together to improve the situation regarding violence among young people, emphasizing the fact that the youths concerned are often immature and need help to avoid getting involved in violence. In January 2009, parents in Villiers-le-Bel took part in a protest march against the proposed reforms of the *Réseau d'aide spécialisée aux élèves en difficulté* (Rased).[34] This network is aimed at supporting students experiencing difficulties at school and the proposed reforms would result in a reduction of teachers in the commune. These examples of parental involvement in community affairs assist in illustrating the sense of solidarity that is shared by local residents. On a larger scale, parents, social workers and members of the local administration are brought together each month at the aforementioned *Conseil de Quartier*. These meetings provide a forum for discussion on pressing social issues, allowing local residents to interact with their elected representatives. Such meetings facilitate dialogue between the local representatives of state and the general population, providing an important means of intra-community exchange.

Between social workers and parents lie another group who play an important role in the dynamic of the *quartier*: the *grand frères*.[35] The *grand frères* are young adults ranging in age from mid-twenties to mid-thirties. These adults, often former delinquents themselves, have grown up in the local area and, as a result, have a profound knowledge of the challenges and problems facing young people in the commune. The *grand frères* are known to the local young people and command their respect. They play an important role in the community, serving as a point of reference for young people. One youth described the *grand frère* as follows:

34   'Une manifestation pour sauver les profs', *Le parisien* (18 January 2009).
35   The literal translation of the term *grand-frère* does not adequately convey the meaning of the term in French.

C'est quelqu'un qui a le respect de tous les jeunes. Quelqu'un qui peut calmer les histoires [...] il connaît les jeunes depuis longtemps [...] c'est ça un grand-frère [...] quelqu'un qui connaît les problèmes, qui a eu les mêmes problèmes que nous.[36]

The *grand frère* represents an important figure in the social trajectory of the young *banlieusard*. Kontos and Brotherton describe these figures as "'charismatic" agents [...], young men who are respected, feared and [...] admired after winning fame and a bit of social honor by exceptional achievement especially in sports or in delinquent activities [...] Such youth are the legitimate embodiment of physical and symbolic authority and become paternalistic figures with an important degree of social capital'.[37] Nadia Kiwan states that the role of the *grand frère* takes on a 'social meaning in the sense that the older inhabitants of the *cité* or the *quartier* are expected to look after the younger residents.[38] The *grand frères* offer advice to young people in order to help them avoid making the same bad decisions that they themselves often made. On 27 October 2008, for a more general example, the Association ACLEFEU (*Association Collectif Liberté Egalité Fraternité Ensemble Unis*) organized a demonstration outside the courts at Bobigny to protest against the delay in the trial of the officers involved in the deaths of the two youths in Clichy-sous-Bois in 2005. The demonstration marked the three-year anniversary of the tragedy. A large number of youths travelled to the event from Clichy-sous-Bois, accompanied by a number of *grand frères* who effectively marshalled the young people as the police looked on. During the protest, which was heavily attended by the local and national media, a *grand frère* from Clichy-sous-Bois took the microphone and addressed the young people of the suburbs. He stated that the older generations had made mistakes that they wanted the youth of the present to avoid, citing education as the way to beat injustice in the suburbs.

36   Interview with Wilfred, twenty-two-year-old French citizen of Sub-Saharan origins (28 November 2008).
37   Louis Kontos, David Brotherton, *Encyclopedia of Gangs* (Westport: Greenwood, 2008), 53.
38   Nadia Kiwan, 'Shifting Socio-cultural Identities: Young People of North African Origin in France', in Gino Raymond and Tariq Modood, eds, *The Construction of Minority Identities in France and Britain* (Basingstoke: Palgrave Macmillan, 2007), 79–97 (87).

Another example, specific to Villiers-le-Bel, of the important role played by the *grand frères* can be seen in the organization of a silent march to mark the one-year anniversary of the deaths of the two teenagers in the commune. The march, which took place on 25 November 2008, was organized and directed by *grand frères* with the help of local parents. On the eve of the march, I attended the final organizers' meeting where it was made clear that, while the local authorities had given the event their approval and support to the event, it was up to them, the adults, to ensure that no violence occurred. The march was attended by approximately one thousand youths and marshalled successfully by the *grand frères* and the parents. It is worth noting that the police maintained a significant distance from the event, leaving the co-ordination and management in the hands of the local adults. Moreover, at the end of the march, the young people were invited to attend discussions with the adults and the elected officials at a sports hall in la Cerisaie (no journalists were permitted to enter). Here, a number of the *grand frères* discussed with young people the events of 2007 and the resultant judicial enquiry. The mayor of Villiers-le-Bel was also present and fielded questions on the riots of 2007 as well as more general questions on unemployment and local development.

These two events illustrate the prominent position occupied by the *grand frères* in the community, especially in the eyes of the local youth. These adults play a decisive role in terms of mediating intra-community disputes among young people and, on a larger scale, influencing the social trajectory of the local youths.

In terms of community development at the administrative level of Villiers-le-Bel, the socialist administration has initiated a number of urban development projects. The commune has been described as a 'fief social-iste' – the last three mayors, for example, have all been socialists over a period stretching back to Louis Perrein in 1953 – and the current mayor, Didier Vaillant, has overseen the implementation of a number of important projects throughout the commune. The renovation of the ZUS designated area, Les Carreaux, initiated by the Mayor in July 2006 in the context of the 'programme national de rénovation urbaine, créé par la loi du 1er août

2003', constitutes a prime example of these efforts.[39] This renovation project, begun in June 2007, in the 'quartier d'habitat collectif le plus ancien de la Ville va permettre de le moderniser et d'y améliorer les conditions de vie, notamment grâce à la réhabilitation de l'ensemble des logements et à la restructuration de son réseau de rues'.[40] The renovations revolve around six primary objectives: the creation of new lodgments; the rehabilitation of existing lodgments; the creation of new streets; the development of new educational facilities; the construction of a more 'harmonious' area, and the development of a dedicated commercial area.[41] In terms of housing, the area, which is comprised entirely of social housing, will see the demolition of 401 existing residences as well as by the construction of 428 new residences, 374 of which will be allocated as social housing. The new streets envisaged for the area will improve traffic and open up the area. In terms of educational facilities, it is envisaged that five schools in the area will be demolished, to be replaced with two state-of-the-art academic institutions which will be 'adaptés aux exigences de l'école du futur (pédagogie, équipement, modularité, nouvelles technologies,...).[42] The renovation project in Les Carreaux is due to be completed in 2014. Similar projects are planned for the areas of Derrière Les Murs and Puits-la-Marlière; these areas are currently being evaluated by the Agence nationale pour la renovation urbaine (ANRU). On a larger scale, the local authorities devote a significant amount of the annual budget to developing educational facilities in the commune. In 2008, a sum of over 500,000 euros was spent on enlarging and refurbishing the Jean Moulin primary school, situated near the commercial district.[43]

---

39 Ville de Villiers-le-Bel, 'Rénovation urbaine du quartier des Carreaux', <http://www.ville-Villiers-le-Bel.fr/renovation-urbaine-du-quartier-des-carreaux/> accessed 3 August 2009.

40 Ibid.

41 Ville de Villiers-le-Bel, 'Les objectifs de la rénovation urbaine des Carreaux', <http://www.ville-Villiers-le-Bel.fr/renovation-urbaine-du-quartier-des-carreaux/les-objectifs-de-la-renovation-urbaine-des-carreaux/> accessed 3 August 2009.

42 Ville de Villiers-le-Bel, 'Objectif n°5: Des équipements scolaires neufs', <http://www.ville-Villiers-le-Bel.fr/travaux-et-urbanisme/travaux-et-amenagements/les-travaux-dans-les-ecoles/> accessed 4 August 2009.

43 Ville de Villiers-le-Bel, 'Les travaux dans les écoles', <http://www.ville-Villiers-le-Bel.fr/travaux-et-urbanisme/travaux-et-amenagements/les-travaux-dans-les-ecoles/> accessed 4 August 2009.

However, while these developments are indicative of a positive dynamic in the commune, the urban regeneration plans are limited in Villiers-le-Bel due to the heavy reliance on state subsidies:

> La ville est en difficulté. C'est vrai que financièrement on est une des villes les plus pauvres d'Ile-de-France. On est toujours classé dans les cinq premiers. [...] On est très dépendant des subventions de l'état. [...] On est pris en tenaille entre les besoins des habitants et ce qu'on peut mettre en place.[44]

In 2007, over 70 per cent of the commune's municipal budget came from state subsidies and allowances.[45] In recent years, the local authorities have signed up to a number of wider departmental and national initiatives, including the *Contrat de Développement Urbain*, the *Contrat d'Initiatives Ville-Qualité*, the *Contrat Urbain de Cohésion Sociale*, the *Programme de Réussite Educative*, and the *Contrat Enfance Jeunesse*. However, the resources of these initiatives are widely spread among communes across the nation and, as a result, there are not sufficient funds to comprehensively address all the issues facing the population of this commune. This issue undoubtedly creates a certain sense of frustration among elected officials:

> Il y a plein de choses qu'il faudrait faire [...] il y a plein de besoins auxquels on aurait envie de répondre [...] mais il y a la gestion, on peut pas avoir plus de personnel, on peut pas avoir plus de locaux [...] parce qu'on a un budget constant, voire avec des charges qui augmentent.[46]

The elected officials are aware of the problems facing Villiers-le-Bel but as a result of these financial constraints, regeneration is somewhat limited.

Ultimately, Villiers-le-Bel is a commune dominated by many of the negative elements that characterize the *quartiers sensibles*, socio-economic difficulty and academic failure constituting two prime examples. The commune benefits from the various departmental and national programmes

---

44   Interview with Marion Petit Jean, Adjointe au maire chargée de la politique de la ville et de la lutte contre les discriminations (24 November 2008).
45   Mairie de Villiers-le-Bel, 'Ville de Villiers-le-Bel' (Internal memo, 2007), 11.
46   Interview with Marion Petit Jean (24 November 2008).

that have been put in place, but in spite of this, a significant gap separates Villiers-le-Bel from mainstream society in social and economic terms. The *Observatoire national des zones urbaines sensibles* (ONZUS) effectively summed up this situation in its 2008 report: 'les Zus restent des territories en grande difficulté sociale. Ainsi, même si les évolutions récentes sont encourageantes, beaucoup reste à faire en vue de réduire les inégalités sociales et les écarts de développement entre les territoires.'[47] In 2010, the ONZUS report included a sixteen-year retrospective panorama which revealed that, although conditions in the *quartiers sensibles* have improved, inhabitants in these areas remained disadvantaged in comparison to mainstream society.[48] The young people of Villiers-le-Bel are among those who suffer most from the current challenging social and economic climate. High rates of academic failure and unemployment provide little hope for the future. As the following sections will demonstrate, these issues have resulted in a growing frustration among the youth in Villiers-le-Bel, particularly those living in the underprivileged areas designated as ZUS. Young people feel marginalized by mainstream society, excluded from the dominant culture represented by the city of Paris. Moreover, the situation of local young people is further complicated by their relationship with the forces of law and order. In Villiers-le-Bel, relations between police and local youths have deteriorated in recent years, a fact that is reflected both in the increase in episodes of collective violence against the forces of law and order, and more obviously in the intensity of the riots of 2007. This growing climate of tension has incontrovertibly provided an outlet for young people to vent their frustration at their current social situation.

In general terms, the pressing social, cultural and economic issues affecting the young people of the area mean that they are subjected to a 'violence sociale et symbolique qui en résulte reste le plus souvent muette, non-dite, cachée, rétournée contre soi ou régulée d'une manière ou d'une

---

47 Observatoire national des zones urbaines sensibles, 'Rapport 2008', <http://i.ville. gouv.fr/divbib/doc/rapport_ONZUS_2008.pdf> accessed 2 May 2009, 3.

48 Observatoire national des zones urbaines sensibles, 'Rapport 2010', <http://www. ville.gouv.fr/?Rapport-2010-de-l-ONZUS-Decembre> accessed 23 February 2011, 8–12.

autre'.[49] This silent, symbolic violence is produced by their social environment and is a key element to be considered in any attempt to understand the causes of the riots that took place in 2005 and 2007. In general terms, this brief exploration of the physical, social and economic environment that constitutes Villiers-le-Bel provides an immediate contextual framework within which expressions of large-scale and collective violence can be studied. This established, the next chapter will explore the violence that occurred in Villiers-le-Bel through the voices and perceptions of those inhabiting the area.

49   Kokoreff, *Sociologie des émeutes*, 180.

Voices of Villiers-le-Bel: Exploring Social Trajectories

The suburban riots of 2005 and 2007 were unprecedented in their scale and intensity. In 2005 the scale of the violence was enormous as the riots spread to all corners of the nation, while in 2007 a new threshold was crossed in terms of intensity, with a number of shots being fired at police. But what were the causes of the violence? Chapter 1 set out the dominant interpretations articulated by various social and political commentators both during and after the events of 2005. This chapter also showed how these interpretations resurfaced during the 2007 riots in Villiers-le-Bel. The more security-oriented and, incidentally, the most dominant of these interpretations viewed the violence of both occasions as an attack on the Republic, a purely nihilistic violence perpetrated by hardened delinquents. Other commentators saw in the riots an ethno-religious revolt that essentially reflected a clash of cultures and highlighted the inassimilable nature of certain populations of immigrant origins. On the other end of the spectrum, certain sociologists interpreted the events as symptomatic of a purely social crisis. Chapter 1 went on to show how each of these interpretations was ultimately insufficient in explaining the scale and intensity of the riots of 2005 and 2007 respectively. Naturally, certain social and economic variables such as academic failure and unemployment have an important impact on the social situation that characterizes life in the *banlieues* – these underlying social issues play a significant role in the construction of a deep-rooted malaise that in turn plays an integral role in facilitating the potential for episodes of large-scale violence. However, despite their ongoing importance in terms of perpetuating the precarious social situation of those inhabiting the *banlieues*, these variables alone do not explain the unprecedented nature of both 2005 and 2007 respectively.

Paradoxically, it is the perpetual nature of these social and economic issues that renders them insufficient in explaining the causes of the riots. The harsh socio-economic climate that reigns in the suburbs has existed since the 1980s, and yet the many documented instances of urban violence that have occurred in the last three decades have remained limited to the immediate locality of the geographical area concerned. In the context of the *banlieues*, the spatial extension of violence has never before constituted a defining characteristic of riots. However, in 2005, the scale of the riots resulted in a state of national emergency, with the violence reaching all corners of the hexagon. And the riots of 2007, the aftershock of 2005, brought yet another new element to the equation. The events in Villiers-le-Bel, while limited geographically, represented the crossing of a new threshold in terms of the intensity of clashes between young people and police. Consequently, a more profound and far-reaching explanation is required to explain the fundamental causes and meaning of these events.

In an analysis of the violence Kokoreff affirms that the riots 'ont marqué une entrée en politique des jeunes non seulement animés par le désir de détruire mais par une volonté de confrontation'.[1] In other words, those youths who participated in the violence were motivated by a desire to confront the exclusion to which they are subject. Lapeyronnie states that 'en absence de mécanismes politiques, l'émeutier "exprime" ses sentiments à propos du monde social et tente de les mettre sur la place publique'.[2] As such, the riots constitute 'une façon d'entrer ou d'imposer sa présence dans l'espace public. Privés d'accès à cet espace et peut-être surtout, privés de représentation, la violence devient pour eux un moyen de "forcer l'entrée", d'exister'.[3] These interpretations, giving strength to the research hypothesis laid out in Chapter 1, explain the riots as a means of confronting and opposing exclusion through the medium of violence. This chapter will thus examine the case of Villiers-le-Bel through an analytical prism that views

1   Kokoreff, 'Sociologie des émeutes. Les dimensions de l'action en question', 528.
2   Lapeyronnie, 'Révolte primitive dans les banlieues françaises. Essai sur les émeutes de l'automne 2005', 443.
3   Ibid.

the riots as a plea for access to French society. More than that, the analysis here will go further, exploring the riots as a form of protopolitics – that is, a primitive attempt by the inhabitants of the French suburbs, exemplified in this case by the population of Villiers-le-Bel, to impose themselves in the public sphere. In this way, the inhabitants of these areas achieved a certain visibility, ephemeral though it was, in the political arena, an arena from which they are normally excluded. This reading of events is in line with the understanding maintained by Didier Lapeyronnie and Michel Kokoreff, among others, and this chapter will attempt to verify this interpretation with reference to the case of Villiers-le-Bel. Crucially, the analysis here will be supported by empirical evidence gained from qualitative research carried out in Villiers-le-Bel. Qualitative fieldwork plays an important role in elucidating the social dynamic of a given community or social group. This has an added importance in the context of urban violence in French suburbs since the voices and perceptions of those involved in the violence are often rendered inaudible by the waves of social and political commentary that inevitably accompany such events. The fieldwork carried out in Villiers-le-Bel allowed me to draw conclusions based on *direct* observation of and interaction with those involved in the riots.

Rebels Without a Cause?

The Riot as a Collective and Political Act

As discussed in Chapter 1, the principal interpretation of the riots of 2005, as well as those of 2007, dismissed the violence as the work of thugs and delinquents, a collective and nihilistic violence that held neither meaning nor message. This interpretation proved to be the predominant one expressed in media reports and analyses. Other interpretations carrying weight in terms of media exposure, such as that which portrayed the riots as an ethno-cultural revolt, also emphasized the collective nihilism of the rioters, revolting against a society whose norms and codes the rioters ultimately reject. Chapter 1 – and, indeed, subsequent chapters – proved these interpretations to be fundamentally flawed. In one respect, though, all of the dominant interpretations identified and insisted upon a crucial characteristic of the riots: the riots of both 2005 and 2007 constituted a collective action on the part of the youth of the suburbs. In relation to 2005, Lapeyronnie affirms that 'quelles qu'en soient les raisons, et quoique les émeutiers avaient voulu exprimer, ils l'ont fait de la même manière dans l'ensemble des villes concernées'.[4] Evidently, the riots of 2007 did not replicate the sheer scale of the 2005 violence. However, while represented on the smaller scale of the commune, the events of 2007 did also share this collective element, in relative terms, as the individual gave way to the collective and youths from various estates within Villiers-le-Bel, as well as a certain number from suburban areas beyond the commune, united in opposition to the forces of order:

> J'avais beaucoup d'amis pendant les émeutes. Il y avait des jeunes de tous les quartiers et même des jeunes que je connais pas. C'était tout le monde ensemble contre la police.
>
> — DRISS, twenty-one years old, unemployed

This collective nature of events is crucial in understanding the causes of the violence, especially when paired with an analysis of the riots as a political act.

In general terms, it can be said that the riots of 2005 and 2007 constituted political acts in the sense that the violence caused by these events propelled the question of the suburbs into the centre of the political stage, forming the focus of debate right up to the highest echelons of political power. However, this immediate and rather superficial observation does not do justice to the complexity of the question of the riot as a political act. Robert Castel gives a more profound analysis in saying that: 'En plus

---

4   Lapeyronnie, 'Révolte primitive dans les banlieues françaises. Essai sur les émeutes de l'automne 2005', 433.

de se trouver dans une situation sociale souvent désastreuse, les émeutiers voulaient aussi régler des comptes avec la société française accusée d'avoir failli à ses promesses'.[5] Castel goes on to say that 'C'est ainsi qu'on peut trouver une signification politique à ces événements, même s'ils n'ont revêtu aucune des formes classiques du répertoire politique'.[6] Essentially, Castel places emphasis on the perspective of the rioters rather than focusing on the politicians who reacted to the events. In this context, the riots can be viewed as political events charged with a symbolic meaning, which, while not clearly articulated, is nonetheless emphatic. Lapeyronnie goes further still in his analysis, offering a more radical interpretation regarding the political significance of the violence:

> Même si [l'émeute] s'accompagne de violences, de destruction et de pillages, même si elle est 'non-conventionnelle', c'est-à-dire qu'elle se déroule en dehors des mécanismes institutionnels légitimes à la différence d'une grève ouvrière ou d'une manifestation, elle relève d'abord de la compréhension des mécanismes sociaux et politiques qui commandent la formation et l'orientation des mouvements sociaux et collectifs.[7]

In this context, Lapeyronnie argues that the riots belong to the 'répertoire "normal" d'action politique'.[8] In other words, the riots present a unique paradox, being at once unconventional and conventional: 'unconventional' in the sense that they do not follow prescribed forms of political action, but 'conventional' in the sense that they are ultimately rooted in the fundamental social and political mechanisms that underlie the emergence of collective social movements. Thus, for Lapeyronnie, the violent and destructive behaviour and actions produced during the riots must be viewed from the *perspective of the riot* and analysed in this context, not the inverse. It is in this sense that the underlying logic of those involved in the violence may be understood. For, while the rioters of 2005 and 2007 failed to express a clearly articulated set of demands, their actions were full of meaning. This proved to be the case in Villiers-le-Bel. One youth who was directly involved in the riots in Villiers-le-Bel claimed:

5   Castel, *La discrimination négative*, 59.
6   Ibid.
7   Lapeyronnie, 'Révolte primitive dans les banlieues françaises', 433.
8   Ibid.

C'est pas qu'on avait rien à dire, c'est qu'on s'est exprimé d'une autre manière tu vois?
C'est pas par hasard qu'on a brûlé le commissariat! C'est comme ça ici...si on va à
la mairie ou...je sais pas où, ils veulent pas nous entendre, mais quand ils voient des
voitures brûlées et tout c'est une autre histoire.

— *ANONYMOUS, twenty-two years old*

In the above quotation, the words of the interviewee are revealing in relation
to the social and political position and status of the rioters, a marginalized
population who regard violence as the only means of making their voices
heard in an institutional system from which they are largely excluded. This
theme proved to be a common one throughout the interview process in
Villiers-le-Bel:

J'en ai marre moi! Les politiques, ils parlent...ils parlent, tu vois? Mais rien ne change
sauf quand on brûle des voitures. Après, les médias viennent et tout le monde voit
qu'on accepte pas ce qui se passe ici.

— *NASSIM, twenty years old, unemployed*

The young people involved in the riots feel excluded by mainstream
society and ignored by the politicians who claim to represent them. In
this respect, Lapeyronnie, drawing on the work of Hobsbawm, labels the
rioters 'primitifs de la révolte'.[9] In his view, the rioters formed part of a
primitive political movement, devoid of structure and a clear ideological
standpoint, since those involved exist outside the political institutions and
often lack the means and the cultural capital (in the Bourdieusian sense
of the term) to access these institutions. The movement is considered as
political since those involved ultimately desire recognition in this social
order that excludes them. However, while Lapeyronnie effectively draws
attention to the political significance of the riots, his description does not
do justice to the complexity of the journey undertaken by the rioters. The
use of the term primitive in the context of the riots implies a normative
political trajectory that would consist in a move from immaturity towards
a more sophisticated political perspective and role. This interpretation
could be viewed as overly deterministic, sharing some of the assumptions

9   Ibid.

underlying the politico-media security-oriented discourse. In fact, interviews revealed an acute awareness of current political developments on the part of many interviewees. Their actions could nonetheless be characterized as proto-political in that they are an attempt to forge a new path that lies both outside and inside conventional political channels: outside in the sense that the riots take an unconventional form that seems alien to conventional forms of political engagement, yet inside in the sense that those involved seek to force their way into the political sphere using alternative means. Paradoxically, the rioters attempt to move away from conventional means of political engagement in an attempt to gain access to a political arena which is structured, to a large extent, by these same channels. Crucially however, the violence and destruction of the riots should not be confused with a lack of understanding of the issues at stake, or indeed, a lack of coherence in terms of the aims of the violence. The interviewee clearly indicated that the choice of public building to be attacked was the result of a conscious decision-making process within the group, revealing an internal logic to the riots. In this respect, Lapeyronnie affirms that 'l'émeute possède sa logique propre. Elle est le fait d'émeutiers dont les comportements [sont] fortement socialisés'.[10] The question of the logic and rational (perceived or otherwise) behind the violence will be explored further at a later stage. However, it is important at this point to emphasize the influence of the underlying processes of socialization highlighted by Lapeyronnie in the production and direction of the riots, given that the outlook and interpretative framework of the rioters is heavily influenced by these processes.

A Culture of Respect: Socialization in Villiers-le-Bel

It has been shown in previous chapters how the social trajectories of many young people in the *banlieues* are negatively influenced by low levels of academic success and high levels of unemployment. In this respect, Villiers-le-Bel exhibits similar characteristics to other *quartiers sensibles*. However,

10   Ibid.

while these issues undoubtedly pose problems in their own right, they are also inextricably linked to deeper processes of socialization. This link is perhaps best explained as a vicious circle where social, economic and cultural exclusion has contributed to the construction of a specific 'street culture' that is based on respect and permeated by violence. Eric Marlière has described how 'la socialisation [...] dans les cages d'escaliers, au stade de football ou même dans des "courses poursuites" avec la police engendre en somme une sorte de "culture de rue" où l'honneur et la fierté sont les éléments moteurs dans les rapports sociaux'.[11] It is important to understand that this street culture forms part of a broader 'us-versus-them' paradigm that is constructed, to a large extent, in opposition to the exclusion and marginalization experienced by inhabitants of the *banlieues*. This paradigm is crucial in determining the fundamental motivations for the riots of 2005 and 2007 and will be explored in greater detail further on. This street culture that exists in the *banlieues*, often marked by violence, has in turn contributed to the negative perceptions of these areas that are circulated in mainstream society, thus reinforcing the social divide that sees the suburbs pushed to the outer limits of French society. Nurmi states that 'adolescents grow up in changing environments that *channel* their developmental trajectories. A variety of socio-cultural factors like cultural beliefs, institutional structures, and historical events form such environments'.[12] Nurmi goes on to affirm that 'such socio-cultural and institutional structures define an opportunity space for the adolescent that channels his or her future-oriented motivation, thinking, and behavior'.[13]

In the suburbs, where socio-economic relegation represents an ever-dominant characteristic amongst the local population, the notion of status (social and/or economic) is a problematic one for many young people, positioned as they are at the limits of mainstream society. In this context, the themes of respect and honour emerge as socio-cultural tools, a means

11   See E. Marlière, *La France nous a lachés*, 180.
12   Jari-Erik Nurmi, 'Socialization and self-Development: Channeling, Selection, Adjustment, and Reflection', in Richard Lerner and Laurence Steinberg, eds, *Handbook of Adolescent Psychology* (Hoboken, NJ: Wiley, 2004), 85–124 (87).
13   Ibid.

of opposing the dynamic of social exclusion that overshadows daily life. Thus, while the broader social and economic processes leading to socio-economic relegation appear to rest beyond the control of the individual, the theme of respect within a broader street culture offers the individual a tangible means of obtaining a social status within the local community that is denied them in mainstream society. Respect in this context is based primarily on physical attributes such as strength and prowess, qualities that have been manifested by physical confrontations with local rivals or during encounters with the police. In addition, the theme of respect is often, but not always, linked to age, with older youths demanding the respect of those younger than themselves. Crucially, this street culture is inextricably linked to territorial concerns:

> Mais concrètement on a des jeunes qui sont en très grande difficulté parce qu'ils ont pas d'horizons, ils ont pas d'horizons, ils arrivent pas à consacrer...Et du coup! Et du coup on les retrouve beaucoup dans des...c'est très, très présent à Villiers-le-Bel, on les retrouve dans des préoccupations de territoire. C'est-à-dire que comme ils arrivent pas à trouver de perspective, concrètement ils se rabattent sur les choses sur lesquelles ils peuvent tenir un peu les choses, concrètement, c'est le territoire. Et donc on les retrouve beaucoup, beaucoup, beaucoup dans les questions d'affrontement.
> — *ALAIN, directeur, Maison de quartier Boris Vian*

In the context of this street culture, Villiers-le-Bel has witnessed significant intra-communal conflict between young people from different areas of the commune. Physical confrontations involving small groups of young people occurred frequently at the local secondary school during the period of fieldwork. These confrontations revolved for the most part around the question of respect, with many originating from an insult, real or perceived. One example saw certain young people in the *quartier* of Derrière-les-Murs-de-Monseigneur (DLM) engaged in a long-running opposition with youths from the neighbouring *quartier* of Puits-la-Marlière (PLM). Numerous accounts on both sides revealed that the root of the conflict was an insult published on a personal blog on the internet.[14] In

---

14 The role of the internet blogs in the construction of the street culture of the suburbs is significant and presents an interesting topic for further research. Examples

any case, immersed in their social setting, the young *banlieusards* absorb this street culture both consciously and unconsciously through their daily interactions within the social networks of the local community.

In relation to these processes of socialization, Bourdieu observes that 'through experience with one's environment and routine performances, strong dispositions develop that may be beyond the grasp of consciousness, relatively impervious to efforts to change them or even to articulate them'.[15] In Villiers-le-Bel, participant observation provided frequent confirmation of the effects of these processes of socialization. A local music association called 'Kings of Hood', for example, based in the quartier of DLM and made up of youths aged between twenty and twenty-five with a keen interest in rap music, has organized a number of concerts at the local community centre.[16] These concerts were organized almost entirely by the youths themselves, from the cover charge of five euros, which goes towards funding the association, to security. Attendance at one of these concerts revealed a well-planned event, hosting over three hundred youths. Security was managed by the young people themselves, with the help of one or two *grand frères* from the local estate and, while local social workers dropped in over the course of the evening, there was no police or parental supervision. This fact proved significant in that the absence of police and institutional figures of authority afforded an unmediated insight into the processes of socialization affecting local youths. The above-mentioned

---

relating to Villiers-le-Bel include: <http://kingsofhood.skyrock.com/> and <http://blackboyzxcv-officiel.skyrock.com/>. These blogs have been created by local self-styled rappers.

15   Pierre Bourdieu cited in Barbara Rogoff et al., 'Children's Development of Cultural Repertoires through Participation on Everyday Routines and Practices', in Joan Grusec and Paul Hastings, eds, *Handbook of Socialization: Theory and Practice* (New York: Guilford Press, 2007), 490–515 (491).

16   The young people involved in Kings of Hood (male and female) are predominantly black and, like many groups before them (most notably the well-known rap group Suprême NTM) have adopted certain characteristics of American rap culture through their form of dress and emphasis, in their lyrics and homemade music videos, on violence and territorial attachment. The issue of territorial attachment will be explored in greater detail at a later stage.

preoccupation with the theme of respect, within the broader framework of a specific street culture possessing its own clearly defined rites and codes, can be effectively exemplified by an extract from field notes relating to attendance at the concert:

> By 7pm there the hall of the Maison de quartier was almost completely full, holding around 300 young people. According to Wilson, those attending came principally from the quarter of DLM. This is not surprising given that the music association is made up of residents from DLM and the Maison de quartier borders the quarter [...] Having interviewed certain group members in private, I made my way to the main hall where I took up a position near the front door. From here, I could observe traffic passing in and out. Shortly afterwards, I noticed that I was being observed by a group of males that I did not recognize. As I made eye contact with one member of the group he moved towards me, followed by his friends. The group formed a semi-circle around me and the young male asked: 'T'es qui toi? T'es journaliste ou quoi? T'as une caméra? Qu'est-ce que tu fais ici?'. These questions were repeated by one or two others in the group. As I began to explain my presence, we were interrupted by my contact, Wilfred, who had just entered and immediately noticed the group (which was beginning to attract more attention). Wilfred pushed through to my side and exclaimed: 'Dégage! Qu'est-ce que tu fais là? Il est avec moi. Dégage!'. In a further conversation, Wilfred explained that I was a guest of Kings of Hood. The group of youths subsequently moved to a different part of the hall. Not, however, before one youth commented: 'Il faut faire attention ici, t'es pas connu. Tu sais pas que c'est le ghetto ici?'. However, I was still evidently the subject of discussion, judging from the frequent glances in my direction.
>
> — FIELD NOTES, *June 2009*

Somewhat paradoxically, the code of respect that has evolved, to a large extent, as an opposition to the social relegation and exclusion suffered by those inhabiting the *banlieues* has also contributed to the suspicion and distrust that 'outsiders' are subject to. Those actors originating outside the *quartier* have no fixed place in the street culture that directs relations within the community. Unknown to the young people of the locality, they cannot be positioned within the interpretative framework that categorizes actors within the community. However, as mentioned above, once it was made clear that I was attending at the invitation of one of the organizers of the event, a known figure commanding the respect of his peers, the interlocutors moved their attention elsewhere.

It is important to note that the intervening youth had previously been interviewed both formally and informally. The informal interviews in particular had revealed that Wilfred, a French citizen whose family origins are in sub-Saharan Africa, had been incarcerated for acts committed during the riots of 2005. In addition, Wilfred himself stated that, having dropped out of school at an early age, he had, in the past, been well-known to police due to his participation in delinquent acts. Thus, Wilfred had progressively gained the respect of his peers in the local community as someone who was not afraid to engage in confrontations with the police. Moreover, in physical terms, Wilfred's imposing figure undoubtedly intimidated potential opponents.[17] However, while the response to Wilfred's intervention reveals much about the social norms influencing behaviour amongst local youths, the parting remark is also significant. In an environment where social norms prioritize respect and pride, the young person concerned felt that a response of some kind was necessary to avoid losing face before the researcher. Moreover, the reference to the 'ghetto' in the parting remark constituted a means of emphasizing the position of the researcher as an outsider, having no status in terms of the local street culture. This reference to the ghetto also represents an example of the strong territorial attachment that exists in the *banlieues*, an attempt to appropriate the negative identity attributed to a marginalized social space and its population by mainstream society. This territorial attachment can also be interpreted as an attempt to ground an identity that is progressively becoming disjointed from that of mainstream society, which refuses to fully incorporate the youth of the *banlieues*. These issues will be developed further at a later stage in the chapter.

17   At the time of interview Wilfred had recommenced his education and was undertaking a two-year business course in order to obtain a professional qualification.

Losing Faith in Law and Order

Fieldwork conducted in Villiers-le-Bel supported the idea that social relations in Villiers-le-Bel are dominated by this street culture that revolves
primarily around the themes of honour and respect. This deeply rooted
culture, which has developed to a large extent in opposition to social, economic and cultural relegation, effectively constitutes a set of social norms
for the young people of the locality, and heavily influences daily interactions
both within and between peer groups. In more general terms, these underlying processes of socialization form the basic contextual framework within
which the aforementioned us-versus-them paradigm develops. However, it
is by examining interactions between the youth demographic of the suburbs
and the forces of law and order that this paradigm begins to take shape as
an interpretative prism through which events are viewed. It is clear that
the hostile relationship between police and local youths plays a dominant
role in the production of large-scale urban violence. It has been shown in
Chapter 3 how police–public relations have been at the heart of civil unrest
in French *banlieues* since the beginning of the 1980s. The violent events
witnessed in Villiers-le-Bel in 2005, and again in 2007, represent a continuation of this trend. Broadly speaking, fieldwork in Villiers-le-Bel has shown
that young people residing in the area regard the police as a corrupt source
of power rather than as a force supporting justice and upholding the law.
When asked about the police during the course of formal and informal
interviews, the interviewees were unanimous in stating their opinion that,
for them, the police do not represent justice:

> La police, pour nous, c'est pas la justice. Ils viennent casser les couilles dans le quar-
> tier, même quand on fait rien...quand on est là, tranquille. Si tu les regardes, ils font
> un contrôle. Ils provoquent les jeunes, ils jettent des insultes. Non, pour moi, c'est
> pas la justice.
> — DALADIÉ, *twenty-two years old, employed in the financial industry on a CDI*

Throughout the commune young people harbour a strong opposition
towards the forces of order. As a result, the concept of justice in Villiers-
le-Bel is somewhat displaced, frequently taking the form of 'street justice',
where the matter is resolved on the streets by members of the public rather

than by the police. This reassignment of the source of justice at once undermines the police as an institution and feeds into the aforementioned street
culture that dominates daily life. This is particularly the case among the
younger residents of the commune. A number of interviewees revealed
that in the case of a problem that would normally be reported to police,
such as an assault, the majority of young people would often settle matters themselves, perhaps through the use of violence, rather than go to the
police for assistance:

> [Les jeunes] vont régler les choses eux-mêmes ici. Ils vont pas à la police. Tu sais
> pourquoi? Parce qu'ils vont rien faire pour nous aider. Personne fait confiance à la
> police, tu vois?
>
> — NASSIM, *twenty years old, unemployed*

Participant observation in the area of DLM confirmed this trend. Violence
among local youths is largely answered with violence; the police are not
seen as a valid alternative. Moreover this perception of the police and their
practical role, shared by all those young people interviewed, is also shared
by a number of parents from Villiers-le-Bel. An example of this lack of faith
in the police can be seen from when the researcher attended a local meeting
organized by social workers and designed to promote discussion between
parents from the different *quartiers* of Villiers-le-Bel.[18] Incidentally, the
meeting was a direct response to increases in intra-communal violence
involving young people, itself engendered largely by the aforementioned
street culture that overshadows social relations in the *banlieues*. During the
course of the often-heated exchanges, one parent recounted the story of
how she had brought her nephew to file a police report after he was attacked
by a group of youths from another *quartier*. According to the parent, the
police dismissed the report saying that the youth in question was as much
a 'voyou' as the rest. The woman emphasized that, while the youth had
gone to the police as a victim, he was treated as a delinquent by the officer
on duty. The parent went on to reveal that, following a second attack, her

18   The meeting between parents, which took place on 22 November 2008, was a col-
      laborative effort organized by social workers from each of the *Maisons de quartier*.

nephew refused to go to the police due to their previous treatment of him. This account was followed by other similar stories, all serving to highlight the fact that young people in the commune do not place any confidence in the police as a force for justice. For many residents in Villiers-le-Bel, the police are perceived as an opposing force, working against the population, rather than a force working with the people to promote justice.

Undoubtedly, residents inhabiting the *quartiers sensibles* of Villiers-le-Bel harbour more resentment towards the forces of law and order than those living in other parts of the commune. In these areas, any mention of the police is sure to provoke heated debate on the part of the local young people. Claims of police provocation and harassment frequently punctuate interviews and conversations. And this resentment is perhaps not unfounded. During a trip to the area of PLM, the researcher was introduced to the maze of basement passages that lie beneath the HLMs. Here, a group of local youths had attempted to create a space for themselves, bringing a sofa, chairs, a television, and even an old computer game console into one of the many disused rooms that form part of the basement area. However, the youths claimed that the police had discovered this room during the course of a raid and had destroyed its contents. Inspection of the room revealed that the television and Playstation had indeed been broken, and the young people present claimed that the police had urinated on the sofa and chairs. Additionally, in response to a comment written on the walls by a local youth – 'nique la police' – the police had responded in kind. The walls of the basement featured a number of racist slurs and insults including: 'nique les arabes et les noirs, Sarkozy va vous casser'; 'sales arabes et noirs, vive la France'; 'Fuck les arabes et les noirs, vive la République'. According to the local youths, the incident had occurred a number of months earlier; however, these insults have remained on the walls of the basement. When asked why nobody had covered them over, one of the youths responded: 'on s'en fout'. It would appear that the youths' sense of pride prevents them from erasing the insults, an act that would constitute acknowledgement of the hurt that the remarks caused. And yet the anger and sense of injustice evoked by the situation was evident:

Tu vois? Tu vois ce qu'ils ont écrit? C'est ça la justice? Quand tu vois ça, comment peux-tu les aimer, la police?

— *CANTON, twenty-one years old,*
employed on a CDI in an air-conditioning business

So the insults remain on the walls, a constant reminder of the racist sentiments harboured by some officers and a visual evocation of the tension between the young people and the police.

The infamous *controle d'identité*, frequently cited in media articles relating to the *banlieues*, represents another key issue in the question of police-public relations in the commune. The *contrôle d'identité* represents a commonly used tactic for the forces of law and order. Interviews with police confirmed the status of the identity check as a crowd-management technique and provided examples of its use:

Si tu veux c'est une technique qu'on emploie, quand les mecs sont dans un grand groupe, dans une cage d'escalier et tout ça, on fait un contrôle d'identité systématique. On sait psychologiquement qu'ils aiment pas ça...et on sait qu'ils vont s'écarter, parce qu'ils vont pas vouloir être contrôlés une deuxième fois. Qu'ils vont partir de la cage d'escalier, qu'ils vont partir du lieu. C'est une technique pour les faire virer...c'est la seule technique qu'on a trouvée pour les faire virer.

— *PIERRE, officer serving with the*
Groupes d'Intervention de la Police Nationale (GIPN)

However, while the police regard the identity check as a necessary crowd-management technique, for the young people of Villiers-le-Bel the *contrôle d'identité* is often at the heart of problems arising between local youths and the police. A number of youths claimed that the identity checks are carried out in a violent and disrespectful manner, even when the young people have done nothing wrong:

Si on est là dans le quartier, ils viennent, s'ils veulent nous faire un contrôle d'identité...s'ils veulent nous contrôler il y a pas de problème, nous on se laisse contrôler... mais après dans le groupe de policiers il y en a toujours un ou deux qui va...qui va faire que les choses vont mal se passer. C'est ça que nous les jeunes on accepte pas ça. [...] Des fois ça se passe mal...'met toi par terre', 'met toi à genoux'...Non, non [*tuts and shakes his head*] on se met pas à genoux dans un contrôle d'identité, on est pas des chiens. Tu veux nous contrôler vas-y, j'ai rien sur moi. Si j'ai fait quelque chose, vas-y, ok...tu mets les menottes, fais ce que tu veux, il y a pas de souci...mais si je suis pas en tort...on se laisse pas faire, on se laisse jamais faire.

— WILFRED, *twenty-two years old, studying for a diploma in sales*

The *contrôle d'identité* represents one of the most common contexts for the expression of this provocation or abuse of power and, as such, plays an important role in the dynamic underlying police-public relations in Villiers-le-Bel. The above quotation is representative of the sentiments of those young people interviewed in Villiers-le-Bel regarding this aspect of police procedures. The statement reveals a profound sense of injustice at the treatment suffered by local youths at the hands of the police. Thus the *contrôle d'identité* represents one of the key elements contributing to the construction of an us-versus-them paradigm within suburban communities. In broader terms, Lapeyronnie affirms that 'le racisme, le harcèlement et la pression des policiers finissent par créer une sorte de "nous" collectif sur la base d'une expérience commune et d'une opposition au "eux" policier' [...] Si les "jeunes de banlieue" ne constituent pas une catégorie sociale ou culturelle, ils partagent largement le sentiment de subir un "traitement" commun, de vivre une expérience commune face à l'institution policière'.[19]

It is important to note that this us-versus-them binary is not limited to the young people directly involved in confrontational situations with the police. In fact, the interpretative framework incorporates a significant proportion of the population, whether through their familial links to those youths who have suffered from police misconduct, or through a shared ethnic background or territory. Lapeyronnie effectively sums up this spread of the us-versus-them paradigm in saying that 'la population dans son ensemble, par son appartenance ethnique et territoriale, se sent directement concernée et visée, cible privilégiée d'une police plus prompte à harceler qu'à réprimer les "véritables délinquants". La police est perçue comme une institution travaillant contre la population plutôt qu'à son

---

19   Lapeyronnie, 'Révolte primitive dans les banlieues françaises', 437.

bénéfice.'[20] The extension of the us-versus-them paradigm is effectively illustrated by the aforementioned incident where a parent was dismissed by police when she attempted to report an attack on her nephew. In any case, the formation of this us-versus-them mentality is crucial in understanding the production of large-scale urban violence. Essentially, the construction of this Manichean opposition between the forces of order and the population of the suburbs results in the creation of an interpretative framework, a '"grille interprétative" des événements et de la situation, chaque incident, chaque difficulté venant le renforcer'.[21]

Two issues are of central importance here. First, the role of memory in this context cannot be overstated. The link between the actions of police and previous tragedies that have occurred in suburban areas since the beginning of the 1980s brings significant weight to bear on the perceptions of the young *banlieusards*. Each event has contributed to a collective and subjective memory which, ultimately, places the blame for all such incidents firmly on the shoulders of the forces of order. In this context, each of these events has constituted yet another building block serving to reinforce this interpretative framework through which subsequent events are viewed:

> Pour moi, il y avait pas besoin d'une enquête [à Clichy-sous-Bois en 2005]. On sait bien comment ça se passe, la poursuite et tout ça. C'est la même chose ici, tu vois? La police ils aiment casser les couilles, faire des contrôles...même quand on a rien fait.
> — *HASSEIN, twenty-one years old,*
> *employed on a CDI in the family-run air-conditioning business*

The above quotation illustrates the effects of this interpretative framework. The weight of similar past events can effectively preclude any alternative interpretation on the part of the young people. The interpretative framework through which events are viewed constructs, in this sense, a context where the results of any inquiry must compete with deeply entrenched perceptions forged over the course of a number of years and based on what is perceived as the repeat of an established pattern of police misconduct. This question of memory will be further discussed in the context of the events that took place in Villiers-le-Bel in 2007.

20   Ibid., 438.
21   Ibid.

Second, as this framework has progressively been reinforced, so too has the sentiment of injustice that is prevalent among the young people of the suburbs. The young people progressively see themselves as victims in a context where the misconduct of police officers appears to go unpunished. Ultimately, this interpretative framework serves to undermine the statements of police who rush to deny culpability on the part of their officers in contexts such as that of the tragic deaths in Clichy-sous-Bois. Politicians have fallen into the same interpretative framework through premature statements that support police actions. The example of Sarkozy's reaction, discussed in Chapter 1, to both the events of 2005 and those of 2007 is particularly relevant here. This situation has been augmented by the fact that the hasty statements published by police management and politicians have often proved to be flawed, thus giving an added legitimacy to the interpretation of the young people:[22]

> On avait même pas besoin de réfléchir. On savait tout de suite que c'était la faute de la police...mais le problème c'est que eux ils ont tout nié, tu vois? Ils auraient dû accepter la responsabilité.
>
> — *NASSIM, twenty years old, unemployed*

Events viewed in the context of this us-versus-them paradigm have a profound effect on the reception of potential police misconduct on the part of the young people. Lapeyronnie states that 'la loi se change en oppression. Un "cadre d'injustice" se substitue ainsi au "cadre dominant" et ouvre l'espace de l'action. Le "nous", victime d'injustice, a soudain la capacité de surmonter l'autorité légitime des institutions qui sont à la source de l'outrage moral qu'il subit. Il offre aussi les critères de condamnation de cet ordre'.[23] Essentially, on the part of the young people concerned, any delinquent behaviour is no longer considered as such, having gained legitimacy as a means of responding to the injustice imposed by the police. Moreover, once this process of legitimization takes place in the collective imagination of the youth of the suburbs, any increase in police repression aimed at quelling the violence is perceived by the young people as yet another injustice, which, in turn,

---

22   See Chapter 1 for a detailed description of the events of 2005 and 2007.
23   Lapeyronnie, 'Révolte primitive dans les banlieues françaises', 438.

nourishes the sense of legitimacy attached to any violence on the part of local young people, particularly in the context of the riot:

> Il y a un sentiment de toute-puissance chez eux. Ils rentrent dans le quartier comme ça, ils font des contrôles...ils insultent les jeunes et tout, tu vois? Sale arabe, petit pédé, des trucs comme ça. Certains ont même tué des jeunes et ils sont toujours là, rien ne change, ils font n'importe quoi...Mais toi, t'as vu ça hier.[24] C'est pour ça qu'on brûle des voitures et caillasse les flics. Il faut faire ça pour leur montrer qu'on accepte pas ce qu'ils font dans les quartiers.
>
> — *DRISS, twenty-one years old, unemployed*

The divide that places police and public, particularly the younger population, on opposing sides is compounded by numerous claims of police provocation and harassment. Allegations of police provocation have severely undermined police-public relations in the commune in recent years, producing a hostile social environment where clashes between local youths and the forces of law and order have contributed to the construction of an us-versus-them paradigm that causes the young people to perceive themselves as victims. The police are regarded as an oppressive and unjust force that must be opposed through what are judged to be the only means available – violence and destruction. This interpretative framework gives legitimacy to acts of violence and delinquency among young people in the *quartiers*. This is especially relevant in the context of the riot where the us-versus-them opposition is crystallized.

It is not enough, however, to limit the study here to the perspective of the young people residing in the *quartiers*. To gain a comprehensive understanding of the situation in the *banlieues*, we must also explore the perspective of those charged with upholding law and order in the suburbs. This is important not only in terms of understanding the challenges facing those police officers working in the *quartiers sensibles*, but also in terms of

---

24 Reference to an incident witnessed by the researcher where the police spoke in a disrespectful manner when ordering a resident to move his car. The resident in question asked the officer why he used the familiar 'tu' in addressing a stranger, adding that this form of address was not polite. The officer laughed and replied: 'On est la police nationale mec, on fait ce qu'on veut'.

understanding how the perceptions of certain officers regarding the young people can feed into a reinforcement of the us-versus-them paradigm in more general terms.

Policing the Quartiers: The View from the Other Side

It is clear that there exists a divide that places the youth of the suburbs in direct opposition with the police. Young people regard the police as an oppressive force. However it is also important to consider the point of view of those officers charged with policing the *banlieues*. Essentially, the working environment of those officers stationed in the suburbs is one dominated by conflict. Just as the young people suffer due to the conflict that defines their relationship with police, police officers also take their place in a circular process that sees both groups affected by the hostile nature of the relationship. Police working in these areas face many challenges, some resulting in bodily harm, as they attempt to impose order amid a tense and hostile climate. Interviews with police officers revealed the nature and extent of these challenges:

> Etre policier, c'est être témoin de la misère sociale, de la détresse humaine, de drames humains, de la violence, de la mort sous toutes ses formes [...] Etre policier, c'est être exposé au danger. J'ai été durant ma longue carrière, blessé à plusieurs reprises, frappé et insulté, mon uniforme souillé par des crachats. J'ai été planté par la seringue d'un toxicomane [...] mon bassin cassé et mon thorax enfoncé.
> — JEAN-LUC, *Brigade Anti-Criminalité (BAC)*

> On reçoit des frigos, des machines à laver sur le camion...oui, c'est déjà arrivé...des cailloux, des cocktails Molotov...tout ça.
> — PIERRE, *Groupe d'Intervention de la Police Nationale (GIPN)*

These difficulties facing the police in the suburbs play an important role in distancing police officers from certain members of the public in the *quartiers sensibles*, thus contributing to the divide that separates police and public. In terms of their perception regarding the young people of the *banlieues*, the latent conflict between the two groups causes the police to identify the young people of the *banlieues* as a collective group, as an enemy. Consequently, relations between the police and the young people are defined by a *rapport de force*, where members of both groups strive to avoid losing face. In an example of a more extreme manifestation of this *rapport de force*, one officer confirmed a report, given by a youth in Villiers-le-Bel, which claimed that police officers and young people frequently engage in a 'tête-à-tête', a one-on-one physical confrontation to establish superiority:

> C'est vrai, je reconnais que ça arrive souvent...j'ai des amis...mais pour les gars...c'est un emploi de force, c'est toujours la force, c'est toujours un conflit. Pour le policier, le mec il dit 'oui, enlève ton uniforme et je vais te péter la gueule'...'enlève ton uniforme et t'es un mec comme moi'. Voilà. Nous, on a un manque de formation au niveau psychologique. On sait pas quoi dire à quelqu'un comme ça.
>
> — *PIERRE, Groupes d'Intervention de la Police Nationale (GIPN)*

The above quotation is particularly interesting due to the fact that it confirms the departure of police officers from the formal codes found in the police deontology – intended to direct the actions of police officers in their dealings with the public – while also pointing towards the underlying reasons motivating this departure. The reference to the training received by police officers touches at an important issue that plays a fundamental role in terms of the conduct of police officers working in the suburbs. All of those interviewed confirmed the inadequate nature of the training provided to police officers working in the suburbs:

> Le plus grand problème avec les gens, c'est que c'est toujours un rapport de force. Que ce soit pour un barrage routier...pour le...le péquin moyen qui va conduire en voiture, c'est un rapport de force systématique [...] Quand on va interroger des jeunes de cité c'est pareil, on a pas encore...l'approche amicale...il faut pas dire amical non plus, on est en train de représenter la loi, la force de la loi. Il faudrait être ferme mais en même temps pas trop autoritaire. Mais on a pas encore trouvé un juste milieu. On manque de formation. On a pas la psychologie...on a des codes de psychologie, mais c'est vraiment à deux balles.
>
> — *MARC, Brigade Anti-Criminalité (BAC)*

The officers working in the suburbs find themselves confronted with situations for which they are not adequately prepared. Insufficient training in terms of inter-personal skills means that these officers often resort to force in order to impose their authority upon hostile situations where it is beyond their capacity to manage them through dialogue. In these situations, force is seen as the only viable option in order to save face and retain their position of authority:

> La formation du policier est théorique. Un policier qui sort de l'école n'est aucunement préparé à vivre et à faire face aux épreuves qui l'attendent dans les quartiers sensibles.
>
> — *JEAN-LUC, Brigade Anti-Criminalité (BAC)*

> A l'école de police on manque de formation sur l'approche des gens. Ça c'est clair, net et précis.
>
> — *MARC, Brigade Anti-Criminalité (BAC)*

Moreover, the officers that are stationed in the suburbs are often newly qualified officers whose insufficient training is compounded by inexperience and a complete lack of knowledge regarding the social and cultural challenges of the areas in which they will be working. Chapter 3 discussed how the young and inexperienced officers who are stationed in the suburbs experience fear upon arriving in the *quartiers sensibles*. These areas, made infamous through sensationalist media coverage, are undoubtedly intimidating for the newly commissioned officer. Unfortunately, the inadequacy of their training means that the young officers lack the skills and experience to positively channel this fear. Thus the officers attempt to compensate for their fear through a show of force, which, in turn, provokes the local youths and contributes to the deterioration of relations between the two groups:

> La plupart des jeunes policiers affectés en région parisienne proviennent de province et ne sont pas préparés à être confrontés à de tels problèmes. De plus, il faut beaucoup de calme, d'expérience pour ne pas commettre de 'bavures' et il y a un gros 'turnover' dans les effectifs policiers qui cherchent à quitter le plus vite possible la région parisienne pour retourner en province. Ils sont remplacés par des jeunes inexpérimentés et non préparés. Ce qui fait que la situation est constamment problématique.
>
> — *LUC, commissaire de police*

In terms of police provocation, a subject frequently raised by the young *banlieusards* interviewed, the majority of those interviewed were reluctant to acknowledge any element of provocation on the part of the police:

> La police veille au cours de ses rondes de sécurité à la tranquillité des citoyens. Ces patrouilles font partie de ses missions de sécurité publique. La présence de jeunes oisifs dans les banlieues attire l'attention des policiers. La prévention de la délinquance oblige ces fonctionnaires à effectuer un contrôle de ces jeunes désoeuvrés. Cette activité n'est pas une agression ou une provocation vis-à-vis des jeunes mais une obligation de service public dans la prévention des crimes et délits. Ces jeunes doivent se soumettre à ces contrôles sans pour cela crier à la provocation ou au racisme. La véritable provocation est l'oisiveté de ces jeunes. Les gens oisifs sont le fléau des gens occupés, de ceux qui travaillent, qui peinent pour gagner leur vie.
>
> — JEAN-LUC, *Brigade Anti-Criminalité (BAC)*

For these officers, the provocation stems not from their actions as members of the police force but rather the sight of the uniform and all it represents in the *banlieues*:

> Il y a pas vraiment de provocation policière. Le fait de rentrer dans une cité, avec une voiture de police, avec l'uniforme, pour eux c'est déjà une provocation. [...] Nous la police on incarne le gouvernement, l'Etat. Tu vois ce que je veux dire? C'est: on a l'uniforme bleu, donc on est l'Etat.
>
> — PIERRE, *Groupes d'Intervention de la Police Nationale (GIPN)*

Undoubtedly, the interpretation of this police officer holds some truth – Chapter 3 showed how the police represent the visible manifestation of an abstract state. Consequently, many inhabitants of the suburbs project their fears and disappointments onto this easily accessible embodiment of the state. The police are viewed by the local population as a physical manifestation of the symbolic violence that dominates life in the suburbs, a violence that governs their position as people who are socially and culturally relegated to the margins of French society:[25]

---

25   See Chapter 4 for a more detailed analysis of this idea of symbolic violence.

On est tout ce qu'ils détestent. C'est-à-dire les gens qui les laissent tomber, l'Etat qui les suit pas...tu vois, [...] le boulot, le chômage...ils voient tout ça dans un uniforme, l'uniforme bleu.

— PIERRE, *Groupes d'Intervention de la Police Nationale (GIPN)*

Additionally, it must be acknowledged that the uniform constitutes a provocation because it is also the emblem of the national police as an institution. Police misconduct has instilled a hatred of the police in the youth of the suburbs, a hatred that stems directly from the actions of individual officers acting as representatives of the police as an institution. Certain interviewees acknowledged that police misconduct occurs; however, this acknowledgement was always accompanied by an attempt to justify any potential wrongdoing on the part of police officers:

Le policier, lui, il travaille tout le temps, tout le temps dans ces conditions-là, on se fait insulter toute la journée...enfin, c'est horrible quoi...je sais pas moi, je dis pas non plus qu'on est tous des saints dans la police, mais travailler avec des insultes, des jets de pierres [...] on joue comme eux, on devient comme eux. A force de les voir tous les jours, on devient comme eux.

— PIERRE, *Groupes d'Intervention de la Police Nationale (GIPN)*

The above quote is particularly interesting as, while it attempts to offer justification for any police misconduct, it also highlights the influence of the working environment on the mentality and actions of the police officer. In other words, the constant exposure to verbal and physical abuse provokes a certain reciprocity on the part of the police. Once again, however, participation in this culture of provocation and violence is undoubtedly facilitated by the inadequacy of the education offered to police officers during their training period:

Il y a donc toujours des jeunes policiers, inexpérimentés, [qui travaillent en banlieue]. Ces policiers ont souvent peur et peuvent se montrer brutaux ou maladroits dans leurs interventions. Par ailleurs, ces jeunes policiers manquent cruellement d'encadrement et le taux de gradés ou de chefs expérimentés et compétents est faible.

— LUC, *commissaire de police*

Effectively, while the populations of the *banlieues* highlight the tense nature of the relationship with the police, the point of view of those charged with policing the suburbs must also be considered. Police officers are introduced at a young age, and with insufficient training, to an extremely hostile social environment where years of reciprocal violence (whether it be verbal or physical abuse) have resulted in what one officer termed a 'décalage énorme entre la police et la population dans certains quartiers'.[26] The early experiences of these officers are governed by a fear of an unknown territory and a population that has been stigmatized by the media and other social and political commentators. This fear is often countered by a display of force on the part of the police officers, which, in turn, contributes to the vicious circle of deteriorating relations and increasing violence.

As previously mentioned, the latent conflict between the police and the young people of the suburbs causes police to perceive the young people as the enemy. In this way, the perceptions of police officers working in the suburbs play their role in reinforcing the us-versus-them paradigm that exists, albeit in a very different way. The binary opposition, as it is perceived by the police, is equally as strong as that constructed by the young people. However, in this case it is reversed. In terms of their self-perception, it is the police who become the victims in the sense of being indiscriminately attacked by young delinquents as they attempt to uphold law and order in areas at the very limits of society. Thus it is clear that the binary opposition that exists in the suburbs is nourished in different ways by both sides of the divide. In this situation, the opposing interpretations of both sides merely serve to reinforce the conflict between them. This is of particular importance in terms of the interpretative framework of the young people, whose self-perception as victims of injustice can, as previously discussed, give legitimacy to acts of violence and delinquency.

The preceding sections have explored the construction of an us-versus-them opposition that dominates relations between the police and the young people of the suburbs. This opposition has become deeply entrenched over a prolonged period of time, resulting in a situation where dialogue

26   Luc, commissaire de police.

between the two groups is quasi-impossible. However, this opposition, in itself, does not explain the spread of the 2005 violence. Nor does it explain the intensity of the 2007 riots. Tragedies involving young *banlieusards* and police officers have produced riotous behaviour in the past, violence that has been largely limited to the suburb in question. Consequently, further explanation is necessary to understand the causes of the national phenomenon that the events of 2005 represented. Thus, to understand fully the shift from the day-to-day opposition between the forces of order and the local young people to the acute expressions of violence and destruction witnessed during the riot, it is necessary to consider the role of emotion in the riot.

Mobilizing Emotion, Mobilizing Solidarity

The events of autumn 2005, which began in Clichy-sous-Bois and consequently spread to all corners of the hexagon, represented a major landmark in the history of French urban violence. As has been discussed in Chapter 1, the scale and magnitude of these events were unprecedented and illustrate the profound malaise that characterizes the French *banlieues*. In 2005, the deaths of two teenagers in Clichy-sous-Bois proved to be the spark that ignited this underlying malaise in the suburbs. Following the tragedy, violent events were reported in suburban areas across the country. With regard to Villiers-le-Bel, a report summarizing the 'faits de violences urbaines recensés dans les zones urbaines sensibles (ZUS), pour la période allant du 27 octobre au 20 novembre 2005', presented to the Directeur central de la sécurité publique, revealed that over the three-week period concerned, the commune reported forty-two vehicles burned.[27] While this figure represented less than half of that reported in Clichy-sous-Bois – where the

---

27   Le Chef du bureau des relations extérieures et du conseil en sécurité urbaine, 'Mémo: Etat des violences urbaines recensées dans les zones urbaines sensibles du 27 octobre au 20 novembre 2005' (Ministère de l'intérieur et de l'aménagement du territoire: 2005), 1 & 40.

amount was ninety-six vehicles – it represented, nonetheless, a significant amount of damage. The report goes on to reveal that the majority of the destruction in Villiers-le-Bel took place in the *Zones urbaines sensibles* of PLM and DLM.[28] In these areas alone thirty-one vehicles were burned. The *quartier* of Les Carreaux witnessed slightly less damage with eleven vehicles destroyed. These figures indicate that Villiers-le-Bel was indeed affected by the spread of the violence and destruction. Moreover, formal and informal interviews produced accounts of sporadic clashes with police, particularly in the *quartier* of DLM. These interviews also revealed that the majority of those involved in acts of violence or destruction during the events of 2005 were young people below the age of twenty-five who had no previous criminal record. Thus an important question remains: With no immediate connection to the dead teenagers in Clichy-sous-Bois, what prompted the young people of Villiers-le-Bel to become involved in the violence? Why did these youths feel compelled to burn cars and clash with the forces of order?

In general terms, the death of a young person in an incident involving police has the effect of crystallizing the above-mentioned 'us-versus-them' opposition among the young people of a locality, evoking a strong emotional response both at the level of the individual and the level of the community. In his interpretation of the 2005 riots, Lapeyronnie claims that the strength of this collective emotion plays an important role as a mobilizing factor in the violence. For Lapeyronnie, the individual emotional response feeds into the collective response as 'l'émotion dissout l'individu et soude la collectivité'.[29] The emotional response thus activates the potential for violence, usually directed at the forces of order. Drawing on the work of Durkheim, Lapeyronnie goes on to show how the emotional response, occurring as it does within the framework of the us-versus-them opposition, is inextricably linked to the themes of respect and moral outrage. The role of protest marches and demonstrations are crucial in this respect. Following the deaths at Clichy-sous-Bois, residents gathered with the families of

28   Ibid., 40.
29   Lapeyronnie, 'Révolte primitive dans les banlieues françaises', 439.

the deceased teenagers for a silent march, a peaceful protest in response to the perceived injustice surrounding the tragedy. Lapeyronnie claims that 'le groupe se soude autour du sentiment d'être victime d'injustice.'[30] For him, this process is central to the outbreak of collective violence. The young people involved in violent clashes with the forces of law and order draw 'une énergie émotionelle' from this highly symbolic act which serves both to nourish the violence and give it legitimacy in the eyes of those involved.[31] The rioter is assured of a certain solidarity based on a shared experience of moral outrage and indignity. In this context, expressions of violence are above all conceived as a struggle, not only against the police – who represent the immediate source of the tragedy – but, on a larger scale, against the social order which the police represent.

On its own, the effect of this emotional response indisputably touched those communities dominated by the aforementioned us-versus-them paradigm. In a context where tense police-public relations represent the norm, many young people were in a position to relate closely to what had occurred in Clichy-sous-Bois; the rumours that spread rapidly after the tragedy told of an unjust police intervention that ultimately led to the death of two teenagers. This was followed by an immediate denial of any wrongdoing on the part of the police, a statement publicly supported by the Minister of the Interior.[32] In Villiers-le-Bel, young people could identify with their peers in Clichy-sous-Bois, having often been subject to police interventions themselves. Moreover, many young people could relate to the sentiment of injustice that consumed the inhabitants of Clichy-sous-Bois when the police publicly refused to accept any responsibility for the tragedy:

> Pour moi, il y avait pas besoin d'une enquête [à Clichy-sous-Bois]. Tout le monde sait que les jeunes sont morts à cause de la police. La poursuite et tout ça, ça se passe souvent à Villiers-le-Bel aussi...c'est toujours à cause de la police mais ils acceptent jamais la responsabilité!
>
> — DRISS, *twenty-one years old, unemployed*

30 Ibid.
31 Ibid.
32 See Chapter 1 for a comprehensive description of events.

This act served to further confirm the perception, held by many *banlieusards*, of the police as above reproach, above the laws that they are employed to uphold. But the spread of the violence may have been limited were it not for certain, broader contextual factors which combined to amplify the generalized emotional response to the tragedy. It has been shown in Chapter 1 how the comments made by the now president, Nicholas Sarkozy, markedly increased the potential for violence. Essentially, through his derogatory comments a number of days before the deaths, Sarkozy elicited a widespread and profound resentment in the *banlieues*. This resentment, further reinforcing the underlying feeling of injustice that pervades life in the suburbs, subsequently served as an emotional springboard on the occasion of the tragedy at Clichy-sous-Bois. Kokoreff states that the remarks made by Sarkozy 'a contribué, selon la formule consacrée, à "jeter de l'huile sur le feu", alimentant le ressentiment de populations des quartiers et l'envie d'en découdre des plus jeunes'.[33] For Kokoreff, 'il s'agit d'un invariant structurel: l'émeute est la cristallisation et le point d'orgue d'un sentiment d'injustice, de mépris et d'humiliation qui la déborde de part en part'.[34] Thus the comments made by this high-ranking Minister of State served to augment the generalized malaise of the *banlieues*, nourishing the underlying sense of injustice that permeates life in these areas. This malaise was then channelled and focused with devastating force in the wake of the deaths at Clichy-sous-Bois. The sense of collective injustice was expressed through violence and destruction:

> Il y a deux jeunes qui sont morts à cause de la police. Il fallait montrer un peu de solidarité quand même! Ils étaient pas de notre quartier mais c'est la police qui les a tués, tu vois? Après, ils ont même pas accepté la responsabilité, tu vois?...et Sarkozy... beh, ils ont toujours le soutien de Sarkozy. Pour lui on est tous des voyous ici! Eh oui, il a dit ça!
>
> — *NASSIM, twenty years old, unemployed*

33   Kokoreff, *Sociologie des émeutes*, 16.
34   Ibid., 17.

During the subsequent violence, this feeling of injustice proved to be a unifying theme as young people from across the nation manifested their opposition to the forces of order, representative of a society that marginalizes and excludes. The police represent a visible aspect of the largely invisible violence that weighs on the *quartiers sensibles*. However, while vehicles formed the principal target for the anger of the young people in autumn 2005, certain interviewees spoke of the futility of destroying the cars of those who live in the community. Driss, for example, revealed that he and his friends decided to express their anger at what had happened in Clichy-sous-Bois by attacking state-owned property rather than that of their neighbours:

> J'ai fait une garde à vue à cause de ça [les événements de 2005]. Nous, ce qu'on, ce qu'on...ce qu'on a essayé de faire, c'était plus les bâtiments municipaux, tu vois, les trucs...de police ou des trucs comme ça. Après ben [...] La révolution, c'est pas...brûler la voiture de ta tante ou de...pour moi c'est une famille. Toute la ville c'est une...Avant c'était le quartier. Parce que le quartier, les autres quartiers, c'était pas la famille. Là maintenant, c'est toute la ville, la famille. C'est la famille, on peut pas...
>
> — DRISS, *twenty-one years old, unemployed*

The discourse of Driss is interesting in that it reveals a strong desire to change the social environment that exists in the suburbs. The use of the term 'revolution' is a powerful indicator of the strength and depth of the young man's feelings. Moreover, the use of this term hints at the proto-political nature of the violence. Subsequent informal discussions with Driss revealed that he saw the riots of 2005 as a way of evoking the spirit of the large-scale revolutionary movements of French history. References to the 1789 Revolution and the events of May 1968 were used by Driss to illustrate the point that violence is often the only means to oppose oppression, the only means to enter the political arena. For this young man, the goal of the 2005 violence was to make a public statement; the riots were a means of expressing the voice of the *banlieues* that is not normally heard beyond the territorial limits of these underprivileged areas. However, it is important to note that these references to revolution did not translate into a broader world view held by this young person. The discourse of Driss was rather that of a young person consumed by a profound *malaise* with respect to his immediate social situation as well as an equally strong desire to oppose what he perceives as a pattern of injustice that characterizes the lives of young people in the suburbs. The desire to attack state-owned property reveals an attempt to target the society that the young man regards as exclusive, while the recognition of community solidarity symbolizes an acknowledgement of the shared suffering experienced by the community as a whole. This idea lends support to the hypothesis that the acts of violence were by no means an inarticulate and nihilistic expression of hatred, but rather a statement of anger at the injustices experienced by inhabitants of the *banlieues*, by the community as a whole. The role of emotion here is crucial in terms of the mobilization of a generalized and violent response to the shared experience of injustice.

Contributing to the Violence: The Media Effect

If a sense of solidarity, motivated by a profound underlying sentiment of injustice, was the dominant motivating factor with regard to the expressions of violence and destruction in 2005 on the part of the young people of Villiers-le-Bel, it is also necessary to recognize the role played by the media in the spread of the violence. Chapter 1 drew attention to the idea, put forward by Jean-Jacques Wunenburger, that the media play a role in the propagation of urban violence through the desire to disseminate sensationalist material to the viewing public, thereby holding their attention and increasing ratings. As mentioned in Chapter 1, this theory suggests that the instantaneous diffusion of graphic images of violence and destruction can provoke an amplificatory effect. In other words, the media become actors involved in the events as they attempt to capture and broadcast sensationalist images, offering young *banlieusards* a national, and international, stage on which to exhibit acts of destruction and violence. As those involved in the riots see their actions televised and widely broadcast alongside the actions of young people from other *banlieues*, the rioters feel themselves to be part of a wider network of disorder. This point is crucial. In creating a network of images that are broadcast on the national and international stage, the media provide a means of amplifying the aforementioned emotional energy that is produced by tragic events of this nature. This emotional energy is thus diffused on a scale much larger than that of the immediate community affected. The amplificatory effect produced by the media unites spatially disparate suburban communities, creating what may be described as a sort of virtual community. In this context, young people from *banlieues* across the nation, sharing similar experiences of injustice and situated firmly within the us-versus-them paradigm, become connected with the original event and gain legitimacy for their violent acts in a manner similar to the local young people who attend protest marches or other demonstrations:

> Y'a eu...parce que les gens d'ici, ils ont fait quoi? Ils ont copié la télé. C'est la télé qui a...qui a fait...le cercle, tu vois. Et moi une fois, j'ai entendu un gars, j'étais avec un gars dans un café, on parlait, tout. Il me disait 'ouais, ce soir on va brûler...le garage' Tu vois...le...quand t'arrives, le garage là, y'avait un truc de voitures Peugeot là. Et donc 'on va le brûler'. 'Ouais, on va le brûler, comme ça, ce soir on passe à la télé, tout. Comme ça ils vont parler.' Je lui ai dit: 'Tu vas le brûler parce que tu veux passer à la télé? Ou tu vas le brûler parce que y'a deux gamins qui sont morts?'
> — DRISS, *twenty-one years old, unemployed*

In this above quotation, Driss both acknowledges the role of the media in the spread of the violence and questions the motives of his peers, making a distinction between what he perceives to be two different and unrelated motives for engaging in violence. However, in reality the reasons motivating the young people concerned form two sides of the same coin. It can be argued that the youths concerned were burning cars both because of the tragic deaths *and* in order to feature on television. In this sense, burning the cars represented an expression of anger at the perceived injustice that the tragedy represented. However, having the results of their destructive acts appear on television provided a means of making their anger visible in the public sphere, a statement of both their support for the dead youths and their opposition to the police. In this respect Lagrange affirms that 'les incendies de voiture ont dans la société des écrans un intérêt évident: ce sont des actes télégéniques susceptibles de donner une visibilité à la colère'.[35]

---

35   Cited in Kokoreff, *Sociologie des émeutes*, 75.

Inside the Riots

Factors Limiting the Violence

While the commune did experience significant levels of destruction during the events of 2005, with a large number of vehicles burned and certain buildings vandalized, what is perhaps most interesting about the case of Villiers-le-Bel is the fact that the violence did not attain the levels of violence and destruction recorded elsewhere in France. In terms of vehicles burned, the forty-two vehicles destroyed in Villiers-le-Bel, while undoubtedly significant, represented but a fraction of the overall number recorded at the departmental level – between 27 October and 20 November two hundred and ninety vehicles were burned across the department. It is interesting that this figure was less than that recorded in departments further removed from the Paris region such as Nord (three hundred and sixty-two vehicles burned), for example. Moreover, while significant clashes with police were recorded in suburban areas throughout France, requiring the deployment of fifty-seven brigades of riots police, the damage in Villiers-le-Bel was limited, for the most part, to the destruction of property.[36] Elected officials confirmed the fact that the violence and destruction in Villiers-le-Bel did not attain the levels reached in other suburban areas:

> Par rapport à d'autres villes et à tout ce qui a été dit sur ce qui s'est passé sur d'autres villes sur Villiers-le-Bel il y a pas eu effectivement grand-chose...quelques voitures brûlées mais malheureusement c'est pas...exceptionnel quoi, ça arrive dans d'autres circonstances et par rapport à ce qui s'était passé à Clichy c'est vrai que sur Villiers-le-Bel ça a pas beaucoup réagi finalement.
>
> — *MARION PETIT JEAN, adjointe au maire chargée de la politique de la ville et de la lutte contre les discriminations*

---

36 'Timeline: French riots. A chronology of key events', *BBC News* (14 November 2005) <http://news.bbc.co.uk/1/hi/world/Europe/4413964.stm> [accessed 10 June 2006].

En 2005 la ville était peu touchée...fin, il y avait quand même quelques feux de voitures et la maison du droit et de la justice a pris un cocktail Molotov dessus...mais bon.
— *JEAN-LOUIS MARSAC, adjoint au maire chargé de finances et de développement social*

Moreover, according to local young people and social professionals working in the area, clashes with police were relatively few in number:

Ça n'a pas vraiment touché ici. Il y avait quelques affrontements entre la police et les jeunes de la Zac mais bon, c'était pas comme à Clichy.
— *HYACINTHE, travailleur social*

Thus, while the motivating factors underlying the instances of violence and destruction that did take place in Villiers-le-Bel reveal much about the more general causes of the 2005 violence and its unprecedented scale, the factors that played a role in limiting the growth and spread of the violence deserve equal consideration. Elements of the hypothesis put forward by Kokoreff are particularly relevant in this context. Kokoreff affirms that while the events of 2005 were undoubtedly motivated by 'le double effet de la solidarité émotionelle et morale et de la médiatisation spectaculaire des événements', it is important to recognize the localized nature of the various manifestations of violence. In other words, numerous territorial, political, and socio-cultural issues exerted their influence on the micro-scale of the locality, producing varying degrees of violence. Kokoreff claims that this point is important in order to understand an aspect of the riots that was largely ignored in analyses of the violence: 'elle permet de saisir les mécanismes qui ont joué un rôle sinon de frein, du moins de régula-teur, en considérant les configurations politiques, les réseaux militants ou la capacité des habitants à se mobiliser pour faire diminuer le cycle des tensions, provocations et violences'.[37] In the case of Villiers-le-Bel, there are a number of reasons underlying this apparent limitation of violence in an area sharing much of the characteristics of other suburban areas that experienced significantly higher levels of violence and destruction.

37 Kokoreff, 'Sociologie de l'émeute. Les dimensions de l'action en question', 531.

As discussed in the previous chapter, Villiers-le-Bel is characterized by a strong social network. In general terms, the various social organizations, funded for the most part by the *Mairie* and the *Conseil général*, work closely with each other and with elected officials to identify and target what they perceive to be the principal problems facing the commune. This system translates into a complex web of social bodies including, to name but a few, the *Maison de quartier*, the *Mission jeunesse* (an organization that provides assistance to young people regarding education and employment, among other matters), and the social actors linked to the *Contrat Local de Sécurité et Prévention de la Délinquance* (CLSPD), whose mandate includes advising the *Mairie* on questions of prevention and security in the *quartiers*. Elected officials and social professionals alike emphasized the importance of this network that has been constructed over a number of years and that forms the basis of the municipal response to the problems facing the population of Villiers-le-Bel:

> Il y a un fort réseau partenaire, un partenariat, chez nous depuis des années qui permet aux acteurs principaux dans leur domaine de compétence d'être réactif immédiatement. Ce réseau s'était construit au cours des années, c'était pas fait tout simplement... et c'est fait parce que je crois qu'à Villiers-le-Bel qui est en fait une ville moyenne [...] quand on habite Villiers-le-Bel ou quand on travaille comme moi à Villiers-le-Bel depuis vingt ans on s'aperçoit que c'est un gros village...qui a un peu des périphéries avec des quartiers qui vivent chacun de son côté. Mais finalement le réseau de partenaires fonctionne grâce aux acteurs sur le terrain...tous les quartiers sont perméables. C'est parce que...je crois qu'on a réussi à bâtir un vrai partenariat parce qu'on est pas resté dans une logique de quartier mais plutôt une logique de ville.
> — *PATRICK DÉCHERY, adjoint des services de direction de l'éducation, de l'animation et de la prévention*

> Il y a beaucoup plus de choses qui sont mis en place pour les jeunes. Si un jeune a un projet ici, on va l'écouter...on va l'écouter pour voir si son projet peut être réalisé, tu comprends? Donc oui, le réseau social ici est très fort...et je pense que les jeunes savent qu'ils sont dans une ville où on essaie de les aider. Ça se sent. A Villiers, il y a vraiment un travail de partenariat.
> — *CÉLINE, educateur spécialisé*

This social network depends heavily on the close interaction of key social professionals who, depending on their individual area of competence, provide an insight into the nature and urgency of problems facing the local population:

On a mené beaucoup de réunions depuis des années...avec des gens pour simplement savoir ce que l'autre faisait dans la ville. Mais pas forcément les services de la ville parce que nous les services de la ville on sait ce qu'on fait, mais les partenaires associatifs ou d'autres institutions présent sur la ville...le club de prévention, à l'époque aussi c'était des maisons de quartier qui n'étaient pas de la ville de Villiers-le-Bel, c'était des associations des maisons de quartier. Donc pour savoir un petit peu qui faisait quoi et comment il le faisait...et en fait, l'idée maîtresse là-dedans c'était de mettre en synergie, de mettre en réseau, tous ces partenaires autour d'une idée principale, c'est comment mieux travailler ensemble et comment mieux appréhender notamment des problèmes de...que pose la jeunesse, problèmes de délinquance notamment où on avait du mal à y répondre [...] Mais ça passait également par tout ce qui concerne l'éducation etc.

— *PATRICK DÉCHERY, adjoint des services de direction de l'éducation,*
de l'animation et de la prévention

The above quotation illustrates the importance of the social partnership that has been developed in the commune: a range of social and administrative bodies share information with the goal of identifying and offering potential solutions to the problems encountered by the population. It is those actors working at the ground level that play a potentially crucial role in limiting or preventing the production of violence among the local young people.

As mentioned in Chapter 4, many of the social professionals working at ground level amongst the young people are natives of Villiers-le-Bel and, as a result, have a comprehensive knowledge of the area and its inhabitants. More importantly, these actors have, for the most part, grown up under the influence of similar processes of socialization to those having an impact on the younger generations. Consequently, these have an intimate knowledge of the street culture that pervades the *quartiers*. This fact was made clear through numerous meetings with them over the course of my fieldwork:

At about 7pm, Emmanuel brought me on a drive around DLM. Emmanuel is a social worker employed under a *Contrat Local de Sécurité et Prévention de Délinquence* (CLSPD). He grew up in Villiers-le-Bel and revealed that, as a teenager, he had been heavily involved in delinquent activity. We stopped beside a group of young people gathered in a car park outside the HLM blocks. Emmanuel got out to speak to the youths, who he obviously knew well. Emmanuel introduced me straight away (in response to a number of questions regarding my presence and identity). Observing the group, I was struck by Emmanuel's immediate and complete engagement with the group, undoubtedly a product of his own socialization in the community. He joined in the light-hearted insults that form part of the everyday interactions between young people. However, at the same time it was clear that the young people of the group respected Emmanuel. This was later confirmed by one of those present who told me that the young people living in the quartier of DLM hold Emmanuel in high esteem. His established reputation, combined with his knowledge of the problems facing the young people, make him a figure of trust and support for local youths. The young person, Hassein, told me that he and his friends knew that Emmanuel had their best interests at heart.

— *FIELD NOTES, August 2009*

This comprehensive knowledge of the social dynamic in operation at the ground level, gleaned from a lifetime spent in the commune, has benefited from the structural and theoretical framework provided by professional qualifications in social work. As a result, these social professionals are well-equipped to interpret the problems faced by local youths and provide a targeted response. More importantly, these actors play a vital role in mediating between the young people and the local and state institutions. Thus the role of social professionals working among the local public undoubtedly represents a central element of the attempts to combat social exclusion in Villiers-le-Bel. Moreover, in the context of the riots, fieldwork has shown that during the events of autumn 2005, the strength of this social network played a significant part in limiting the violence in Villiers-le-Bel:

Il y a un travail professionnel qui a été fait sur la ville, associatif et professionnel, parce qu'il y a beaucoup d'associations pour la ville qui se mobilisent, qui font beaucoup de choses, accompagnés par la mairie, et qui étaient sur place, et puis bon...voilà, il y a eu beaucoup de prévention dans ce sens là. Pour ne pas que...et on a beaucoup discuté avec les jeunes: 'Oui, bon, on a qu'à faire attention, on a qu'à attendre la vérité, et ainsi de suite, on va pas faire pareil, on va pas brûler notre ville', voilà. Donc ça a calmé beaucoup de choses, et les jeunes ont pas bougé, quoi. Le soir, en 2005, pendant le mois de novembre, on est allé dans les halls, pour discuter avec eux...c'était pour discuter avec eux, pour calmer...et eux discutaient avec nous aussi. Ils disaient: 'Oui regarde, c'est pas bien'. Oui c'est pas bien, mais il faut qu'on sache la vérité aussi, on sait pas dans quel camp...Donc faut pas aller se battre s'il y a pas de cause. On va entendre la vérité d'abord, et après on verra bien. [...] Et grâce aussi aux adultes de la ville, il y a eu beaucoup de discussions et ça s'est calmé grave. Calmé rapidement, il y a pas eu d'échauffourées.

— *HYACINTHE, Travailleur social*

Of course, in terms of objectivity, it is important to recognize the interests shared by the various social actors, at all levels, in promoting the effectiveness of their operations. At the level of the community centre, which represents one of the primary points of interaction between the local population and the political and bureaucratic structure of Villiers-le-Bel, the realization of successful and efficiently managed objectives ensures continued and possibly increased funding from the town hall. At the level of the town hall and the dominant political actors of the commune, successful strategies, or indeed the successful promotion of strategies, can result in re-election or political advancement on the national stage. Elected officials thus have a clear interest in championing the measures taken by the commune to resolve social problems. However, fieldwork has revealed that during the events of 2005, there was a potent mobilization on the ground in Villiers-le-Bel as local social centres remained open late into the night, while social workers, and many local parents, descended into the streets and attempted to reason with the young people angered by what had happened at Clichy-sous-Bois. This mobilization of Villiers-le Bel's social network undoubtedly played a role in limiting the violence and destruction witnessed by the commune.

Where Crime Pays:
The Role of the Underground Economy in Limiting Violence

The presence and strength of an underground economy can potentially exert an influence on the expression of urban violence. The success of the underground economy is inextricably linked to the level and nature of police activities in a given area; a strong police presence could prove detrimental to the deals and transactions that represent the fundamental structure of this economy. Consequently, expressions of large-scale urban violence, such as those witnessed in 2005, may be unwelcome in those areas featuring a significant underground economy. In the case of Villiers-le-Bel, social professionals and elected officials were, for the most part, reluctant to comment on the influence exerted by the underground economy on the commune. However, certain interviewees did allude to this issue when discussing the factors that limited the spread of violence in 2005, acknowledging the possibility of such a scenario:

> Ou, l'autre supposition, l'autre hypothèse, c'est que ça aurait porté préjudice à des intérêts annexes. C'est-à-dire, que c'était peut être pas profitable à tous qu'on ait les yeux rivés sur Villiers-le-Bel, au niveau des quartiers, alors qu'il y en a qui travaillent peut être un marché parallèle. C'est une supposition...parce qu'il y a des gros quartiers, en France, par rapport aux événements de 2005, où ça a pas éclaté. Où on aurait pu penser que ça allait...je sais plus, je crois que c'était les 4000 à la Courneuve, où il y a pas eu beaucoup d'événements en 2005, les Francs Moisins à Saint Denis...même si on sait que ces territoires-là...il y a beaucoup de marchés parallèles en termes de trafic, etc. Peut être que les grosses têtes, c'était pas à leur avantage que d'attirer l'œil des forces policières, judiciaires et autres, sur ces territoires.
>
> — *SAMIR BRAHMI, coordonnateur d'un Contrat Local de Sécurité et Prévention de la Délinquance*

The general reluctance of political actors to discuss this scenario may stem from a reluctance to acknowledge failures in the strategic approach adopted by the *Mairie* in previous years, such as the failure to adequately address the concentration of underprivileged populations in specific geographical areas, for example. In any case, it was through interviews with local youths that a more direct insight into the social processes in operation in the suburbs was obtained. One youth revealed that the *quartier* of PLM was almost completely untouched by any violence or destruction during the riots. The interviewee concerned, an active participant in the drugs trade in Villiers-le-Bel, explicitly attributed this absence of civil unrest to the control exerted over the *quartier* by local drug dealers:

> Nous, chez nous, tu vois, après avoir fait un tour, moi et toi, je vais te montrer vraiment mon...mon autre petit coin, aucune voiture brûlée [...] Parce que nous, on est là, déjà d'une. On laisse pas faire n'importe quoi. Parce qu'à cette époque on, tu vois, on...ça dealait. On voulait pas que les clients ils viennent, ils voient des voitures brûlées, ils viennent plus.
>
> — *BEN, twenty-two years old, drug-dealer*

This information, coming as it did from an actor directly involved in the underground economy in the commune, provides clear evidence of the influence of the underground economy in limiting the production of large-scale urban violence in the area in question. Moreover, this information was later confirmed during the course of several informal discussions with other young people from the *quartier*:

> C'est vrai que des fois quand ça prend trop d'ampleur il y en a qui veulent que ça se calme parce que c'est vrai que s'il y a trop de police partout...beh...on peut pas faire du bizness.
>
> — *NIAYE, eighteen years old, student on a work-placement as part of his Bac Professionel*

This information proves useful in so far as it assists in explaining, to a certain extent, the limited levels of violence witnessed in Villiers-le-Bel in 2005. However, it must be noted that the influence of the underground economy on the expression of violence and destruction in other *quartiers* of the commune could not be satisfactorily quantified. For example, while the majority of interviewees from the *quartier* of DLM denied the presence of any underground economy in their area, two interviewees from this same area acknowledged the presence of what they termed a growing drugs trade. Furthermore, the researcher witnessed evidence of the presence of the drugs trade in the quarter of DLM, as illustrated by an extract from the researcher's field notes:

> After a number of meetings with Ben, I broached the subject of the drugs trade in the local area. The son of Algerian parents (his father had been dead for a number of years), Ben was unemployed with no formal academic qualifications. Ben had entered the underground economy for financial reasons, although his attitude when speaking of his ability to procure drugs indicated a certain pride in this position of privilege. Ben was initially very reluctant to reveal any information regarding his own role and refused to have any such information recorded. However, he did reveal that there was a relatively strong drugs trade in Villiers-le-Bel, that it was possible to get 'anything you want' if you know the right people. Ben was known as a source of drugs among his peers. This was made clear by a number of light-hearted references made within the group. 'This is the man that you need to see if you want a fix!'; 'Why don't you pay for us to go to London, you have the money!'; 'Don't you know that Ben is a businessman around here!'
>
> — *FIELD NOTES, July 2009*

The above extract represents a clear indication of the presence of a drugs trade in Villiers-le-Bel. Evidently, the responses of the first group, who denied the existence of a drugs trade, may have represented a reflection of the suspicion that dominates relations between the young people of DLM and those coming from outside the commune, thus presenting a distorted picture of the situation in the *quartier*. However, the varying responses make any conclusions in this regard incomplete.

Finally, while many young people empathized with their peers in Clichy-sous-Bois and expressed their solidarity through acts of violence and destruction, fieldwork revealed that certain youths did not feel concerned by the affair, immersed as they are in their own immediate social environment, and thus felt no need or desire to become involved in the events that were spreading across the nation:

> Je sais pas pourquoi ça a pas vraiment explosé en 2005...peut-être parce que on se sentait pas trop concerné...même s'il y avait des cadavres là-dedans...d'enfants en plus.
> — *NIAYE, eighteen years old, student on a work-placement as part of his Bac Professionel*

> En 2005 c'était pas chez nous. Ça s'est passé à Clichy. Moi, je connais pas les gens là-bas donc, voilà. C'est comme ça.
> — *DALADIÉ, twenty-two years old, employed in the financial industry on a CDI*

In this case, it would appear that the concerns of the immediate social sphere surrounding the individual outweighed any desire to become involved in the violence and destruction. It is worth noting that both of the above interviewees are currently engaged in employment or education: Niaye is attempting to continue his education with a view to securing full-time employment, while Daladié has already successfully entered the employment market. Both youths are self-professedly focused on their personal trajectories, and thus less susceptible to provocation by affairs occurring outside of their immediate social environment. Clearly this is not the case for all those young people who abstained from the violence and destruction in 2005. However, it does provide an example of how the immediate personal concerns of the individual can influence involvement in events such as those that took place in 2005. Moreover, the above factors reveal the important influence of intra-community elements in the more general production of urban violence. In 2005, the violence that occurred in Villiers-le-Bel was undoubtedly limited by two important factors: the presence of a strong and deeply rooted social network, and to a lesser extent, the presence of a potentially lucrative underground economy.

2007: C'était chez nous

While the above-mentioned factors played a role in limiting the scale and extent of the violence in Villiers-le-Bel in 2005, the events that unfolded in the commune in 2007 represented a different story. The deaths of Moushin and Larami, in a context extremely similar to that of the tragedy that occurred in Clichy-sous-Bois in 2005, touched the community directly and immediately crystallized all the underlying tensions and problems facing this *banlieue*. In particular, the tragedy galvanized the deep-rooted us-versus-them paradigm that places the young people of the commune in sharp opposition with the forces of law and order. In the immediate aftermath of the tragedy, rumours began to spread rapidly among the local population, particularly the young people, regarding the role of police in the deaths. In a situation similar to that of 2005, a significant number of those interviewed stated their belief that the incident was not an accident and that the police had in fact killed the two young people. This despite the fact that they had not witnessed the events themselves and, in some cases, had received second and even third-hand information:

> Quand ils disent que la police...que c'est les jeunes qui sont rentrés dans le véhicule de police, c'est faux. On a tous eu des motos quand on était petit. Quand un policier veut t'arrêter, il te dit pas 'arrête-toi', il te met un coup de pare-choc et la...pour t'arrêter c'est comme ça. Sinon il peut pas t'arrêter...en moto ça va trop vite. Il est obligé de mettre un coup de pare-choc...voilà. C'est ça qui s'est passé, il y a même pas besoin de savoir...il y a même pas besoin de réfléchir. On sait, on sait. On a tous eu des motos, on a tous fait de la moto on s'est tous fait arrêter en moto...on sait comment ça se passe. Sauf que là ça s'est mal passé et ils veulent pas admettre la vérité. C'est dommage. C'est dommage.
>
> — WILFRED, *twenty-two years old, studying for a diploma in sales*

The situation deteriorated further when the police released a statement on the very evening of the tragedy renouncing any responsibility:[38]

> Après il y a eu effectivement des déclarations...de la police, du procureur, des différents ministres qui sont venus...peut-être un peu rapide, peut-être pas très équitable. Voilà, on a eu l'impression d'une justice à deux vitesses. On fait monter les choses en terme

---

38   See Chapter 1 for a detailed description of the events of autumn 2007.

de révolte face aux institutions. C'est ça qui a un petit peu marqué Villiers-le-Bel, c'est que bien sûr il y a eu des voitures brûlées, mais je crois que vraiment il y avait presque une rage vis-à-vis de l'institution.

> — *MARION PETIT JEAN, adjointe au maire chargée de la politique de la ville et de la lutte contre les discriminations*

The immediate and emphatic denial of guilt on the part of the police, intended to pre-empt potentially violent repercussions by acquitting the police officers involved of all responsibility regarding the tragedy, had the opposite effect. As rumours spread placing blame on the police officers involved, the rapid official denial of responsibility, based on the subjective interpretation of events by the police, was viewed as confirmation among the local young people of a two-tier justice system that places the representatives of justice above the system that they are employed to uphold:

> Et puis très vite, le soir même il y avait des rumeurs...les policiers qui étaient dans la voiture...ils ont pas été enquêté, il y avait pas de contrôle d'alcool...si nous, on est amené à avoir un accident, évidemment tout de suite ça sera garde à vue, mais là les policiers sont partis...il y a pas eu de suite. Et puis après on a senti une révolte contre tout ce qui pourrait représenter l'état.
>
> — *MARION PETIT JEAN, adjointe au maire chargée de la politique de la ville et de la lutte contre les discriminations*

> Donc là y'a deux jeunes, la police en plus. Tu vois, moi je sais pas, comment ça s'est passé, tu vois. Je sais juste que la police avant de...avant de les percuter leur ont dit: 'Bientôt, on va vous rentrer dedans'.
>
> — *DRISS, twenty-one years old, unemployed*

The rumours regarding the role of the police in the deaths, impossible to quantify as the enquiry into the causes of the tragedy is ongoing, undoubtedly played a significant role in the instigation of the violence. As the perceived culpability of the police in the tragedy took root, the anger of the local population spilled onto the streets. For many young people, the restraint that had been shown in 2005, when social workers and parents descended into the streets to prevent the spread of violence, now gave way to a deep-rooted rage as the commune was faced with the deaths of two local youths, well known to their peers:

Moi j'étais en colère...j'étais en colère. Il y avait de la colère, voire même de la haine.
— *NIAYE, eighteen years old, student on a work-placement*
as part of his Bac Professionel

En 2007 c'était autre chose parce que les deux petits venaient d'ici. C'était chez nous, c'était deux jeunes du quartier! La cause du truc c'était ici. C'était pas pareil. C'était direct!
— *ANONYMOUS, twenty-four years old*

It is important to note that this anger was not limited to the young people of Villiers-le-Bel. Formal and informal interviews carried out with young people and social professionals have revealed that the expressions of violence and destruction involved local residents of all ages and ethnic backgrounds:

En fait, c'était pas que des jeunes de douze, treize, quatorze, quinze ans, mais au-delà de trente-cinq, quarante ans, ça a été prouvé, et c'est la vérité!
— *HYACINTHE, travailleur social*

C'était pas que nous [les jeunes]. Il y a avait des grands frères de trente-cinq ans et des papas en plus! Il y avait tout le monde, des noirs, des blancs, des arabes...tout le monde. On était tous ensemble contre la police. Même les mamans...elles étaient sur les balcons et elles nous disaient 'va te cacher, il y a la police qui arrive!'
— *NASSIM, twenty years old, unemployed*

The involvement of older generations is particularly interesting as it provides further support for the hypothesis put forward by Lapeyronnie regarding the role of emotion in legitimizing the riots. The emotional response to the deaths had an effect throughout the community – similar to the sequence of events at Clichy-sous-Bois, a protest march was held the day after the deaths of the teenagers – feeding into the us-versus-them paradigm that exists in Villiers-le-Bel and giving the violence a powerful legitimacy in the eyes of those involved:

Deux jeunes, ben oui, deux jeunes du quartier. On peut pas laisser. Faut aider, faut aider, faut aider. On est entre pauvres. Mais faut s'aider, comme on dit.
— *DRISS, twenty-one years old, unemployed*

Moreover, the involvement of such a range of generations effectively counters the theory put forward by President Sarkozy in the aftermath of the violence: the actions of a hardened core of young delinquents, a 'voyoucratie' attempting to wreak havoc throughout the commune.[39] The majority of those participating in the violence were distanced by age and background (both socio-economic and ethnic). The range in age and ethnic origins of those involved in the riots also assists in deconstructing another interpretation widely articulated in the wake of the events of both 2005 and 2007, an interpretation that posited religion as a major factor motivating the violence and destruction. In Villiers-le-Bel, fieldwork has shown that religious orientation did not represent a motivating factor for those involved in the riots. When interviewed, social workers and young people from different religious backgrounds were all united and emphatic in their claims that religion played no part in the violent events:

> La religion n'a rien à voir avec ça…mais vraiment rien à voir. La religion a strictement aucun rapport avec les événements.
>
> — *NIAYE, eighteen years old, student on a work-placement as part of his Bac Professionel*

> Non, ça n'a rien à voir. Moi je suis pas musulman, j'ai des amis qui sont musulmans, j'ai des amis qui pratiquent pas. Ca n'a rien à voir, on est tous ensemble. C'est vrai qu'il y a des musulmans et qu'il y a des chrétiens mais il y a pas de problème. On est tous pareil. On est tous ensemble, c'est la même chose.
>
> — *WILFRED, twenty-two years old, studying for a diploma in sales*

> Ben pour calmer, la religion musulmane ils faisaient du porte à porte, pour discuter dans le quartier, avec les jeunes, y compris nous, pareil. Tout le monde discutait avec les jeunes. Ce jour là c'était l'union sacrée. Il y a pas de religion, c'est tous ensemble. Tous ensemble pour parler avec tout le monde. Voilà. C'est pas les Catholiques qui vont aller parler aux Catholiques, non c'est tous ensemble, on parle aux Musulmans, aux Bouddhistes, voilà. Voilà, ça…ça joue beaucoup ici.
>
> — *HYACINTHE, travailleur social*

---

39   See Chapter 1 for further information regarding the interpretation of the violence as the work of delinquents and thugs.

These opinions were confirmed by a number of social workers during the course of informal discussions. These remarks are significant in that they directly contradict one of the dominant interpretations of the riots mentioned in Chapter 1: the idea of the riots as an ethno-religious uprising. Moreover, extensive fieldwork, especially participant observation, indicated that Villiers-le-Bel does not appear to harbour any obvious or significant divisions amongst the population based on religious grounds. Participant observation has revealed a close and unmarked interaction between adherents of different religious faiths. Positive interaction between adherents of the Christian and Muslim faiths was particularly apparent among the peer groups observed.

Urban Echoes: The Influence of Memory

The majority of those involved in the events of 2007 took part in order to express their anger at the injustices that they perceive to dominate their community. Within a context where social, cultural and economic issues form a background to frequent police misconduct, the violence of 2007 constituted the expression of a profound underlying anger on the part of the population. The deaths of the two local teenagers undoubtedly served to channel the underlying tensions and anger within the community. However, the immediate cause of the violence does not, in itself, adequately account for the intensity of the subsequent violence. The riots that occurred in Villiers-le-Bel in 2007 represented the first time that firearms played a significant role in clashes between young *banlieusards* and the forces of law and order. These episodes of violence crossed a new threshold in terms of police-youth conflict in the suburbs, going beyond similar previous events with regard to intensity. The role of memory, discussed earlier, plays a central role in any analysis of the violence. In general terms, Lapeyronnie argues that 'la longue litanie des incidents et des morts constitue une sorte de "mémoire identitaire" des quartiers, mémoire de relations très dégradées avec la police'.[40] In the context of this collective and almost organic memory, each new episode of violence is viewed through the interpretative framework that situates the youth of the *banlieues* as victims and reinforces the us-versus-them paradigm. Consequently, any official response or attempt to refute culpability, whether legitimate or not, must compete with deeply rooted pre-existing perceptions, themselves formed over a period of years and travelling through different generations. However, the role of memory takes on an added importance in the context of Villiers-le-Bel and the intensity of the police-public confrontation in 2007.

Essentially, the enormous social and cultural impact of the 2005 riots, which provoked intense media coverage and debate, as well as an emphatic political response in the form of the declaration of a state of national emergency, constituted an important moment in the collective imagination of the youth of the *quartiers sensibles*. The nationwide and unprecedented episodes of violence and destruction, represented primarily through clashes with the police and the destruction of mostly state-owned property, signalled a new stage in the production and expression of suburban violence. The violence that occurred in the wake of the deaths at Clichy-sous-Bois symbolized an almost simultaneous manifestation of a wide-ranging solidarity and revolt born of shared suffering, a deep-rooted sense of injustice and, more tangibly, a profound opposition towards the forces of law and order. The extent of the violence revealed the depth of the malaise that dominates the social dynamic in many *quartiers sensibles* and effectively expressed the growing anger of the residents of the *banlieues* at their socially and economically relegated position. In this context, the events of 2007, coming as they did so soon after the violence of 2005, were viewed by the young people of Villiers-le-Bel as the aftershock of 2005. The temporal proximity of both events ensured that the imprint of the events of 2005 had not faded from the collective memory of the inhabitants of Villiers-le-Bel. Connerton states that 'our experience of the present very largely depends upon our knowledge of the past. We experience our present world in the

40   Lapeyronnie, 'Révolte primitive dans les banlieues françaises', 436.

context which is casually connected with the past events and objects.'[41] In other words 'the beliefs encased in collective memory help to make sense of the present reality.'[42] Consequently, the deaths of Larami and Moushin, linked as they were to the tragedy of 2005 in contextual terms, reignited and amplified the anger provoked by the deaths at Clichy-sous-Bois:

> On s'est dit ça recommence encore 'deux jeunes à Clichy, deux jeunes à Villiers-le-Bel...la police là-bas, la police ici'...oui, oui, de ce côté-là on a pensé à 2005.
> — WILFRED, *twenty-two years old, studying for a diploma in sales*

> C'est vrai qu'il y avait...c'était très similaire par rapport à ce qui s'est passé en 2005, oui. Ca m'a fait penser à 2005.
> — NIAYE, *eighteen years old, student on a work-placement as part of his Bac Professionel*

As previously noted, the contextual similarity of both events was indeed striking: in both cases a direct causal link, whether perceived or real, between the actions of the police and the deaths of two local youths was denounced by the local community. It has already been described how in 2005, certain youths engaged in acts of violence and destruction in order to express their solidarity with their peers in Clichy-sous-Bois and, on a larger scale, as a means of opposing the injustice that forms part of daily life in these areas. Thus in 2007, the apparent repeat of the pattern so recently seen in Clichy-sous-Bois was interpreted as a continuation and reinforcement of the processes that produced the violence of 2005, in this case amplified by the direct link to the local community. For the young people involved in the riots in Villiers-le-Bel, the escalation in the intensity of the violence represented a logical progression within the context of the revolt of 2005:

41 Paul Connerton, *How Societies Remember* (Cambridge: Cambridge University Press, 1989), 2.
42 Daniel Bar-Tal, 'Collective Memory of Physical Violence: Its Contribution to the Culture of Violence', in Ed Cairns and Mícheál Roe, eds, *The Role of Memory in Ethnic Conflict* (London: Palgrave Macmillan, 2002), 77–93 (85).

Oui, bien sûr on a pensé à 2005 au moment des événements. Ce qui s'est passé ici, c'était la même chose à Clichy en 2005, tu vois? Deux jeunes qui sont morts à cause de la police...Ils changent pas, la police, ils font ce qu'ils veulent. C'est pour ça ils se sont fait tirer par-dessus, tu vois, ils ont un sentiment de toute puissance. Ils font ce qu'ils veulent.

— *NASSIM, twenty years old, unemployed*

Thus the memory of 2005, combined with the immediate events of 2007, had an amplificatory effect on the violence, contributing to a marked increase in the intensity of the clashes with police in comparison with those witnessed across the nation in 2005.

While it is clear that the memory of 2005 did indeed represent a factor influencing the intensity of the violence witnessed in Villiers-le-Bel in 2007, the link between the events of Clichy-sous-Bois and those of Villiers-le-Bel in the collective imagination of the local community was tangibly confirmed during the remembrance march held in November 2008, one year after the deaths of Moushin Sehhouli and Larami Samoura. As mentioned in the introduction, a number of youths sported homemade t-shirts bearing the slogan 'Morts pour rien', the same slogan adopted by the population of Clichy-sous-Bois in 2005. However, other branded t-shirts displayed more explicitly the link between both sets of events in the imagination of local youths: 'Z et B (27/10/05) L et M (25/11/07)' was handwritten onto a number of plain white t-shirts, for example, thus clearly expressing the presence of this link in the consciousness of the local young people.[43] It is worth noting that this march, although it took place one year after the violence, was clearly emotionally charged. The strength of the turnout (over 500 youths) was a testament to this fact.

Ultimately, the link between the events of 2005 and 2007 in the collective imagination of the young people of Villiers-le-Bel had an important impact on the processes underlying the production of violence in 2007. In addition, the perceived continuity evoked by the memory of

---

43   'Z' and 'B' evidently refer to Zyed and Bouna, the names of the teenagers who died in the tragedy at Clichy-sous-Bois, while 'L' and 'M' represent those of Larami and Moushin, the two youths from Villiers-le-Bel.

Clichy-sous-Bois exerted a significant influence on police-public relations in more general terms. Chapter 3 has shown how tense police-public relations have, for many years, constituted a major issue in relation to the underlying social dynamic of the *banlieues*. In 2005 this oppoxsition to the police was expressed on a national scale during three weeks of riots. These events represented yet another link in a chain, real or perceived, of police misconduct stretching back to the 1980s. Each incident, since the riots of Vaulx-en-Velin at the beginning of the 1980s, has served to confirm and strengthen the negative perceptions harboured by the populations of the *banlieues* regarding the forces of law and order. This progressive construction of the police as a negative force in the suburbs has been accompanied by a concomitant growth in anger towards the police. The violence of 2005, as well as that of 2007, significantly contributed to this negative perception and further distanced the local populations from the police. On a larger scale, this process has undermined the entire justice system as it is perceived in the *banlieues*.

The Internal Outsider

Having explored the social, cultural and economic issues that form part of the underlying dynamic of Villiers-le-Bel, it is clear that the riots were a manifestation of 'profound feelings of injustice and a collective demand for respect'.[44] The violence at this time reflected the crystallization of a deeply rooted binary opposition, an us-versus-them paradigm that posits the youth of the *banlieues* as victims of oppression. Preceding sections have shown how this opposition took shape in the riots and gained legitimacy from the emotional energy produced by the tragic deaths of local youths. Moreover, this emotional energy gave the violence an added legitimacy in the eyes of those involved, since they interpreted their actions as a means

---

44   Michel Kokoreff, 'The Political Dimension of the 2005 Riots', in D. Waddington, F. Jobard, and M. King, eds, *Rioting in the UK and France: A Comparative Analysis* (Uffculme: Willan Publishing, 2009), 147–156 (147).

of opposing the injustice represented by the forces of law and order. The widespread sentiment of injustice that found expression in the riots of 2005 and 2007, coupled with the collective demand for respect, are undoubtedly produced by the social, economic and cultural exclusion to which the population of the banlieues are subject. Thus, on a larger scale, and in the context of the relationship between the populations of the underprivileged *banlieues* and French society at large, the violent events witnessed in 2005, and again in 2007, reveal much about the question of belonging within the Republic.

Both during and after these instances of rioting, social commentators aired a variety of interpretations. These interpretations, discussed in detail in Chapter 1, had, for the most part, a common underlying link – that of a rejection of French society and the Republic at large. Moreover, the ethno-religious interpretation of the riots explicitly evoked the ethnic background of those involved and an opposition to the Republic stemming from religious and cultural issues. It was shown how Robert Redeker, for example, attempted to draw a link between the malaise of the suburbs and what he regards as the refusal of immigrants to integrate into mainstream French society. Chapter 2 went on to explore, in more detail, the establishment of this link between immigration and the social problems of the *quartiers sensibles* in the popular imagination. Interpretations such as these have brought about claims of the failure of the Republican model of integration, the traditional engine of assimilation within the French Republic, in terms of its capacity to integrate those populations of immigrant origins.[45] However, with the passing of generations, the issues at stake have changed, reflecting social and cultural developments among populations of immigrant heritage. Chapter 3 showed how the challenges in terms of integration that applied to immigrants who arrived in France from elsewhere, such as the conflict posed by the consequent dual identity,

---

45   See Raphael Canet, Laurent Peche and Maura Stewart, 'France's Burning Issue: Understanding the Riots of November 2005', Social Science Research Network, <http://papers.ssrn.com/sol3/papers.cfm?abstract_id=1303514> accessed 12 August 2009.

have essentially lost their relevance with the emergence of new generations, each more firmly rooted in French culture and society. Thus for the
descendents of those migrants who established themselves as permanent
residents in France, while undoubtedly guarding traces of their ancestral
heritage, particularly in terms of somatic difference and religious heritage,
French society constitutes the dominant frame of reference within which
their social and cultural norms have developed:

> Nos parents, nos grands-parents sont des immigrés. Nous, on est né ici, on est fran-
> çais. On a la carte, on est français. Nos parents sont des immigrés mais nous, nous
> sommes des français. On est né ici...voilà!
> — WILFRED, *twenty-two years old, studying for a diploma in sales*

> Mais 'immigré', c'est un terme pour qualifier les gens qui sont pas de couleur blanche
> quoi, pour moi c'est ça. Ils s'en foutent de savoir si t'as les papiers ou pas. Si t'es noir,
> t'es un immigré pour eux. C'est ça.
> — NIAYE, *eighteen years old, student on a work-placement*
> *as part of his Bac Professionel*

In terms of identity and belonging, these young people of immigrant
origins are French, especially in terms of their self-perception. The first
quotation illustrates the change effected by the passing of generations, while
the second quote draws attention to one of the primary challenges facing
populations of immigrant origins in terms of their perceived position in
society – the challenge of overcoming the barriers posed by their somatic
difference. It is important to note that all those young people interviewed
described their identity as French. They regard themselves as members of
French society, or, to draw on the language of Benedict Anderson, members of the imagined community that constitutes the French Republic.[46]
In this context, the question of integration inevitably evokes a profound
confusion and, ultimately, frustration for these youths:

---

46 See Benedict Anderson, *Imagined Communities* (London: Verso, 1983).

Moi, je comprends pas ce qu'ils veulent dire par intégration.[47] Ça je comprends pas. C'est quoi l'intégration? C'est d'être né en France, d'avoir grandi en France? C'est ça l'intégration? ...parce que là je suis intégré alors. Je suis né en France, j'ai grandi en France...je suis intégré! C'est quoi alors? C'est travailler pour la France? C'est payer ses impôts et tout?

— *MOHAMMED, twenty years old, unemployed*

Beh, l'intégration...ça veut dire quoi? Ça veut dire que...ça veut dire quoi? L'intégration c'est...je sais pas!

— *ROMARIC, twenty years old, employed as a delivery boy in Paris*

Moreover the concept of integration, presented by mainstream society as the obligation for young people of immigrant origins to assimilate into French society, poses problems for the young people of Villiers-le-Bel in the sense that complete social access to the Republic appears to be denied. This interpretation was pointed out by a number of interviewees:

On dirait que nous on doit s'adapter à eux alors que peut-être qu'eux...peut-être c'est eux qui doivent changer, qui doivent nous accepter. Peut-être c'est pas qu'à nous de faire des choses...

— *NIAYE, eighteen years old, student on a work-placement as part of his Bac Professionel*

Ils parlent beaucoup d'intégration dans les médias. Mais pour qu'on s'intègre il faut qu'ils veuillent qu'on s'intègre. Nous, on veut s'intégrer dans la société. Le problème c'est eux, ils nous laissent pas s'intégrer, tu vois? Dans les médias ils parlent de l'intégration et tout mais en réalité ils nous rejettent. C'est comme ça.

— *HASSEIN, twenty-one years old, employed on a CDI in the family-run air-conditioning business*

Essentially, this interpretation challenges the conventional dynamic of integration, whereby the host society calls for those of immigrant origins to adopt the dominant cultural and social norms. In the situation that faces

47   It should be noted that the term 'integration' was introduced to the discussion by the interviewee on a number of occasions. Having thus established that the term forms part of the repertoire of vocabulary employed by the interviewees, the researcher then referred directly to the term in subsequent interviews.

the youth of the suburbs, it is the perceived outsider (perceived as such by mainstream society) who desires access to the Republic while mainstream society effectively refuses this access. The context here is made more complex by the fact that those being refused access are French citizens, both officially and in terms of self-perception. In the case of Villiers-le-Bel, this situation was confirmed through interviews with social professionals working in the commune:

> Alors, il est là le problème. C'est que la société française, moi je l'appelle le petit hypocrite en référence à une chanson que j'ai déjà entendue. C'est-à-dire que on va dire 'mais on vous donne la possibilité de vous intégrer et on va faire des lois d'intégration' mais au bout d'un moment quand un môme, ça fait trois générations que sa famille elle est en France...que lui il est né en France...pourquoi est-ce qu'on lui demande de s'intégrer? ...et un petit môme tout blond de Paris...la seizième...on va pas lui demander de s'intégrer! Ça se pose pas cette question-là. Mais les jeunes, ici, on leur demande encore aujourd'hui de s'intégrer à la société française. Mais ils en font partie! Ils ont la carte d'identité française, ils sont nés en France, et ça aujourd'hui on leur reconnaît pas. C'est ça qui est compliqué.
>
> — *OLIVIER, educateur spécialisé*

> Tous les jeunes qui sont là, la plupart sont français. Ils sont nés en France. Mais dans le regard de l'autre ils sont des immigrés. Voilà, c'est le regard qui compte. Je sais pas qui dit ça...je me souviens pas...il disait on est juste dans le regard de l'autre. Donc on est arabe ou musulman ou banlieusard dans le regard de l'autre. Ce que je veux dire c'est qu'il y a un certain nombre de gens qui passent à la télé, ils disent mais c'est la banlieue, c'est des immigrés...Si quelqu'un me voit, pas tout le monde mais un certain nombre de gens vont me voir et ils vont penser que je suis musulman... parce que j'ai un visage qui est d'origine maghrébine je suis musulman. Donc dans le regard de l'autre je suis musulman. Mais qui sait si je suis musulman sans me voir pratiquer [...] Mais dans la société française d'entrée les gens te mettent dans une case malgré toi. Tu es musulman, tu es arabe, tu es immigré, tu es étranger dans le regard de l'autre. C'est ça qui est problématique. C'est pas tant la personne comme elle se pense, comme elle se vit...ces jeunes ils sont nés là, ils connaissent de moins en moins leurs origines, ils les connaissent pas. Mais la personne qui les regarde elle veut pas savoir. Tu t'appelles Abdel ou Mahmoud donc tu es immigré...et c'est un vrai problème de mentalité des français.
>
> — *KHADER, directeur, IMAJ*

Thus it can be asserted that the Republican model of integration has indeed encountered failure. Crucially, however, this failure is not on the part of the youth of the suburbs but rather stems from the failure of mainstream French society to consider and adapt to the socio-cultural evolution of the *banlieues*. Successive generations have become progressively more immersed in the norms and social codes of French society. With the passing of generations, the immigrant origins of young *banlieusards* have progressively faded, in many cases recollected only by somatic and religious difference. The label of 'immigrant' is, in this context, obsolete. In contemporary society, French *banlieues* are populated by French citizens, who regard themselves as such in terms of identity and belonging. Nonetheless, French society has failed, or refused, to fully recognize and accept the progression from immigrant to citizen *of immigrant origins* and the distinction that this progression entails in terms of belonging to the national community. Physical and cultural differences marking these youths as having ancestral roots in other nations continue to form a cultural barrier in terms of how these young people are perceived by mainstream society. These developments have formed a background to the already present social and economic malaise that dominates many suburban areas, all combining to produce a potent social mix that exploded into violence during the events of 2005 and 2007.

A Plea for Access

This chapter has shown that, far from representing nihilistic expressions of violence and destruction, the riots of 2005 and 2007 did indeed hold a message. The populations of the *banlieues* are marginalized and excluded from mainstream society. Socially and economically disadvantaged, the difficulties of these populations are compounded by a profound sense of injustice. The deadly pattern of violence and death or injury that has, since the 1980s, placed the inhabitants of these areas in staunch opposition with the forces of law and order has resulted in the construction of an us-versus-them paradigm. This binary opposition, expressed primarily through the relationship between the *banlieusards* and the police, also serves as an interpretative prism through which everyday events are viewed. Joly sums up this position in saying: 'le désavantage de ces jeunes est découplé par l'échec scolaire, le chômage, la pauvreté, un avenir sans issue, ainsi que par le racisme et la discrimination avec leurs cortèges d'humiliations quotidiennes et les injustices qui en découlent'.[48] The situation here, perceived as beyond their control, induces a profound malaise among the inhabitants of the *banlieues*, particularly the young. These young people thus experience 'un fort sentiment d'impuissance généré par l'impossibilité de se faire entendre'.[49] In this context, violence appears to be the only means of making their voices heard, of becoming visible in the public sphere. Violence provides a means of focusing media attention on the suburbs, which, in turn, brings the problems of the *banlieues* to the attention of public and politicians alike. Fieldwork in Villiers-le-Bel has shown that the violence did not represent the destructive tendencies of young delinquents, expressive of a hatred of French society. Rather, the violence constituted a form of protopolitics: a means of breaking the silence that is imposed upon the *banlieues* and entering, albeit somewhat unconventionally, into the political arena. The significance of the riot as a political act has already been discussed and in this respect, Castel draws on the work of Abdelmalek Sayad who 'parlait déjà en 1985 [...] de la "violence la plus violente" à laquelle "une jeunesse interdite de parole" serait renvoyée si aucune issue politique ne lui était offerte'.[50] In this context, the riots can be viewed, not as a rejection of French society by young people of immigrant origins, but rather as a plea for access to mainstream society on the part of French citizens who are excluded from the society of which they are legally members.

48   Danièle Joly, *L'émeute: ce que la France peut apprendre du Royaume-Uni* (Paris: Éditions Denoël, 2007), 293.
49   Ibid.
50   Cited in Castel, *La discrimination négative*, 61.

Conclusion

Taking an analysis of both the violence of autumn 2005 and the aftershock of 2007 as a starting point, the preceding chapters have explored the social, cultural and economic situation that exists in the *quartiers sensibles*. The study has sought to deconstruct popular interpretations of the violence and reveal the underlying motivating factors that prompted youths from suburban communities across the country to engage in acts of violence and destruction of an unprecedented scale over a three-week period in autumn 2005. The aftershock of 2007, where the intensity of the violence reached new heights, added a new element to the equation. In order to do this, the book offered a general study of the founding principles and ideals of the French Republic, forged in the period following the 1789 Revolution and consolidated as the republican model cemented its position as the political and social framework within which France would develop as a nation-state. This provided a historical, social and political background to the republican conception of citizenship and the emergence of the model of integration that exists in contemporary French society.

Building on this historical and ideological overview, the book proceeded to examine the challenges brought to bear on the Republic by changes in international migratory flux, especially in the second half of the twentieth century. In this context, the debate focused on the challenges associated with reconciling cultural and ethnic difference with the dominant norms and perceptions of French society, or indeed vice versa. Issues such as education, religion, unemployment, and law and order all occupy a place at the centre of this debate. The book then moved from the general to the specific — that is, from a more wide-ranging exploration of republican ideology and the challenges posed by immigration, to the specific context of the *quartiers sensibles*, areas that have been directly and significantly influenced by the anthropological, social and political changes stemming from immigration and, more importantly, changing perceptions of immigrants in French society. Chapter 3 documented the development of suburban areas in post-war France, charting the progression of the *banlieues* from areas representing modernity and progress to zones concentrating populations of immigrant origins, areas of relegation existing at the periphery of French society widely regarded as microcosms of the problems facing French society. Issues of discrimination and racism were shown to be paramount in the social mutation of the *quartiers sensibles* as changing economic conditions and the rise of the far right impacted on perceptions of immigrants in the public sphere.

More importantly, the analysis laid bare the changes that have taken place in the *banlieues* in terms of identity, thus revealing the fundamental paradox that threatens the continuation of the republican model. With the passing of generations, inhabitants of immigrant origins have acculturated to the dominant French identity. Moreover, the majority of the youth now residing in the suburbs have been born and raised in France and are French citizens, in legal terms and, crucially, in terms of self-perception. The discussion showed how mainstream society has failed to recognize these socio-cultural developments, denying these legitimate members of the citizenry full social acceptance. It has also been shown how the accumulated frustration and anger that has resulted from this denial has expressed itself through large-scale episodes of violence. The police represent an important factor in this equation that has seen the *banlieues* become disjointed from French society and develop as areas characterized by exclusion, discrimination and sporadic outbursts of violence and destruction. The relationship between the inhabitants of these areas and the forces of law and order has impacted significantly on the deterioration of the social situation in the *quartiers sensibles*. The police are seen as unjust and discriminatory by the population of the suburbs, a viewpoint that has important implications for how the state in general is perceived by these populations. Additionally, the trajectory of the riots in both 2005 and 2007, like other similar instances of violence, was significantly influenced by the actions of police in these areas.

In Chapter 4, the focus of the book moved to the empirical and an in-depth exploration of life in the *banlieues*. Drawing upon the results of participant observation and in-depth interviews, the analysis offered a comprehensive insight into the social processes that govern Villiers-le-Bel, and, on a larger scale, the French *banlieues*. This information provided conclusive evidence to support the working hypothesis laid out at the start of the book – that the violent events of 2005 and 2007 did not represent a rejection of French society and the Republic at large, but rather represented a call for access on the part of the youth of the suburbs.

In 1997, Michel Wieviorka evoked the urgency of the problems facing the French Republic in relation to the growing issues of multiculturalism and social integration.[1] Part of a collection of essays debating multiculturalism and social fragmentation in France, Wieviorka's assertions emphasized the new challenges facing the Republic as it moved towards the dawn of a new millennium, challenges brought by multiculturalism and the problems of reconciling an abstract republicanism with a rapidly evolving social and cultural reality. Now, over a decade later, France is still faced with the same questions. However, the situation has degenerated, the social gap separating the suburbs from mainstream society is wider than ever, and as the malaise of the suburbs is expressed ever more violently, repression seems to be the basis for action on the part of the government – increasing police presence in the suburbs and calling for tougher sentences to be handed out to young offenders.

The growth of the theme of insecurity in the political sphere, and consequently in the media, has fostered a widespread fear among the general public, for whom the media often provide the only means of gaining an insight into the world of the *quartiers sensibles*. Moreover, a definitive link has been forged in the popular imagination between the theme of insecurity that permeates discourse relating to the *quartiers sensibles* and the subject of immigration, a link that leads to discrimination based on what Dubois terms 'real or supposed origins'.[2] These damaging links have served to further distance the inhabitants of the *banlieues* from mainstream society. On the part of those living in the suburbs this divide has been further widened

---

1   Michel Wieviorka, ed., *Une société fragmentée: le multiculturalisme en débat* (Paris: La Découverte, 1997).

2   Jean-Pierre Dubois, 'Violences et politiques', in Clémentine Autin, Stéphane Beaud et al., eds, *Banlieue, lendemains de révolte* (Paris: La Dispute, 2006), 73.

through the many years of tense police relations that have eroded faith in the justice system, a central element of republican ideology. However, for Beaud and Pialoux, what is perhaps most striking about the situation in the suburbs is the apparent incapacity on the part of those in power to comprehend the social fragility of the inhabitants of the suburbs.[3]

The social problems that face the inhabitants of the *banlieues* are further compounded by the cultural issues that stem from questions of identity and belonging. Following the riots of both 2005 and 2007 there was widespread criticism of the Republican model and its failure in relation to the integration of the *quartiers sensibles*. In spite of this, closer examination of the situation in the suburbs reveals that it is not the nature of the Republican model and its ideals that is in question, but rather the failure to extend this model to all parts of society that is at the heart of the divide separating the *banlieues* from mainstream society. Danièle Joly cites the work of Wieviorka in asserting that 'l'Etat français est le seul en Europe à promettre de garantir la liberté, l'égalité et la fraternité à ses citoyens. Ces idéaux sont louables mais il y a loin de la cuillère à la bouche'.[4] In other words, the proclamations of liberty, equality and fraternity that are the foundations of the French republican model have failed to successfully penetrate all corners of the hexagon. This study has shown how the suburbs exemplify this failure, representing the blind spot of the Republic, a social space embodying all the social, cultural and economic challenges facing the Republic. Joly effectively sums up the situation in saying 'Les jeunes des cités ont intériorisé les valeurs fondamentales proclamés par la République française et s'insurgent contre l'iniquité et l'humiliation qu'ils subissent quotidiennement. Ils expriment une frustration relative, en rapport avec ce que d'autres obtiennent, attisée par leur désenchantement vis-à-vis d'une République mensongère'.[5]

The continued failure to fully face the worsening situation in the suburbs has resulted in a vicious circle where certain inhabitants have come

3   Beaud and Pialoux, 'La "racaille" et les "vrais jeunes"', 27.
4   Joly, *L'Emeute*, 282.
5   Ibid., 283.

to see violence as possibly the only way to draw attention to the urgent social issues that dominate these areas. For the rioters, acts of violence and destruction present themselves as a sure means of drawing attention to their situation, of imposing their problems on a political landscape where their voices are not heard. The riots represented an attempt to forcefully enter the political arena – the desire being not to destroy for the sake of destruction, but rather to use the violence and destruction as a means of confronting the exclusion to which they are subject. Paradoxically, the young people involved in the violence felt that, in order to make themselves visible in the political sphere, it was necessary to circumvent the conventional channels that help shape the political arena as a whole. Of course, these arguments raise questions as to how the inhabitants of the *banlieues* can move beyond the protopolitical form of protest and channel these expressions of anger through more conventional vehicles and forms of political action.

With regard to the 2005 riots, Jobard states that 'the memory of the riots remains extremely vivid, however, both in marginal public spaces, and in alternative spaces, such as blogs, Internet sites, and rap or hip-hop songs, albeit without ever achieving a univocal interpretation of the disorders and the action required in their aftermath'.[6] A similar situation followed the 2007 violence in Villiers-le-Bel where internet sites, for example, still display videos of rap songs dedicated to the memory of the teenagers who died. Jobard goes on to point out that there were a number of 'more formal political responses' such as a grievance book recording the complaints of residents in underprivileged *banlieues* and the setting up of social forums in other neighbourhoods. In Villiers-le-Bel, Ali Soumaré, a young man who acted as a spokesperson for the families of the dead teenagers in the immediate aftermath of the tragedy and also organized a peaceful protest, subsequently entered the political arena and appeared on the Socialist list for the legislative elections of 2009. However, Kokoreff reveals that these isolated acts, while hinting at potential paths that residents could follow,

6   Fabien Jobard, 'Rioting as a Political Tool: The 2005 Riots in France', *The Howard Journal*, 48 (2009), 235–244 (239).

do not offer any sort of 'alternative vision' for the future.[7] In Jobard's analysis, the indication is that 'there has been no long-term gain or positive impact on policy, but rather an external negative reinforcement of political polarisation'.[8] Jobard draws on Murray Edelman's seminal work, which was published in the 1970s, to illustrate the illusory nature of political promises with regard to the suburbs.[9] However, while the next stage in the evolution of the *banlieues* is not yet clear, the absence of new forms of engagement with conventional political structures does not undermine the political significance of the events that took place in 2005 and 2007.

Traditionally, the motto 'one and indivisible' has formed a cornerstone of the French Republic. Despite this, at the beginning of the twenty-first century, the social geography of France reveals a significant divide that poses a serious threat to this proclamation. French society has reached a crossroads in its social development; if the Republic is to progress as a whole, the suburbs must be embraced by mainstream society. Begag affirms that public institutions 'can no longer survive on the basis of a republican sclerosis wrapped up in mythical past glories'.[10] These institutions must recognize the potential of these areas to positively contribute to French social and economic progression, and invest in the development of the suburbs. In the words of Alec Hargreaves, 'Many years that could have been used to build greater social cohesion have nevertheless been wasted [...] If politicians had spent their time applying republican principles instead of building what many regarded as discriminatory barriers, such as the nationality law reform of 1993 and the anti-headscarf law of 2004, the banlieues might not have lapsed into despair'.[11] The events of 2005, as well as the aftershock of 2007 represent a stark warning. The malaise of the suburbs is growing and the current trajectory cannot hold; unless the social

---

7   See Kokoreff, *Sociologie des émeutes*, 260–270.
8   Dave Waddington and Mike King, 'Identifying Common Causes of UK and French Riots Occurring Since the 1980s', *The Howard Journal*, 48 (2009), 245–256 (256).
9   Jobard, 'Rioting as a Political Tool', 242.
10   Azouz Begag, *Ethnicity and Equality. France in the Balance* (Lincoln and London: University of Nebraska Press, 2007), 123.
11   Hargreaves, *Multi-ethnic France*, 210.

and cultural trends that govern life in the suburbs are altered for the better, French society may see a repeat, perhaps intensified, of the violence and destruction witnessed in 2005 and 2007. The dynamic of exclusion that has split the Republic must be reversed or France will move divided into the future. In this context, the *quartiers sensibles* would appear to be the testing ground for the Republic of the future.

Bibliography

Agulhon, M., *The French Republic: 1879–1992* (Oxford and Cambridge, MA: Blackwell, 1993).

Amiraux, V., and Simon, P., 'There Are No Minorities Here: Cultures of Scholarship and Public Debate on Immigrants and Integration in France', *International Journal of Comparative Sociology*, 47 (2006), 191–215.

Aron, R., *France, the New Republic* (London: Atlantic Books, 1960).

Autin, C., Beaud, S., Bertho, A., et al. (eds), *Banlieue, lendemains de révolte* (Paris: La Dispute, 2006).

Barou, J., *La Place du Pauvre: Histoire et géographie sociale de l'habitat HLM* (Paris: L'Harmattan, 1992).

Barrett, P., *La République et l'école* (Paris: Fayard, 2006).

Baubérot, J., *Histoire de la laïcité francaise* (Paris: PUF, 2000).

Beaud, S., and Pialoux, M., *Violences urbaines, violence sociale: Genèse des nouvelles classes dangereuses* (Paris: Fayard, 2003).

Beaud, S., and Pialoux, M., *Retour sur la condition ouvrière* (Paris: Fayard, 1999).

Becker, H.S., *Outsiders: Studies in the Sociology of Deviance* (New York: Free Press of Glencoe, 1963).

Begag, A., *Ethnicity and Equality: France in the Balance* (Lincoln and London: University of Nebraska Press, 2007).

Black, D., *The Manners and Customs of the Police* (New York: Academic Press, 1980).

Bleich, E., *Race Politics in Britain and France: Ideas and Policymaking since the 1960s* (Cambridge: Cambridge University Press, 2003).

Body-Gendrot, S., and Spierenburg, P. (eds), *Violence in Europe: Historical and Contemporary Perspectives* (New York: Springer, 2008).

Body-Gendrot, S., Wihtol de Wenden, C., *Sortir des banlieues. Pour en finir avec la tyrannie des territoires* (Paris: Editions Autrement, 2007).

Borgmann, A., *Holding On to Reality* (Chicago: University of Chicago Press, 1999).

Bourdieu, P. (ed.), *La Misère du monde* (Paris: Le Seuil, 1993).

Bourdieu, P., and Wacquant, L., *An Invitation to Reflexive Sociology* (Chicago: University of Chicago Press, 1992).

Bourdieu, P., and Passeron, J.-C., *Reproduction in Education, Society and Culture*, trans. R. Nice (London: Sage, 1996).

Bowen, J., *Why the French Don't Like Headscarves: Islam, the State and Public Space* (Princeton: Princeton University Press, 2007).

Brogan, D., *The Development of Modern France (1870–1939)* (London: Hamish Hamilton, 1949).

Brubaker, R., *Citizenship and Nationhood in France and Germany* (Cambridge, MA, and London: Harvard University Press, 1994).

Bui Trong, L., *Violences Urbaines. Des vérités qui dérangent* (Paris: Bayard, 2000).

Cairns, E., and Roe, M. (eds), *The Role of Memory in Ethnic Conflict* (London: Palgrave Macmillan, 2002).

Castel, R., *La discrimination négative. Citoyens ou indigènes?* (Paris: Seuil, 2007).

Censer, J., and Hunt, L., *Liberty, Equality, Fraternity. Exploring the French Revolution* (University Park: Pennsylvania State University Press, 2001).

Cesari, J., and McLoughlin, S. (eds), *European Muslims and the Secular State* (Aldershot: Ashgate, 2005).

Cole, A., and Raymond, G. (eds), *Redefining the French Republic* (Manchester: Manchester University Press, 2006).

Coolsaet, R., *Jihadi Terrorism and the Radicalisation Challenge in Europe* (Aldershot: Ashgate, 2008).

Connerton, P., *How Societies Remember* (Cambridge: Cambridge University Press, 1989).

Crook, M., *Elections in the French Revolution: An Apprenticeship in Democracy, 1789–1799* (Cambridge: Cambridge University Press, 1996).

Curtis, W., *Le Corbusier, Ideas and Forms* (London and New York: Phaidon, 2001).

Delsol, C., *La République: une question française* (Paris: Presses Universitaires de France, 2002).

De Maillard, J., 'The governance of safety in France: Is there anybody in charge?', *Theoretical Criminology*, 9 (2005), 325–343.

De Maillard, J., and Roché, S., 'Crime and Justice in France: Time Trends, Policies and Political Debate', in *European Journal of Criminology*, 1 (2004), 111–151.

Derderian, R., *North Africans in France: Becoming Visible* (New York: Palgrave Macmillan, 2004).

Devereux, E., *Understanding the Media* (London: Sage, 2007).

DeWalt K., and DeWalt, B., *Participant Observation: A Guide for Fieldworkers* (Walnut Creek, CA: Altamira Press, 2002).

Dikeç, M., *Badlands of the Republic: Space, Politics and Urban Policy* (Oxford: Blackwell, 2007).

Donzelot, J., *Quand la ville se défait* (Paris: Seuil, 2006).

Doyle, W., *The French Revolution* (Oxford: Oxford University Press, 2001).

Draï, R., Mattéi, J. (eds), *La République brûle-t-elle? Essai sur les violences urbaines françaises* (Paris: Editions Michalon, 2006).

Dubet, F., and Lapeyronnie, D., *Les quartiers d'exil* (Paris: Seuil, 1992).

Dubet, F., *La galère: jeunes en survie* (Paris: Fayard, 1987).

Duprez, D., and Kokoreff, M., *Les Mondes de la drogue* (Paris: Odile Jacob, 2000).

Elliott, J., *Using Narrative in Social Research: Qualitative and Quantitative Approaches* (London: Sage, 2005).

Esposito, J., and Burgat, F. (eds), *Modernising Islam: Religion in the Public Sphere in Europe and the Middle East* (London: Hurst, 2003).

Evans, M., and Godin, E., *France. 1815–2003* (London: Hodder Arnold, 2004).

Fassin, D., and Fassin, E. (eds), *De la question sociale à la question raciale* (Paris: La Découverte, 2006).

Favell, A., *Philosophies of Integration. Immigration and the Idea of Citizenship in France and Britain* (Basingstoke and New York: Palgrave, 2001).

Feagin, J., Orum, A., and Sjoberg, G. (eds), *A Case for the Case Study* (North Carolina: University of North Carolina Press, 1991).

Feldblum, M., *Reconstructing Citizenship: The Politics of Nationality Reform and Immigration in Contemporary France* (New York: SUNY Press, 1999).

Fortesque, W., *The Third Republic in France, 1870–1940: conflicts and continuities* (London: Routledge, 2000).

Fourcaut, A. (ed.), *Un siècle de banlieue parisienne, 1859–1964* (Paris: L'Harmattan, 1988).

Freedman, J., *Immigration and Insecurity in France* (Aldershot: Ashgate, 2004).

Furet, F., *La Révolution* (Paris: Hachette, 1988).

Fysh, P., and Wolfreys, J., *The Politics of Racism in France* (London: Macmillan, 1998).

Geddes, A., *The Politics of Migration in Europe* (London: Sage, 2003).

Gerring, J., *Case Study Research: Principles and Practices* (New York: Cambridge University Press, 2007).

Glazer, B., and Strauss, A., *The Discovery of Grounded Theory: Strategies for Qualitative Research* (Chicago: Aldine, 1967).

Gorgeon, C., 'Socialisation professionnelle des policiers: le rôle de l'école', *Criminologie*, 29 (1996), 141–163.

Goulbourne, H. (ed.), *Race and Ethnicity: Critical Concepts in Sociology* (London: Routledge, 2001).

Guénif-Souilamas, N. (ed.), *La république mise à nu par son immigration* (Paris: Fabrique éditions, 2006).

Gueniffey, P., *Dictionnaire critique de la République* (Paris: Flammarion, 2002).

Hargreaves, A., *Multi-Ethnic France. Immigration, Politics, Culture and Society* (London and New York: Routledge, 2007).

Hargreaves, A., *Immigration, 'Race' and Ethnicity in Contemporary France* (London and New York: Routledge, 1995).

Hargreaves, A., McKinney, M. (eds), *Post-colonial Cultures in France* (London: Routledge, 1997).

Hazareesingh, S., *The Jacobin Legacy in Modern France. Essays in Honour of Vincent Wright* (Oxford: Oxford University Press, 2002).

Hazareesingh, S., *From Subject to Citizen: The Second Empire and the Emergence of Modern French Democracy* (Princeton: Princeton University Press, 1998).

Hallam, E., and Street, B. (eds), *Cultural Encounters. Representing 'Otherness'* (London: Routledge, 2000).

Hayward, Jack, *The One and Indivisible French Republic* (London: Weidenfeld and Nicolson, 1973).

Hiddleston, J., *Reinventing Community: Identity and Difference in Late Twentieth-Century French Philosophy and Literature* (Oxford: Legenda, 2005).

Holstein, J., and Gubrium, J., *The Active Interview* (Thousand Oaks, CA: Sage, 1995).

Hunt, L. (ed.), *The French Revolution and Human Rights. A Brief Documentary History* (Boston: Bedford/St Martin's, 1996).

Janoski, T., *The Ironies of Citizenship: Naturalisation and Integration in Industrialised Countries* (New York: Cambridge University Press, 2010).

Jarvinen, M., 'The Biographical Illusion: Constructing Meaning in Qualitative Interviews', *Qualitative Inquiry*, 6 (2000), 370–391.

Jenkins, P., *God's Continent: Christianity, Islam and Europe's Religious Crisis* (Oxford: Oxford University Press, 2007).

Jobard, F., *Bavures policières? La force publique et ses usages* (Paris: La Découverte, 2002).

Jobard, F., 'Rioting as a Political Tool: The 2005 Riots in France', *The Howard Journal*, 48 (2009), 235–244.

Joly, D., *L'émeute: Ce que la France peut apprendre du Royaume-Uni* (Paris: Editions Denoël, 2007).

Joly, D., *International Migration in the New Millennium* (Aldershot: Ashgate, 2004).

Jorgensen, D., *Participant Observation: A Handbook for Human Studies* (Thousand Oaks, CA: Sage, 1989).

Kaës, R., *Vivre dans les grands ensembles* (Paris: Editions Ouvrières, 1963).

Kelly, J., *Borrowed Identities* (New York: Peter Lang, 2004).

Kepel, G., *Les banlieues de l'Islam* (Paris: Seuil, 1991).

Khosrokhavar, F., *L'islam des prisons* (Paris: Balland, 2004).

Kiwan, N., *Identities, Discourses and Experiences: Young People of North African Origin in France* (Manchester: Manchester University Press, 2009).

Kokoreff, M., *Sociologie des émeutes* (Paris: Payot, 2008).

Kokoreff, M., *La Force des quartiers* (Paris: Payot, 2003).

Kvale, S., Interviews: *An Introduction to Qualitative Research Interviewing* (Thousand Oaks, CA: Sage, 1996).

Lagrange, H., and Oberti, M., *Emeutes et protestations. Une singularité française* (Paris: Presses des Sciences Po, 2006).

Landes, J., *Visualizing the Nation: Gender, Representation and Revolution in Eighteenth Century France* (Ithaca, NY: Cornell University Press, 2001).

Lane, J., *Pierre Bourdieu: A Critical Introduction* (London: Pluto Press, 2000).

Lapeyronnie, D., *Ghetto urbain. Ségrégation, violence, pauvreté en France aujourd'hui* (Paris: Robert Laffont, 2008).

Lapeyronnie, D., 'Révolte primitive dans les banlieues françaises. Essai sur les émeutes de l'automne 2005', in *Déviance et Société*, 30 (2006), 431–448.

Laurence, J., and Vaisse, J., *Integrating Islam. Political and Religious Challenges in Contemporary France* (Washington, DC: Brookings Institution Press, 2006).

Le Goaziou, V., and Mucchielli, L. (eds), *Quand les banlieues brûlent. Retour sur les émeutes de novembre 2005* (Paris: La Découverte, 2006).

Lepoutre, D., *Coeur de Banlieue, Codes rites et langages* (Paris: Odile Jacob, 2001).

Lerner, R., and Steinberg, L. (eds), *Handbook of Adolescent Psychology* (New Jersey: Wiley, 2004).

Lofland, J., and Lofland, L., *Analyzing Social Settings: A Guide to Qualitative Observation and Analysis* (Belmont: Wadsworth, 1995).

Marlière, E., *La France nous a lâchés: Le sentiment d'injustice chez les jeunes des cités* (Paris: Fayard, 2008).

Marlière, E., *Jeunes en cité: Diversité des trajectoires ou destin commun?* (Paris: L'Harmattan, 2005).

Marlière, E., 'La police et les jeunes de cité', *Agora*, 39 (2006), 90–100.

Marliere, P., 'La mémoire socialiste. Un cas d'étude sociologique du rapport au passé' (doctoral thesis, European University Institute, Florence, 2000).

Marlière, P., 'The Rules of the Journalistic Field: Pierre Bourdieu's Contribution to the Sociology of the Media', *European Journal of Communication*, 13 (1998), 219–234.

Marshall, C., and Rossman., G. (eds), *Designing Qualitative Research* (Thousand Oaks, CA: Sage, 2006).

Martinet, G., *Une certaine idée de la gauche (1936–1997)* (Paris: Odile Jacob, 1997).

Mauger, G., *L'émeute de novembre 2005: une révolte protopolitique* (Broissieux: Editions du Croquant, 2006).

Maurin, E., *Le ghetto français* (Paris: Seuil, 2004).

Maurin, E., *l'Egalité des possibles: La Nouvelle Société française* (Paris: Seuil, 2002).

Maurin, L., and Savidan, P. (eds), *L'état des inégalités en France, 2007* (Paris: Belin, 2006).

May, T. (ed.), *Qualitative Research in Action* (London: Sage, 2002).

McQuail, D., *Mass Communication Theory* (London: Sage, 1994).

McQuail, D., *McQuail's Mass Communication Theory* (London: Sage, 2000).

Ménanteau, J., *Les Banlieues* (Paris: Le Monde Editions, 1997).

Mendès-France, P., *La république moderne: propositions* (Paris: Gallimard, 1962).

Mendras, H., and Cole, A., *Social Change in Modern France. Towards a Cultural Anthropology of the Fifth Republic* (Cambridge: Cambridge University Press, 1991).

Merlin, P., *Les Banlieues* (Paris: Presses Universitaires de France, 1999).

Mignard, J.P., and Tordjman, E., *L'Affaire Clichy. Morts pour rien* (Paris: Stock, 2006).

Miles, M., and Huberman, M., *Qualitative Data Analysis: An Expanded Coursebook* (Thousand Oaks, CA: Sage, 1994).

Miller, M., *The Representation of Place: Urban Planning and Protest in France and Great Britain, 1950–1980* (Aldershot: Ashgate, 2003).

Monjardet, D., *Ce que fait la police. Sociologie de la force publique* (Paris: La Découverte, 1996).

Monjardet, D., 'Police and the Public', in *European Journal on Criminal Policy and Research*, 8 (2000), 353–378.

Mucchielli, L., *Violences et insécurité. Fantasmes et réalités dans le débat Français* (Paris: La Découverte, 2001).

Mucchielli, L. (ed.), *La frénésie sécuritaire. Retour à l'ordre et nouveau contrôle social* (Paris: La Découverte, 2008).

Muncie, J., and Goldson, B. (eds), *Comparative Youth Justice* (London: Sage, 2006).

Noiriel, G., *The French Melting Pot: Immigration, Citizenship and National Identity*, trans. Geoffrey Laforcade (Minneapolis and London: Minnesota University Press, 1996).

Padgett, D., *Qualitative Methods in Social Work Research* (Thousand Oaks, CA: Sage, 2008).

Palier, B., Hall, P., and Culpepper, P. (eds), *La France en mutation 1980–2005* (Paris: Presse des Sciences Po., 2006).

Péguy, C., *Notre jeunesse* (Paris: Gallimard, 1957).

Pena-Ruiz, H., *Qu'est-ce que la laïcité?* (Gallimard: Paris, 2003).

Piotrowski, P. (ed.), *Understanding Problems of Social Pathology* (Amsterdam: Rodopi, 2006).

Pogrebin, M. (ed.), *Qualitative Approaches to Criminal Justice: Perspectives from the Field* (Thousand Oaks, CA: Sage, 2003).

Power, A., *Hovels to High Rise: State Housing in Europe since 1850* (London: Routledge, 1993).

Price, R., *The French Second Republic: A Social History* (London: Batsford, 1972).

Rachid, '"Génération Scarface". La place du trafic dans une cite de la banlieue parisienne', in *Déviance et Société*, 28 (2004), 115–132.

Raleigh Yow, V., *Recording Oral History: A Guide for the Humanities and Social Sciences* (Walnut Creek, CA: Altimira Press, 2005).

Raoult, E., *SOS Banlieues* (Paris: L'Harmattan, 1993).

Rapport, M., *Nationality and Citizenship in Revolutionary France* (Oxford: Clarendon Press, 2000).

Raymond, G., and Modood, T. (eds), *The Construction of Minority Identities in France and Britain* (Basingstoke: Palgrave Macmillan, 2007).

Rémond, R., *L'invention de la laïcité. De 1789 à demain* (Bayard: Paris, 2005).

Rey, H., *La peur des banlieues* (Paris: Presses des Sciences Po, 1996).

Rigouste, M., 'Le langage des médias sur "les cites". Représenter l'espace, légitimer le contrôle', in *Hommes et Migrations*, 1252 (2004), 74–81.

Ritchie, J., and Lewis, J., *Qualitative Research Practice: A Guide for Social Science Students and Researchers* (London: Sage, 2003).

Roché, S., *Police de proximité. Nos politiques de sécurité* (Paris: Seuil, 2006).

Roché, S., *Le Frisson de l'émeute. Violences urbaines et banlieues* (Paris: Seuil, 2006).

Sadoun, M. (ed.), *La Démocratie en France. Idéologies* (Paris: Gallimard, 2000).

Sarkozy, N., Collin, T., and Verdin, P., *La République, les religions, l'espérance* (Paris: Pocket, 2005).

Schneider, C., 'Police Power and Race Riots in Paris', in *Politics and Society*, 36 (2008), 133–159.

Shields, J., *The Extreme Right in France: From Pétain to Le Pen* (Abingdon and New York: Routledge, 2007).

Sieffert, D., *Comment peut-on être (vraiment) républicain?* (Paris: La Découverte, 2006).

Sieyès, E., *What is the Third Estate?*, trans. M. Blondel (New York: Praeger, 1963).

Silverman, M., *Deconstructing the Nation: Immigration, Racism and Citizenship in Modern France* (London: Routledge, 1992).

Silverstein, P., *Algeria in France: Transpolitics, Race and Nation* (Bloomington: Indiana University Press, 2004).

Stébé, J.-M., *La crise des banlieues* (Paris: Presses Universitaires de France, 1999).

Susser, I. (ed), *The Castells Reader on Cities and Social Theory* (London: Blackwell, 2001).

Talmon, J.L., *The Origins of Totalitarian Democracy* (New York: Praeger, 1960).

Thody, P., *The Fifth French Republic: Presidents, Politics and Personalities* (London: Routledge, 1998).

Thomson, D., *Democracy in France: The Third Republic* (London: Oxford University Press, 1946).

Tissot, S., *L'Etat et les quartiers. Genèse d'une catégorie de l'action publique* (Paris: Seuil, 2007).

Triandafyllidou, A., and Gropas, R. (eds), *European Immigration: A Sourcebook* (Aldershot: Ashgate, 2007).

Tribalat, M., *Faire France. Une enquête sur les immigrés et leurs enfants* (Paris: La Découverte, 1995).

Van Maanen, J., 'Police Socialization: A Longitudinal Examination of Job Attitudes in an Urban Police Department', in *Administrative Science Quarterly*, 20 (1975), 207–228.

Viard, J. (ed.), *Aux sources du populisme nationaliste* (Paris: L'Aube, 1996).

Vieillard-Baron, H., *Banlieue, ghetto impossible?* (Paris: Editions de l'Aube, 1996).

Waddington, D., and King, M., 'Identifying Common Causes of UK and French Riots Occurring Since the 1980s', *The Howard Journal*, 48 (2009), 245–256.

Weber, E., *Peasants into Frenchmen. The Modernization of Rural France 1870–1914* (London: Chatto & Windus, 1977).

Weil, P., *La République et sa diversité: Immigration, intégration et discrimination* (Paris: Seuil, 2005).

Weil, P., *Qu'est-ce qu'un Français? Histoire de la Nationalité Française depuis la Révolution* (Paris: Grasset, 2002).

Wieviorka, M., *The Arena of Racism*, trans. Chris Turner (London: Sage, 1995).

Wolf, P., and Macedo, S. (eds), *Educating Citizens: International Perspectives on Civic Values and School Choice* (Washington: Brookings Institution Press, 2004).

Yang, P., *Ethnic Studies: Issues and Approaches* (New York: SUNY Press, 2000).

Yin, R., *Case Study Research: Design and Methods* (Thousand Oaks, CA: Sage 2003).

Zauberman, R., and Lévy, R., 'Police, Minorities, and the French Republican Ideal', *Criminology*, 41 (2003), 1065–1100.

Index